Culture and Enchantment

CULTURE *and*
Enchantment

MARK A. SCHNEIDER

The University of Chicago Press
Chicago and London

Mark A. Schneider teaches in the Department of Sociology,
University of Michigan.

The University of Chicago Press, Chicago 60637
The University of Chicago Press, Ltd., London
© 1993 by The University of Chicago
All rights reserved. Published 1993
Printed in the United States of America

02 01 00 99 98 97 96 95 94 93   1 2 3 4 5

ISBN: 0-226-73927-9 (cloth)

    0-226-73928-7 (paper)

Library of Congress Cataloging-in-Publication Data

Schneider, Mark A.
    Culture and enchantment / Mark A. Schneider.
        p.   cm.
    Includes bibliographical references and index.
    1. Culture—Philosophy.   2.   Culture—Semiotic models.
    3.   Mythology.   4.   Structural anthropology.   5.   Knowledge, Theory of.
    I.   Title.
    GN357.S36   1993
    306'.01—dc20   93-10216
                                                                              CIP

⊚ The paper used in this publication meets the minimum
requirements of the American National Standard for Information
Sciences—Permanence of Paper for Printed Library Materials,
ANSI Z39.48-1984.

Contents

Preface and Acknowledgments

Max Weber saw history as having departed a deeply enchanted past en route to a disenchanted future—a journey that would gradually strip the natural world both of its magical properties and of its capacity for meaning. Yet if for many the Book of Nature has been closed and certain realms abandoned to the mere "hurrying of material" of which Whitehead (1925:80) complained, it does not follow that we have been disenchanted. Of course we are aware that tabloids still hawk marvels, that astrology sometimes has sway in the corridors of power, and that a "new age" thrives outside the academy: but enchantment persists closer to home, as we shall see, in the work of the academy itself. Advances in sociological understanding since Weber's day make this now theoretically to be anticipated, but it takes some getting used to.

How might this be argued? Disenchanting the world, as a social process, involves sorting its behavior into mundane and magical categories—and stigmatizing the latter, making it a disreputable object of inquiry. We become disenchanted only when this invidious distinction is developed, and remain so only while it lasts: in its absence, by contrast, the magical and the mundane appear to us largely indistinguishable. This is clear when we look far enough into the past: in the seventeenth century, for instance, Joseph Glanvill could proceed in one year from his *Plus Ultra* (1668), a propaganda tract for empirical natural philosophy, to *A Philosophical endeavor in the defence of the being of witches and apparitions* without batting an eye. To him the "defence" of apparitions was not all that different from defending "minute bodies" or "animacules"—the microscopic bugs of Hooke's *Micrographia* (1665) and of van Leeuwenhoek's *Anatomia* (1687). Because we think him mistaken in this regard, Glanvill—like his better-known colleague John Aubrey—appears credulous, and we congratulate ourselves on being above his naïveté. Yet our self-satisfaction here is anachronistic: as K. Theodore Hoppen (1976) has argued, even the most "hard-nosed" empiricists in the seventeenth century gave some latitude to phenomena we would today deem peculiar, and Glanvill's case is thus more modal than extreme. In fact he was not particularly anomalous, and we think him naïve only because research into the being of witches and apparitions has since been stigmatized. The interesting, if unsettling, question is whether we will ourselves be found naive for having failed to segregate phenomena that will some day cleave "naturally" into magical and mundane categories, as apparitions and animacules do for us. We argue in what follows that strong grounds for this judgment exist, but that whether it will ever be rendered remains very much in doubt. At issue, essentially, is whether "mature" sciences—we mean the term descriptively rather than evaluatively—will some day grow where our immature ones currently struggle: if so, we will appear as "credulous" as Glanvill; if not, we won't.

Perhaps this is an odd way to frame our problem, but it gets quickly to its core. Enchantment, we suggest, is part of our normal condition, and far from having fled with the rise of science, it continues to exist (though often unrecognized) wherever our capacity to explain the world's behavior is slim, that is, where neither science nor practical knowledge seem of much utility. Epistemic immaturity and enchantment are thus deeply intertwined, and we illustrate this by analyzing academic inquiry into one particular phenomenon, *culture*. Systematic thought about culture, though of ancient lineage, is largely a twentieth-century endeavor and still in a condition it might, for all we know, not escape—an estimate we might also have made, were we alive in the seventeenth century, of natural philosophy. Consequently, we are no more able today to distinguish the culturally magical from the mundane than Glanvill could separate apparitions from microbes.

To demonstrate this, however, involves us in a curious rhetorical bind, since it presumes a judgment that could only be fully persuasive in retrospect—and not just in *any* retrospect, but from the vantage point of precisely the "mature" understanding of culture we presently lack. (We are forced here, it seems, into a type of prospective Whiggishness.) Whether this can be finessed, and enchantment "materialized" where little extraordinary is now remarked, remains to be seen. Obviously, we need to defamiliarize current habits of thought, though this is easier said than done. Parallels with early natural philosophy aid us here, however, for just as in the seventeenth century some investigators found Glanvill's open-mindedness about apparitions misguided, today qualms about the results of cultural inquiry are occasionally voiced, though infrequently on the basis of their enchantment. Strategically, we need to reinforce these qualms, though this consistently involves pulling ourselves down by our bootstraps—that is, becoming literal-minded and pedestrian even when we are unsure this is appropriate. Only if we establish a threshold low enough, however, will the strangeness of cultural inquiry momentarily appear like an "apparition"—and not on Glanvill's terms but our own.

We set about this by mustering tools from sociology, philosophy, literary theory, and the history of science, and putting them to work on a spectrum of inquiries into culture, though anthropology soon becomes our focal concern. (The variety of tools employed has yielded a text that facets its subject, approaching it from several different but compatible angles, rather than seamlessly developing it. The main line of argument extends over chapters 1, 5, 7, and 8, while chapters 2 and 6 address background methodological or philosophical issues, and chapters 3 and 4 provide case studies. Though the chapters were deployed in this fashion quite deliberately, readers are encouraged to read them in the order that best suits their needs.) In chapter 1 we argue that, whether belonging to culture or nature, phenomena that commonly give rise to enchantment share certain properties. Normally, for instance, their behavior is highly mercurial. Such things prove inhospitable to explanation, and mature sciences normally avoid them—sometimes even claiming they are not really *phenomena* in the first place, but merely figments of our imagination. Yet some mercurial phenomena have had an enduring and understandable fascination for students of culture, who risk investigating them for the potential payoff to be had. Among these is the *meaning* of objects or events. Two very different examples are taken up to illustrate why certain species of meaning prove both elusive and enchanting. They are elusive because consensus about them is difficult to achieve, and enchanting because their behavior is accounted for in startling though ultimately obscure ways. Indeed, if we take these accounts seriously, we find ourselves in the grip of forces equal in peculiarity to apparitions.

Chapter 2 refines this argument. Phenomena can be interpreted so as to yield several types of meaning, some of which may be subject to explanation—and thus disenchantment—and some not. We analyze the latter to reveal features they share with other enchanted phenomena, and then isolate the specific interpretive practices that discover enchanted properties in them. Essentially, what happens is that things previously thought to be without meaning are found to possess it, and to explain how this can be, interpreters locate its source in strange entities like the unconscious or other ghostly agents. In result, it behaves in (quite peculiar) ways we can appreciate but not really explain, since it arrives from domains that are beyond our current understanding.

Chapters 3 and 4 present extended case studies of this. We wonder first about the implications of finding nonlinguistic culture to be a "text." In viewing certain customs or events this way, for instance, Clifford Geertz discovers meaning where none has been seen before. Yet how this was produced remains unclear, since it seems to have neither an empirical author nor an easily discernable readership. Thus though seeming unexceptionable in almost every way, the notion of culture-as-text proves, upon mundane interrogation, quite full of mystery. We turn in chapter 4 to Claude Lévi-Strauss. His structural analyses reveal entirely novel messages in myths, conveyed by means not previously seen as having semantic potential. To account for this the universal structuring activity of the unconscious is brought into play. On the one hand all myths are seen as structural transformations of one another, transformations Lévi-Strauss often suggests are regulated by innate mental capacities; whereas on the other, each myth addresses a unique sociocosmological conundrum presumed to afflict its tellers. Myth thus "writes itself" while paying attention to the specific social and cognitive milieu in which it comes to be told—all this without conscious intervention. Mundane queries once again outline the mystery in this. Reflecting on both cases we are struck that the two most broadly influential anthropologists of the past quarter-century should both have been drawn to enchanted realms.

In chapter 5 we explore parallels between this and early natural philosophy. Whether "enchanted" phenomena were to be investigated by the Royal Society in Restoration England was at issue just much as it is for students of culture today. Indeed, this is not surprising, since the study of nature was then organized upon the same pattern as the study of culture today. In such circumstances it proves impossible to form an invidious, disenchanting boundary, a fact we explain by drawing on a sociological theory of genre discrimination. Fields like cultural anthropology, sociology, and literary studies, it turns out, are so organized that they have difficulty agreeing on a boundary in the first place. Before investigating this further, however, we pause momentarily to ask whether there is something about culture that prevents this, making the field somehow "inherently" enchanted.

To answer this, we turn in chapter 6 to address debates in literary theory. There, realists and relativists have disagreed over the nature of culture as an object of inquiry, and in ways that illuminate its explicability (and thus its status as a possible subject for a mature discipline). We conclude from analyzing these debates that it would be reasonable to separate the many forms of meaning into two general types: one, which we continue to call "meaning," can be seen as "metaphysically enchanted" and incapable of explanation; the other, which we designate "intention," is explicable in principle by empirical inquiry. We wonder whether inquiry into *meaning* is perhaps best considered an edifying enterprise subject to one set of evaluative criteria, and inquiry into *intention* a naturalistic discipline using quite different evaluative standards. Employing a thought experiment borrowed from Richard Rorty, we argue that these pursuits share little common ground, appearances not withstanding.

In chapter 7 we examine the organization of cultural disciplines and compare them with mature sciences. The differences explain why enchantment (though unrecognized as such) continues to inhabit cultural inquiry—indeed, is often highly valued there. We discuss some developments, such as the spread of "postmodernist" vocabularies and the growth of an empirical sociology of culture, that favor reorganizing cultural studies in a way inimical to enchantment, but conclude that countervailing factors in all likelihood preclude this.

Thus we arrive at a vision somewhat different from Weber's. In the face of the seemingly relentless advance of science and bureaucratic social organization, he believed, enchantment would be hounded further and further from the institutional centers of our culture. Carried to an extreme, this process would turn life into a tale which, whether told by an idiot or not, would certainly signify nothing, having been evacuated of meaning. Yet he understood as well that meaning was crucial to human sustenance and thus could never be eliminated by science. In a sense, then, enchantment was guaranteed a future. Indeed, we find it to have one as well, uneasy in some places but secure in others. In taking this view we adopt Weber's own ambivalence: enchantment is something we intend to disenchant . . . yet know we will remain enchanted by.

Acknowledgments

This book grew out of a 1985 Yale dissertation in sociology under the direction of David Apter. The support and latitude he offered were most beneficial, as were the comments and advice of Kai Erikson, Jeffrey Sammons, and Jonathan Rieder. Since then, a slightly different version of what is now chapter 3 appeared as "Culture-as-text in the work of Clifford Geertz" in *Theory and Society,* whose editors have graciously granted permission to reprint it. Ellen Idler, Richard Ochberg, Sylvia Tesh, Leslie Rado, Steven Brint, Scott Boorman, Charles Perrow, Robert Farris Thompson, and especially Paul DiMaggio aided in the evolution of that article. A portion of chapter 5, under the title "Boundary Problems in Seventeenth-Century Natural Philosophy," was presented for various audiences at Princeton and Michigan as well as at the annual meeting of the American Sociological Association. Robert Wuthnow, Michèle Lamont, Walter Wallace, Anne Harrington, and Michael Hunter all helped with versions. Bennett Berger and an anonymous reader for the University of Chicago Press had helpful comments on the manuscript as a whole. Special appreciation to Suzanne Keller and Charles Lindblom, whose kindness remains inexplicable, and to Paul DiMaggio, whose support eased the way throughout; and even more to my wife, Patricia Simpson, whose enthusiasm made the journey seem shorter. None are to be burdened with failures that remain; all are most deeply thanked.

1   The Logic of Enchantment

Anno 1670, not far from Cyrencester, was an Apparition; Being demanded, whether a good Spirit or a bad? Returned no answer, but departed with a curious Perfume and a most melodious Twang.

Aubrey, Miscellanies (1696)

John Aubrey (1626–1697) may strike us today as quaint. Certainly his *Miscellanies,* a compilation of odd phenomena either encountered personally or gathered from correspondents, has about it an air of credulity we imagine long-abandoned. In fact so capacious is it in this regard, so open to marvels and peculiar goings-on, that it suggests a naïveté nearly prelapsarian in character.[1] It may seem incongruous, then, that Aubrey was an early and vigorous participant in the Royal Society—the first organization devoted exclusively to the empirical study of nature and one we think of as the institutional birthplace of the very skepticism that makes him now seem so antiquated. To imagine him in the company of Boyle, Hooke, or the other early scientists seems somehow inappropriate, for they had passed beyond his Apparitions, Knockings, Blows Invisible, and Glances of Love and Malice into less-enchanted terrain. How could such divergent investigative attitudes be accommodated in the same scientific organization?

In chapter 5 we will look into the circumstances of the early Royal Society to probe this question in detail, but here we confine ourselves to very general reflections. To begin with, the "credulity" we find in Aubrey is often simply a characterization attached in retrospect to open-mindedness that seems unwarranted. Unless people are somehow undone by it, they cannot easily tell which is which. Thus in pursuing apparitions and other strange phenomena Aubrey may have labored in a frame of mind similar to that of his contemporaries who investigated meteorites: the objects in question, whether apparitions or stones from the sky, were indeed odd—but not the less to be investigated for that.

---

1. This is additionally encouraged by Aubrey's literary style, since its period properties and idiosyncracies can be taken to indicate innocence. Specific images contribute to the effect: he records in a section on animal precognition, for instance, that in County Donegal, Ireland, "a party of the Protestants had been surprised, sleeping by the Popish Irish, were it not for several wrens that just wakened them by dancing and pecking on the drums as the enemy were approaching" ([1697] 1784:65). This image is no more easily forgotten than the melodious twang of the Cyrencester apparition.

Both later came to be condemned, though meteor hunting was in the course of time rehabilitated.[2] By and large, Aubrey was not: his particular miscellanies were in this regard ill-chosen.

Yet we do not want to paint him as an intellectually cautious man poorly served by the subsequent development of knowledge—on the contrary, his want of skepticism was noted even by contemporaries.[3] Rather, we need to see credulity as a function not just of individual character but of community norms, which vary across time and from one endeavor to another. In this regard what is initially puzzling is not Aubrey's personal fondness for odd goings-on, but, as we noted, his participation in the Royal Society, of whose motto *Nullius in verba*—which urged him to accept nothing without demonstration—he was well aware. Yet what we see as an inconsistency here, as also in the relation between Newton's science and his alchemy, was not universally recognized as such then. In fact the norms that give such apparent contradictions their current flavor of scandal had not fully developed in the community of seventeenth-century natural philosophers. Consequently, the line between what was "science" and what was not, or simply between what was a likely topic for study and what promised only frustration and eventual disappointment, was then both differently and less firmly drawn (see Hoppen 1976).

In this respect early modern natural philosophy was like the study of culture today. What perplexes us about Aubrey or Newton has not so much disappeared from the scene as simply migrated from an old subject of inquiry to a new one, from nature to culture. And we accept the result with the same equanimity Aubrey showed in the face of apparitions. Those of us who study culture operate in an enchanted milieu because we have not yet broadly accepted (or perhaps even developed) the craft intuitions that would discriminate between "magical" and mundane objects of inquiry, and in this regard we are little different from predecessors who lacked grounds to dismiss Blows Invisible while accepting stones from the sky.

We turn in a moment to illustrations, but it will first help to be clear about what we mean by enchantment. For our purposes, the many uses of this term all have their origin in certain experiences occasioned by events in the world around us. We become enchanted, it can be argued, when we are confronted by circumstances or occurrences so peculiar

2. Meteorites were only rehabilitated in the first decade of the nineteenth century, after a long period as a disreputable object of inquiry (see Ley 1963:232–236; Westrum 1978).

3. Anthony Wood, for instance, uncharitably mocked Aubrey for his credulity (see Powell 1948:130; and for further contemporary views, Hunter 1975:229–231).

and so beyond our present understanding as to leave us convinced that, *were* they to be understood, our image of how the world operates would be radically transformed. To be enchanted is thus different from being "deeply delighted" or "charmed"—dictionary synonyms for the word—since we are faced with something both real and at the same time uncanny, weird, mysterious, or awesome. Consequently, it is not a condition apt to be produced by fairy tales, at least for adults.

How deeply enchanted we become quite likely depends upon how fundamentally our understanding of the world is challenged: certainly a melodious sound and fragrant scent from a departing apparition would today pose for the majority of us just such a challenge. Presumably to be confronted in this way is exciting and perhaps even thrilling, though the uncanny flavor will add a tincture of unease. The excitement comes from being lifted out of our mundane existence and situated on the verge of a new understanding of our world, while the unease derives from the assault upon our prior sense of how that world works—and thus upon our practical competence in dealing with it. Should we be unable to recapture this, the world around us may never again acquire the solid and predictable form that allows us to rest comfortably within it.

Though initially intense in proportion to the challenge, enchantment quite likely diminishes with familiarity, since it is evoked in part by the novelty of our circumstances and must gradually fade as we become acclimated to them. Even when the initial thrill and unease are gone, however, one might refer to our condition as enchanted as long as no explanation for what we have encountered has come forth. Similarly, repeated exposure to novel occasions of enchantment (as with Aubrey) may make us blasé about it, unable to quite recapture the pristine wonder, and yet we would still call this condition enchanted. In this case, our failure to register astonishment may be an index of the pervasiveness of provocation, for the more there is of this, the less gripping will any particular instance of it be.

By extension, we can think of a given culture (or subculture) as enchanted when it customarily traffics in the odd and unexplained. *Miscellanies* does this, for instance, just as do some of the more serious offerings in occult sections of bookstores today. Enchantment, in other words, can be something of a commodity, and we are concerned with its production and consumption. But further, we are interested in how the experience itself, had either first- or secondhand, is responded to. At least two possibilities in this regard suggest themselves: in the first, we directly confront the challenge novel phenomena present and set about seeking explanations for them, while in the second, we are so taken with the experience itself that we seek to preserve or renew the circumstances that evoked it. "Scientists," one might argue, customarily react in the first manner: for them the experience of enchantment spurs a quest for explanation, which, when successful, brings with it "disenchantment"—by which we mean not some emotional letdown, but rather a return to intelligibility and practical competence. Successful explanation domesticates the uncanny by revealing the engines behind it. Like Toto in *The Wizard of Oz*, it demystifies events by drawing back the veil that obscured their causes.[4]

One might thus characterize science as aimed at experiencing enchantment as often, but also as *briefly,* as possible. This was not what Aubrey sought. Rather than dispel enchantment by seeking to explain it, he hastened to generate it anew. "I think," John Ray wrote to him, "that you are a little too inclinable to credit strange relations . . . or delight to teratologize, (pardon the word) & to make shew of knowing strange things" (cited by Hunter 1975:133–134). With singular exceptions such as his investigation of the Avebury megaliths—research that allows us to view him as the father of British archeology—he was content to collect and catalog the peculiar phenomena he took pleasure in making "shew of knowing." Indeed, for the most part Aubrey's researches were geared to luxuriate in wonder, and though his promiscuity in this regard may somewhat have weakened the enjoyment of any single case, the sum of them, so energetically added to, must have proven satisfying. Nor was he alone in this, for he was a "virtuoso," a species of natural philosopher relatively common in the seventeenth century, whose investigations sought more to preserve than to dispel enchantment (see Houghton 1942).

We will return to these early virtuosi in chapter 5, where we examine the social circumstances in which they flourished. For now, we need only borrow the term itself, so as to designate a class of investigators

4. Even when a new and revolutionary picture of the world retains perplexing features—think of the paradoxes of quantum mechanics—our capacity to predict and explain on its basis generally convinces us that our residual impression of weirdness derives less from the world around us than from ourselves. In other words, our inability to grow comfortable with the "paradoxical" quantum description of things is chalked up to the way our brains are wired rather than to the obdurate uncanniness of the world. (The latter would simply be at odds with the precise predictions such a theory allows us to make.) This is not to say that a sense of uncanniness is ever entirely eliminated by scientific explanation, for in the end we probably all must share Einstein's puzzlement over the relative goodness of fit between the structure of the world and our capacity to explain it. In this sense the goal of science is to sequester *enduring* sources of enchantment at a "philosophical" level, having eliminated them from the empirical one.

who promote enchantment as a condition to be enjoyed in its own right. Of course few works today directly resemble Aubrey's *Miscellanies*,[5] and yet the tradition they represent has modern analogues. Today many virtuosi labor in what are called "interpretive" disciplines, investigating odd or uncanny cultural phenomena and reporting their findings to us. In fact, so common is this that the very uncanniness they uncover may well go unremarked, being difficult to perceive in a context of similarly odd phenomena. Such virtuosi are variously received: admired by many for both the depth and substance of their work (as well as for the stimulation to be had), they are thought by others, to borrow Ray's characterization, "a little too inclinable to credit strange relations." In this regard, at least, the milieu of seventeenth-century natural philosophy is with us again in the interpretive study of culture, and we would like to understand why.

A reasonably full answer to this must await chapters 5 and 7, but it will help to sketch its framework here, even before we turn to examples. For instance, that a particular field of investigation is enchanted seems to be a function both of its subject matter and of the way inquiry into it is organized. In fact these two aspects of the problem are apt to interact in mutually determining ways: the tractability of a subject matter (that is to say, the ease with which it gives itself to explanation) may well influence the organization of inquiry, often creating circumstances in which disenchantment is diligently pursued and handsomely rewarded; whereas organization may (in turn or independently) influence the relative tractability of the subject matter. Phrased somewhat differently, we can say that the relative enchantment of an area of study—a subdiscipline, say—is a function of both its referential ecology and of the organization it develops to support and govern inquiry. Let us take these up in turn.

The notion of referential ecology, which we borrow from Donald Campbell (1986), invites us to conceive of phenomena, any and all phenomena, as constituting a system of "niches" differentiated according to the ease or difficulty of developing referential consensus about them—the latter being a first step to acquiring pragmatic competence in dealing with them. Some phenomena, for instance, are simple, regular in their behavior, and easily observed. By and large we find these

5. Direct equivalents to *Miscellanies* can be found today, but only in a subterranean vein best represented by Charles Hoy Fort and his intellectual descendants. Fort's *The Book of the Damned* (1919), a "procession of data that science has excluded," illustrates the beleaguered circumstance in which an interest in startling curiosities must be expressed. Similar works are today found in the "occult" section of bookstores.

relatively easy to describe, achieve communal consensus about, and perhaps eventually explain. Were we somehow thrown among people whose language we did not speak, these are the sorts of things—trees, animal species, characteristic human actions like eating or walking, and so on—we would point to in our first groping attempts to establish communication. They are prime candidates for a translational bridge, the preliminary links we would need to enter a foreign language. Other phenomena, in contrast, are highly complex, irregular in their behavior, and observable only with the aid of expensive and perhaps undependable equipment, whether physical or conceptual. Should we try to establish a translational bridge with them, we would likely fail—and never be understood. In terms of our metaphorical ecology, these two sorts of phenomena (those easy and those difficult of communal referential access) constitute very different niches (strictly, categories of niche) that are normally occupied by quite different species of inquiry.

In the next chapter we will develop this notion, but even in this vague and intuitive condition it can be of service. It is sometimes suggested, for instance, that classical mechanics be thought of as the study of a single referential niche characterized by the regularity and simplicity of its constitutive phenomena. Undoubtedly this is too glib and crude, but it contains a grain of truth. In like fashion we can suggest that many of the phenomena Aubrey and his fellow virtuosi encountered constituted a specific referential niche: among other qualities they were highly irregular and unpredictable in their occurrence, only sporadically observed among witnesses, and apt to suffer attenuation over time—which is to say to disappear under extended or repeated observation. Gradually this niche ceased to be considered fit for investigation by mainstream science, though those who continue to explore it sometimes employ impeccably scientific procedures (see Collins and Pinch 1982).

If the study of culture is today enchanted, then, this implies that many of the phenomena of interest to us inhabit niches where our referential competence is problematic. To see what this means, however, we have first to consider in what sense cultural artifacts or processes—the products of our expressive life—should be taken as phenomena. It usually is obvious that they do not concern us as purely physical objects or activities (in which case they would pose few referential problems), though exactly what in addition to this they *are* is unclear. Normally, they are taken to be *meaningful*—though this term covers so much territory as to be nearly useless. Leaving specification of it for later, we can simply note that it is the difficulty of getting the physical dimension of culture to line up in any stable way with its meaning that causes us problems.[6] Sometimes the trouble here is thought so radical as to force a conclusion that the study of culture is generically distinct from that of nature, a hermeneutic rather than an explanatory discipline. However this may be, we need remark only that the difficulty of attaching meanings to the appropriate physical vehicles is empirically variable and reflects differences in the referential ecology of the phenomena with which we deal. In some cases we have few problems: in *The Expression of the Emotions in Man and Animals,* for instance, Darwin (1872) noted the cross-cultural uniformity with which we interpret certain facial gestures. Within the domain of expressive phenomena, these would be good bets upon which to construct the sort of translational bridge referred to earlier. Many other phenomena, however, are of contested or enigmatic meaning—perhaps the specific smile of the Mona Lisa could serve as an example—and would be poor bets in terms of their translational serviceability. In fact these latter are in many ways similar to Aubrey's apparitions: they are often irregular and unpredictable in their occurrence, visible only to certain spectators, and apt to suffer attenuation of sorts upon closer (perhaps "deconstructive") inspection. Yet, quite in contrast to the case with mainstream science, cultural investigators frequently gravitate to these phenomena and the niche they define, finding the latter's intractability compensated for by its fascination. A space is thus established for virtuoso endeavor.

No doubt this way of putting things sounds a bit strange initially, yet it only redescribes familiar features of our experience. Referential competence and the explanatory success that can eventually grow from it are things we can have more or less of, as ultimately revealed in the ease or difficulty we have coping pragmatically with the world. Limited competence causes us to behave clumsily, suffer misunderstandings, be surprised by events, and fail to predict outcomes beyond chance. Yet with these difficulties comes an opening for enchantment: our very awkwardness can suggest powers or principles at work that are not just beyond our ken but quite possibly of another order. In contrast, where we are fully competent not only does our awkwardness disappear, but the enchantment along with it. The ease with which we negotiate the world and our failure to be surprised by its behavior underscore the ultimate intelligibility of the circumstances in which we live. Whether or not the assumptions that allow us to operate deftly are "true" in any ultimate sense, the facility they afford us indicates they work. Hence our compe-

6. A broad-ranging consideration of the problems of meaning as an object of inquiry will be found in Wuthnow (1987).

tence is defined pragmatically and is symmetric with disenchantment. Where well developed, it does not allow for things like apparitions.

Differences in referential ecology, then, are a factor in our problem—but not the only one. These differences both influence and are influenced by the social organization of inquiry. The products of inquiry in general—reports about the world—are always too many and too mutually contradictory to allow a stable and coherent picture of that world to develop. Without the organizational capacity to manage the glut and distinguish warranted from unwarranted reports, the systematic exploitation of referential ecologies so as to explain their constitutive phenomena would be severely handicapped. Yet communities vary in the extent to which they are organized for this purpose and thus in their ability to discriminate on the basis of relative warrant. Think of peasant communities, in which reports of prodigies and monstrosities are common, and presumably serve as a form of cultural capital.[7] Of course in peasant societies (as today) prodigies rarely occur in one's own community; rather, they usually are found beyond a radius marking the limits of customary travel. Nothing happens *here*, but much to marvel at goes on in the next-village-but-one.[8] This phenomenon, locally plausible but impossible as a generality, is easily understood in terms of the geographical limits of social control over information. Assuming that peasants are individually no more credulous than we are and have just as much to gain from discrediting hyperbole, they are nevertheless often prevented from doing so by the narrow spatial scope of their experience. Consequently, unusual events can easily suffer inflation as they travel (or be manufactured out of whole cloth), since the capacity of eyewitnesses to monitor retellings decreases with distance. The profusion of prodigies in peasant societies is thus partly a function of structural limits to their systems of

7. This was true at the elite as well as the popular level in the seventeenth century. As Park and Daston (1981:39) have noted, the "wonder books" of the period purveyed material "prized for its social as well as its intellectual benefits." In them a reader might find "accounts of storms, earthquakes, floods, volcanoes, and a selection of the most famous monsters of the day"—all of which could be used as conversational prestige items illustrating, as one guide had it, "the passages and occurrences of the world, the creatures thereof, and the casualties therein."

8. Examples from Mexico will be found in Foster (1967:113–114). The social location of prodigies in modern industrial society has not to our knowledge been much studied, but a casual inspection of the tabloids that report them suggests similar principles may be at work. At least for those published in the United States, many reports are of oddities occurring in Europe or South America (see also Bogdan 1988). Of course there may be alternative explanations for this, but it does correspond with the peripheral origins of phenomena like psychic surgery. For an interesting example of differences between first and second or third worlds in this regard, see Hess (1991).

communication: it is not so much that inflationary pressures are built in—this is true universally—as that brakes upon them are lacking. In fact, reflecting back on Aubrey's credulity, it is not unlikely that we see a similar structural limit exerting some influence. In any event, wherever the capacity to exercise social control over reports is weak—which is to say the more autonomous the conditions in which they are produced—the prospect of enchantment is enhanced.[9]

In the traditional view of the development of disciplines, consensus over the standards for warranting reports and the authority to enforce them are normally seen as outgrowths of referential competence. The better our reports and construals, in this view, the greater our agreement over them, as well as over the methods that produced them. An important contribution of the so-called strong program in the sociology of science, however, has been to suggest that the direction of influence is sometimes the reverse: social control, exercised through disciplinary organization, is perhaps responsible for the development of (what appears as) referential competence in the first place.[10] One instance in which this may have been the case is the growth of modern medicine. During the latter half of the nineteenth century, high-status physicians used the standards of scientificity associated with universities to discredit the practices of their competitors, despite an inability to demonstrate any association between scientificity and increased medical competence (see R. Collins 1979; also Starr 1982). This came only later, when the norms adjudicating claims to medical knowledge had already changed. Thus one can plausibly suggest that the slowly increasing referential competence of doctors around the turn of the century was less a cause than an effect of a disciplinary consensus that had its origins in the status concerns of the wealthier practitioners and was brought about only by an efficient political campaign for monopoly control over medical services.

Despite occasional problems in determining the direction of influence, however, we can say that enchantment results from an interplay

9. David Hess (1991) also finds generally weak control mechanisms among intellectuals involved in the Brazilian "science" of spiritism, which views many personal problems and ailments as caused by the malign influence of "obsessing" spirits.

10. The recognition that disciplinary consensus is partly a function of social control has led some strong programers (e.g. Woolgar 1988) to argue it might be entirely independent of referential competence. Other strong programers allow referential competence to exercise some constraint. For an appealing presentation of the strong program, see Bloor (1991); for a balanced analysis of the possible referential independence of science in light of a particular scientific controversy, see Rudwick (1985:439–445); and for a discussion and critique of the strong program, see Roth (1987).

between, on the one hand, certain niches in our referential ecology and our want of pragmatic competence in dealing with them, and, on the other, our organizational incapacity to discriminate between more and less reputable reports, that is, to reward skepticism if warranted. Where referential incompetence and credulity (or "open-mindedness") are combined, phenomena are encountered that behave so wonderfully and mysteriously as to raise the prospect of an order as yet unfathomed, familiarity with which would fundamentally alter our understanding of the world.[11] Of course the matter is by no means this simple, but a rough sketch of this sort gives us a preliminary sense of the location of enchantment, as well as a viewpoint on it which has the specific advantage of revealing similarities between various of its manifestations. Returning to our subject now, we can simply suggest that where culture behaves like Aubrey's apparition—as a function both of referential ecology and the organization of inquiry—we should expect it to be enchanted.

It remains to be noted that reports on enchanted phenomena have to be made in particular "epistemic registers," a term we introduce to mark distinctions customarily made between, for instance, the "fictional" and the "factual," or between the imaginative on the one hand and the instrumental on the other. None of the traditional ways of putting this are entirely satisfactory, but we need some distinction capable of recognizing that if Aubrey had only "made up" his miscellanies and frankly admitted this, their power to enchant would evaporate. This power depends upon our conviction that what is being reported could be encountered in a very practical way—if not exactly as Dr. Johnson's foot encountered a stone, then in some other sense "unavoidably." Had we been at the right spot at the right time, for instance, we presumably would have encountered Aubrey's Cyrencester apparition. This restriction is necessary because where no referential claim is being made, our pragmatic competence is simply not challenged—and only where competence is challenged is a sense of wonder evoked.

Note that the issue is not whether reports are in fact empirically warranted—research in the sociology of science (e.g. H. M. Collins 1985) has shown how difficult this may be to establish—but only whether we are invited to bring the machinery of empirical warrant into play.[12] This

11. We should add "and vice versa" here: where mysterious and wonderful phenomena are normally encountered, referential incompetence and open-mindedness (or "credulity") will be high.

12. Even the more relativist proponents of the strong program in the sociology of science, who question the "factual" bases for the resolution of scientific disputes (and

seems a simple matter, but like many issues of "tone," it is occasionally quite difficult to decide. Present-day virtuosi, as we shall see, often prefer to leave their epistemic registers ambiguous, putting us in doubt as to how their claims are to be taken. In part this is because the nature of the niche with which they are concerned often makes straightforward substantiation even more difficult than usual. Apparitions, to cite an analogy, simply *appear;* they cannot readily be summoned. Thus as a purely practical matter, enchanted reports must forestall requests of the *hic Rhodus, hic salta* variety—which are grossly insensitive to the character of the niche in which their subject resides. But, just as clearly, the generic legitimacy of requests for demonstration must be recognized as well, at least if suspicions of pure fictionality are to be forestalled. The difficulty here is finessed sometimes by obscuring one's epistemic register and hoping that questions about it will not arise, and sometimes by arguing that enchanted reports are indeed referential, but of a character that allows one to ignore normal standards of evidence. In this case special dispensation is sought; but whichever option is taken, some room for maneuver is generated in dealing with requests for warrant.

Suppose for the sake of convenience we call an epistemic register inviting requests for empirical demonstration a "naturalistic" one.[13] Again, the issue is not whether such requests can be satisfied—the phenomena with which we are concerned may not easily permit this—but whether they are welcome in principle. People who use this register would prefer to deal with doubting Thomases by producing the phenomenon in question and allowing it to be palpated (though, admittedly, they are often unable to: see again H. M. Collins 1985). Yet there are many phenomena for which empirical strategies are inappropriate—moral or aesthetic ones, for instance—and about which one would thus warrant claims quite differently. We can think of these as forming a residual category where phenomena not suitable to naturalistic treatment reside, but it will help to give it a name. Borrowing from Richard Rorty

thus of their warrant), agree that the overall practices and procedures of warrant in the sciences, though ultimately rhetorical, differ substantially from those in non-naturalistic disciplines.

13. We cannot stress too much that by "naturalistic inquiry" we mean something much broader than mainstream natural science. It is at work as much in putting your hand out the window to see if it is raining as in investigating ion channels in a cell; and as much in North American parapsychology as in standard social sciences. As suggested in n. 12, forms of naturalistic inquiry show family resemblances in their general strategies for warranting claims—resemblances that remain real even when one questions (e.g. Shapin and Schaffer 1985) the "sleight of hand" through which they produce "facts."

(1979), we will designate such phenomena "edifying."[14] Though not trouble free, these terms have conveniences that will become apparent later. They differentiate between various strategies we use to warrant claims about the world. Those that are meant to be edifying, for instance, can be challenged as perverse, internally inconsistent, trite, and so on, but we do not ask naturalistic warrant for them.

(Unfortunately, "edifying" carries a slightly pejorative connotation through its use in phrases like "merely edifying." We follow Rorty, however, in insisting that edifying knowledge is indispensable to our lives and coeval with naturalistic knowledge. Though the emphases of our argument may occasionally make it seem "scientistic," it is not—as will become more apparent in chapter 6.)

Returning to our broader concerns, we would now say that for best effect reports on enchanted phenomena—the substance of what we might call "enchanted discourse"—have to be in a naturalistic register.[15] Yet this register will often prove uncomfortable: practically speaking, enchanted phenomena often behave so quirkily that the idea of accumulating naturalistic evidence for them seems quite foolhardy. This difficulty may encourage us to conceive of registers in which we underscore our *desire* to assemble naturalistic evidence, but find no fair and reasonable way to do so. Or we may retreat further from naturalistic criteria, suggesting that our reports should not be subject to them, and yet still be permitted a naturalistic register. Possibly they could be assessed in terms of the standards we use for edifying discourse, while their impact would occur in the naturalistic domain. For instance, they could be judged by "hermeneutic" criteria—in terms, say, of their "insight" or capacity to "make sense" of things—and nevertheless assume a place alongside naturalistic reports as over against edifying ones. This sugges-

---

14. We note that Rorty's primary concern is to oppose edifying discourse to systematic philosophy, and switching the disjunction to one between edifying and naturalistic discourse has consequences of which he would likely not approve. Rorty also associates edifying discourse with "revolutionary" discourse in naturalistic disciplines, but we see no reason to view it this way: it should be quite possible to have edification in a "normal" as well as in a "revolutionary" mode.

15. This is not a matter of fiat but a consequence of the psychology of enchantment: again, where we are confronted with no pragmatic difficulties—where no lacunae in our competence are identified—the prospect of another order at work simply is not raised. And incompetence can only be demonstrated to us through our failure to explain or predict how the world works. This happens, however, only in a naturalistic mode, since edifying discourse does not explain or predict. Any enchantment to be found in it must therefore be metaphysical (and thus pragmatically avoidable). As we shall argue in chapter 6, this is not to diminish the "reality" of metaphysical enchantment (which it has been the purpose of "deconstruction" to explore), but only its coercive purchase upon us.

tion, cases of which we will meet shortly, has been hazarded more and more by today's virtuosi as those who police naturalistic registers (e.g. Grunbaum 1984) have become more aggressive.

To secure an ambiguous register that combines features of both edifying and naturalistic discourse has thus been an aim of contemporary virtuosi. Of late, for instance, this problem has received increasing attention from proponents of so-called interpretive social science. Despite its attractions and despite the influential work done under its aegis, however, it is open to several criticisms. From a naturalistic viewpoint, the special dispensation sought here seems a license for mischief: it permits problems to be discovered where none perhaps exist and thus diminishes our hard-won referential competence, awakening suspicions of mystification. From an edifying viewpoint, on the other hand, such an ambiguous register seems needlessly confined by its referential ambitions. In those modes of edification where claims are assessed simply for the play of imagination involved, for instance, these ambitions can act as a drag, just as programmatic realism in literature can eventually seem stultifying. Thus from either viewpoint ambiguity here yields a troubled product: it is, so to speak, either poor science or tepid edification—a sort of epistemic "near beer." Perhaps this is simply the fate of enchanted discourse today.

However this may be, we can now conclude that in addition to flowing from the conjunction of a particular referential terrain with certain features of social organization, enchantment requires as well an epistemic register that is either directly naturalistic or ambiguous in the sense outlined above. When all three—terrain, organization, and register—are right, the result is enchanted discourse—a way of construing the world that generates marvel.

We have argued this too long in the abstract, however, and must now turn to a few examples that will illustrate it. We draw these from different disciplines so as to exemplify the variety of niches in which enchantment occurs, as well as some similarities among them. They come from two scholars—Oliver Sacks, a neurologist, and Charles Taylor, a political philosopher—chosen for specific reasons: Sacks because of his unusual popular influence (see Kael 1991), and Taylor because the particular essay we will examine has acquired the status of a foundational document for the interpretive study of culture (see Rabinow and Sullivan 1979, 1987). Two notes of caution before we begin, however. The first is that because Sacks and Taylor are important and because we wish to do them justice, our treatment will be moderately detailed and thus a bit slow to develop: some patience is required. The second is that to identify some discourse as enchanted does not mean it will suddenly appear as odd as Aubrey's, while only the moment before having appeared commonplace. The "oddness" of *Miscellanies* is a product of the disenchantment of the general terrain in which Aubrey labored, and the examples we take up will appear similarly quaint only if and when the terrain they investigate has been successfully colonized by naturalistic inquiry. Barring this, enchanted discourse merely presents one way of looking at the world among others, and we no more think it odd than Aubrey would have thought meteors implausible. In other words, the prejudicial component to our phenomenon, which makes us feel superior to the credulous, is an artifact of the progress of knowledge, and where this has not occurred enchantment is both more pristine and less remarkable. In this circumstance it envelops us without our being aware, exploiting a credulity that is indistinguishable from open-mindedness. Nonetheless it *is* identifiable, as our first example will show.

This comes from a field—neuropathology—that will at first seem distant from our interest in culture. Yet it is not, and has the added advantage of showing that virtuoso inquiry, if rare in the more mature sciences, is occasionally present where these address the interface between nature and culture. In the work of Oliver Sacks a bent in this regard is consistently and vividly expressed—and has proved to be of quite unusual appeal.[16] In two sets of case studies (1974, 1985), he has chronicled the startling, bizarre, and often tragic consequences of neurological deficit—as well as the sometimes equally tragic consequences of its treatment. In *Awakenings*, for instance, Sacks describes the effects of administering L-dopa to patients who were victims of parkinsonism pursuant to *encephalitis lethargica* (sleeping sickness), a disease epidemic in the early part of this century. Many of these men and women were profoundly handicapped by their condition, with bodies frozen, extremities deformed, and both cognitive and affective lives muted. Some had been thus stricken for as long as forty years. Upon administration of L-dopa, they "unfroze," experiencing sudden liberation from the prisons in which their neurological disorder had locked them. In most cases, however, this liberation gradually devolved into a manic, tic-ridden existence so threatening that treatment had to be discontinued, whereupon an even more profound paralysis ensued.

Reflecting on these striking "awakenings" and the quite extraordinary experiences his patients had undergone, Sacks (1974:194) characterizes L-dopa therapy as: "the most enchanting of subjects, as dra-

16. *Awakenings*, for instance, had several radio and stage adaptations, among them one by Harold Pinter, before serving as the basis for Penny Marshall's successful movie by the same name. The essay "The Man Who Mistook His Wife for a Hat" served as the basis for an opera, which itself later became a movie (see Kael 1991).

matic, and tragic, and comic as any. My own feelings, when I first saw the effects of L-dopa, were of amazement and wonder, and almost of awe. Each passing day increased my amazement, disclosing new phenomena, novelties, strangenesses, whole worlds of being whose possibility I had never dreamt of." This statement could stand as paradigmatic for our subject: in Sacks's case L-dopa has been a key to a new realm of phenomena whose generative principles are obscure to him but whose workings are, in the old-fashioned sense of the term, wonderful. We need to be precise, however, about just what these phenomena are, for if we read carefully we notice that Sacks is not amazed by events at the neurological level—here the effect of L-dopa, though by no means well understood, is similar to temporarily repairing a short-circuit—but at the experiential one, where they are felt and lived. The "whole worlds of being" that fascinate him are not those of the nervous system, but rather those in which his patients come to live in result of their condition. These are worlds of unusual experiences rather than of strange physiological goings-on; of experiences that are tied together so as to constitute a unique modality of being (or *idioculture*) we can understand only second-hand because of our own neurological normality. In sum, it is the extraordinary oddness of his patients' *worlds,* and not the peculiarities of their physical condition, that awakens in Sacks the sense of enchantment. In this circumstance he is more like an anthropologist astonished by the habits of an exotic tribe than a physical scientist baffled by the improbable behavior of matter.

This is true as well of Sacks's later encounters with patients afflicted with right-brain abnormalities. Like the visual agnosia that allowed one patient to confuse his wife's head with his hat, these abnormalities cast people into life worlds that can only seem deeply foreign to us. Such benighted individuals can be thought of, Sacks (1985:xv) suggests, as "travellers to unimaginable lands—lands of which otherwise we should have no idea or conception. This is why their lives and journeys seem to me to have a quality of the fabulous." It is not just that they have traveled in exotic experiential climes, however; they have "gone native" as well, and incorrigibly so. Consequently they are often unable even to recognize those peculiarities in their activity that make them appear so profoundly other. To imagine our way into their skins, to be able to grasp even momentarily what it "means" to be them, would be a singular adventure, comparable in many ways to being transmogrified into another species: as Sacks notes, the behavior with which we are confronted is sometimes "positively Martian."

In neuropathology, then, Sacks has discovered engines of otherness always potentially within ourselves. Between being who we are and "being" some creature perhaps quite alien, there lies only a brain lesion, a tumor, or an imbalance of neurotransmitters. In each case the cause, if still little understood, seems incommensurate with the effect: a simple lesion on the one side; an incomprehensible transformation of experience on the other. The former can be understood by the standard methods of science, but the latter seems quite beyond them. For Sacks, this points to a flaw in science itself, for it is unable to deal with the phenomenology of illness, to enter into the existential world where the alien actually resides.[17] This leaves him in some perplexity, however, as to the epistemic location of his subject matter: does it belong to neurology or philosophy, science or metaphysics?[18]

This confusion is instructive. If Sacks manages to project a vivid a sense of mystery and of uncharted realms, it is in part because the phenomena in question appear at first so firmly situated within "nature." They are "out there" and quite unavoidably confronting us, rather in the way we are confronted by disease. Such a large portion of his analysis employs the terminology of conventional neurology that we are apt to assume his fascination is with phenomena of this sort—physical pathologies on the one hand and their behavioral manifestations on the other—whereas what has captivated him actually belongs in the domain of philosophical anthropology. For the issue soon becomes not what it *is* to be sick in the exotic fashion of his patients—in principle this could be exhaustively cataloged by the sort of science Sacks finds inadequate—but rather what it *means* or *feels like* to be so stricken, which may be another thing entirely. At any rate, the latter domain is one in which our referential competence proves thoroughly problematic.

Perhaps we can best illustrate this with a specific example from Sacks—that of the calculating twins (1985:195–213). Like many other investigators, he was fascinated by these idiots savants with unusual

17. His prosecution of conventional neurology in this light is quite vigorous: conventional neurology is guilty of "folly," a part of the "madness of the last three centuries . . . which reduces men to machines, automata, puppets, dolls, blank tablets, formulae, ciphers, systems, and reflexes . . . [and] which has rendered so much of our recent and current medical literature unfruitful, unreadable, inhuman, and unreal" (1974:191).

18. Sacks originally argued (1974:191) for a reformed, phenomenological neurology open to the metaphysical domain, because "although the workings of the world never contravene mechanical considerations, they only make *sense,* and become fully intelligible, in the light of metaphysical considerations." But in a later essay on color vision (Sacks and Wasserman 1987:32), he wonders whether "the experience, the phenomenon, of color can ever be explained (or explained away) by physiology or science: it retains a mystery, a wonder, that seems inaccessible." Yet if the "experience" of color belongs in the same general domain as the experiences of neuropathology—and it seems to—then this would put both similarly beyond the bounds of naturalistic description and thus of science.

powers of recall and calendrical abilities. (They could, for instance, easily determine the date on which Easter would fall for any year in the past or future.) During an interview with them he was startled when, a box of matches having spilled, they both immediately registered their number—one hundred and eleven—and saw this as a multiple of thirty-seven, though they could not possibly have counted them in the time elapsed and were further "incapable" of multiplication or division. Deeply puzzled, Sacks queried them as to how their discernment operated, but found them unable to shed much light on the matter. Later, in writing about the problem, he tries out various analogies, attempting to fathom what it could be the twins "saw" that we can't, but as the metaphors grow more conjectural we gradually understand that he has no positive image of what passed before their minds. The subject of his inquiry, which is the twins' experience of "one-hundred-and-elevenness" in a clump of matches, can never really be made present. He has been able to acquire, in other words, almost no referential competence with regard to it.

Thus what it means or feels like to be the twins remains a matter of somewhat distant conjecture. Had we the tools to analyze the brain structures responsible for their remarkable feats, we might discover that these are different from ours—that the twins are, so to speak, differently "wired." Yet this neurological knowledge would give us no clue as to the nature of their experience. And here a deflating thought is apt to intrude: the twins could be differently (at least more powerfully) wired for visually discerning quantity—rather as a bloodhound's nose and brain are more powerfully wired for discerning smells—without their experience of visual "insight" being any different from our own. We are all able to "see" the number of matches in a relatively small clump, after all, and presumably do this by an intuitive judgment that operates beneath awareness. Need it be different for the twins? Need the quantitative superiority of their performance be reflected in a qualitative difference in their experience? Not at all—though if this were the case it would lessen our enchantment, our sense that the twins are unfathomably weird. So it turns out that, being demanded whether alien or not, these curious creatures prove no more forthcoming than Aubrey's spirit—a difficulty that often bedevils the hunt for the Other in philosophical anthropology.[19]

19. After this was written, David Perlmutter published a review of Sacks's new book *Seeing Voices: a journey into the world of the deaf* (1989) that arrives at conclusions similar to ours. He writes (1991:72) that "astounded by its 'unique linguistic use of space,' Sacks saw ASL [American Sign Language] as a miracle different in kind from any oral language. Analysis of its structure [however] could have made this perception of differentness give

The same criticism could be leveled at most of Sacks's case studies: in the end we find that the very experiential foreignness responsible for our sense of wonder proves elusive, behaving in some respects like an apparition. It exists in a difficult referential niche, and we can see in Sacks's work how this has both limited his competence and encouraged him to adopt an ambiguous register, couched between neurology and metaphysics, in which to present his reports. Held to naturalistic standards, his interpretations would prove difficult to substantiate, while offered purely to edify, they would be insubstantial—a sort of science fiction. With these registers played off against each other, however, "positively Martian" states of being can be empathically encountered and written about for a general audience—one not organizationally equipped (unlike neuroscience and the scientific community more widely) to evaluate the result.[20] It seems, then, that referential ecology, organizational milieu, and epistemic register cooperate here to produce enchantment, and in this respect Sacks's collections of case studies nicely illustrate our thesis about its origins—while their unusual popular reception illustrates its appeal.

Indeed, in their function and reception they recall the "wonder books" of the sixteenth and seventeenth centuries. As Park and Daston (1981:37–39) have written: "Much of the wonder literature shows strong affinities to the popular sixteenth-century genre of *divers leçons*. . . . [B]ooks concentrated on fields of general interest, like medicine, natural history and geography [that] tried to render their material more palatable by singling out extraordinary or astounding effects, often including monsters." Monsters, in Sacks's collections, have been replaced by Martian states of being, but with no less astounding result. And just as wonder books promised to elevate their readers above popular ignorance without the expense and boredom of scholarship, Sacks's efforts consistently inform, entertain, and startle while pointing out the dryness and sterility of traditional science.

way to a deeper appreciation of the ways it is like oral languages." Perlmutter analyzes in detail the assumptions which cause Sacks to conclude the signing deaf are "other" in their use and experience of language.

20. Some of these conventions have been brought into play in reviews of Sacks's books in science journals. While these are uniformly appreciative, they make a variety of criticisms. With regard to Sacks's second collection, for instance, they point out that he (1) is concerned with the phenomenology of illness and not neurology proper; (2) is either surprisingly ignorant of the literature or, more likely, playing neurological *faux-naif* for dramatic purposes; (3) is often given to contentious interpretations; and (4) consistently romanticizes the pathological. See, among others, Sutherland (1985), Brandt (1987), and Newman (1987).

In one respect, however, they are not entirely satisfactory for our purposes, since the supposedly exotic life worlds occasioned by neurological disorder, while taxing our empathic powers, pose no great challenge to our overall pragmatic competence. One way or the other, we are little affected by whether the twins are truly "alien" or not, with the consequence that the whole subject is apt to be dismissed as a curiosity. Certainly it seems pale when compared to features of Aubrey's landscape or the wonder books, many of which would shatter the foundational assumptions by which we live our lives. To make our case it would be nice to have an example both as exotic and as challenging as an apparition. But recall that the latter's effect for us results in large part from the disenchantment of the terrain it occupied; and that though an apparition posed certain pragmatic difficulties for Aubrey, it by no means challenged his understanding of the world in the way it would ours. By the same token, enchanted phenomena that today *do* pose pragmatic difficulties for us are often encountered simply as unusual but at the same time rather unremarkable features of our world. Appreciating their true strangeness would require that we shed the some of the conventions that make the world seem normal to us in the first place. To *really* sense the peculiarity of our own circumstances, in other words, we would first have to defamiliarize them—a trick not easy to accomplish. Nevertheless, we will try to isolate in our next example both its occult dimension and its fundamental challenge to our picture of the world.

Whereas Oliver Sacks is interested in what it means or feels like to participate in the idiocultures of his patients, political philosopher Charles Taylor has drawn our attention to phenomena occurring within the realm of "intersubjective meaning."[21] By this he refers not to those beliefs and dispositions of which the individual members of a society are aware or which they could be caused to articulate through questioning, but rather to ideas so foundational to and constitutive of a society's articulated values that they exist and function beneath awareness. Intersubjective meanings thus comprise a sort of collective unconscious and are taken for granted in everyday experience, functioning in this regard like Kantian categories, organizing and giving meaning to our experience, though with the difference that they are less abstract and more given to change, varying from time to time and from one society to another. So hidden are the workings of intersubjective meanings, Taylor argues, that should social scientists seek to investigate them by empirical

21. Taylor's essay "Interpretation and the Sciences of Man," originally published in *The Review of Metaphysics* in 1971, is reprinted in Rabinow and Sullivan (1979), which will be cited in the text.

means the project would necessarily fail: they cannot be teased out of individual consciousness because they are the background of all perception and experience in a society. Without them it would be impossible even to imagine the practices and articulated values of the society in question. Thus they can be supposed "real" even though they do not show up in the sorts of data that commonly warrant findings in naturalistic disciplines (which today have a near monopoly over the definition of the real). Reflective intuition, however, equipped with knowledge of various cultures and ages, can infer their presence, so Taylor argues, by mapping the temporal and geographical boundaries of intelligibility, that is, the borderlines at which the practices or values of a particular culture become opaque to its neighbors.

Such a mapping, he suggests, would be one objective of a hermeneutic social science aimed at comprehending the workings of intersubjective meaning and, through this, of society in general. Like a book whose rationale is unclear to us, social events can remain confusing until the application of insight reveals plausible relations among them, thus giving them sense. For instance, certain phenomena of the sixties—to wit, the "strains in contemporary society, the breakdown of civility, the rise of deep alienation, which [was] translated into even more destructive action" ([1971] 1979:61)—proved enigmatic not just to society at large, but to the social scientists of the period. The narrow regard of the latter, confined as they were by empiricist methodological strictures, prevented them from identifying the sources of these events in the domain of intersubjective meaning. To track these down, Taylor provides us with a historical perspective on the meanings which underlie our own culture.

These are in part constituted, he argues ([1971] 1979:58), by the values and imagery of "the society of work," that is to say:

the vision of society as a large-scale enterprise of production in which widely different functions are integrated into interdependence; a vision of society in which economic relations are considered as primary, as it [sic] is not only in Marxism . . . but above all with the tradition of Classical Utilitarianism. In line with this vision there is a fundamental solidarity between all members of society that labor . . . for they are all engaged in producing what is indispensible to life and happiness in far-reaching interdependence.

This vision, Taylor argues ([1971] 1979:59), "presided over the integration of the working class into industrial democracies," while at the same time functioning "polemically against the 'unproductive' classes." So fundamental was this conceptual and evaluative matrix that it marked the temporal and geographical border of the civilization of the industrial revolution. But two decades ago something went wrong with this matrix, though this failed to register on mainstream political science, which saw in the period's turmoil merely individual pathology, rather than, as Taylor does ([1971] 1979:62), "a malady of society itself, a malaise which afflicts its constitutive meanings":

No one can claim to begin to have an adequate explanation for these major changes which our civilization is undergoing. But in contrast to the incapacity of a science which remains within the accepted categories, a hermeneutical science of man which has a place for a study of intersubjective meanings can at least begin to explore fruitful avenues. Plainly the discipline which was integral to the civilization of work and bargaining is beginning to fail. The structures of this civilization, interdependent work, bargaining, mutual adjustment of individual ends, are beginning to change their meaning for many, and are beginning to be felt not as normal and best suited to man, but as hateful or empty.

Thus the vision of a world of labor, which at its inauguration could symbolize a radical break with the past as well as a promise for the future, and which continued into the sixties to marshal the energies of our civilization, was beginning to fail. Why? Taylor suggests that such a vision could only serve as a basis for community and discipline in the process of its realization. By dynamics that sound rather Spenglerian, once its promise of a general accumulation of wealth had been satisfied, a sort of decay set in: the material and moral ambitions of the society of work "could only sustain man as a goal, not a reality." There was, then, a sort of teleological necessity in this: achieving the goal compromised the values that made its discipline meaningful in the first place, with results seen first in the disaffection of the young, who were (in 1971 at any rate) experiencing "an identity crisis of frightening proportions" ([1971] 1979:63). Potentially, then, the turmoil of the sixties "meant" the demise of the old cultural order, just as it heralded some new world of intersubjective meanings on the horizon.

We should pause here briefly to reflect on the character of this report and on the challenge to us it poses. Somewhere at a level beneath everyday consciousness but above Kantian structures of perception, Taylor has discerned a realm of phenomena which, in the present case at least, is subject to a Spenglerian dynamic whose effects run broad and deep. If an understanding of plate tectonics allows us to grasp the pattern to and causes behind earthquakes, midocean trenches, the Rift Valley, and so on, an understanding of intersubjective meanings reveals a deep pattern in otherwise obscure sociopolitical events. Taylor's hypotheses are so inconspicuously stated and presented so plausibly that we are apt to ignore both how challenging and how extraordinary they are. Yet Aubrey, for instance, might find the notion that political change is an effect of dynamics internal to "intersubjective meaning" as difficult to countenance as we find his Blows Invisible. Certainly it would not easily connect with his matrix of assumptions about how the world works. We are apt to take this as a measure of our superiority to him, and yet Taylor's "intersubjective meaning" behaves in most respects, as we shall see, like the occult subjects of Aubrey's research.

Though Taylor's diagnosis of the sixties perhaps appears dubious today, our concern is not with whether his discoveries proved true, but rather with the nature of the referential niche he explored. For, as we might expect, this was quite difficult to probe and populated by highly unstable phenomena. It was difficult to probe because the phenomena involved—intersubjective meanings—were defined so as to be unobservable by empirical means. Though happenings within this realm indeed leave traces that are part of our common experience (as was, for instance, the turmoil referred to above), and though some rough cartographic sense can be made of it by determining the boundaries of cultural intelligibility, what goes on there is always a matter of somewhat protracted inference. Furthermore, hermeneutic science has as yet developed no norms to ensure that its inferences are systematic and apt to meet with broad acceptance. In fact, Taylor suggests ([1971] 1979:66–67) that the process is "unformalizable," and goes on to note that

this is a scandalous result according to the authoritative conception of science in our tradition. . . . For it means that this is not a study in which anyone can engage, regardless of their level of insight; that some claims of the form "If you don't understand, then your intuitions are at fault, are blind or inadequate," some claims of this form will be justified; that some differences will be nonarbitrable by further evidence, but that each side can only make appeal to deeper insight on the part of the other.

There is, then, no more reason to expect agreement about readings of intersubjective meaning than there is about readings of literary texts. Referential competence is thus quite meager, a difficulty compounded by the fact that intersubjective meaning behaves in unpredictable ways: it is, Taylor suggests, an "open system" as little given to consistency as the weather—apt not just to change quite unexpectedly, but so radically as to alter the very terms in which it must be understood.[22] Thus, both because the subject matter of hermeneutic science behaves so capriciously and because hypotheses with regard to it are thoroughly context

---

22. This seems somewhat at odds, for reasons Taylor does not explicate, with his perception of long-term stability in and an organismic dynamic to the "society of work."

dependent, predictions are not in the offing. On the other hand, "*ex post* understanding" is, Taylor claims, to be expected.

Granted the problematic nature of his referential niche, it is not surprising that Taylor, like Sacks, falls into an ambiguous register when couching his program for hermeneutic science. His use of the term "science" here, combined with his consistent prosecution of conventional social science as narrow and sterile—which seems to indicate they are competing over roughly similar territory—suggests that his hermeneutic insights might be meant naturalistically. As if to emphasize this, he proposes a pragmatic function for them, since his "principle claim is that *we can only come to grips with* this phenomenon of [cultural] breakdown by trying to understand more clearly and profoundly the . . . intersubjective meanings of the society in which we have been living" ([1971] 1979:64, emphasis added). Like a medical diagnosis, hermeneutic vision reveals to us the causes of the cultural disorder whose symptoms vexed us; and, thus equipped, we might be better able to respond to it. Evidently, then, Taylor is exploiting rhetorical markers that customarily designate naturalistic discourse.

So clearly do his hypotheses appear to belong in this domain that we are apt to be confused when he insists just as clearly that they do not: for, as we have already noted, no observational data are permitted to bear on their validity, which must be judged within the hermeneutic circle. Thus though "the ideal of a science of verification is to find an appeal beyond differences of interpretation. . . . [A] hermeneutic science cannot but rely on insight. It requires that one have the sensibility and understanding necessary to be able to make and comprehend the readings by which we can explain the reality concerned" ([1971] 1979:66). The criterion here is the "depth" of the reading, not its capacity to survive efforts at verification, and real depth can only be evaluated by those with the broadest and most discerning sensibilities. Indeed, this is just what we would expect of insights presented to us for their capacity to edify, yet if we take Taylor's this way, the great civilizational divide he discovered in the sixties is robbed of an important basis for the compliment of "factuality" that would give it purchase on us. Taylor's argument thus seems to encounter an epistemic dilemma.

However this might be resolved, let us assume we have defamiliarized Taylor's findings enough to make their enchantment apparent. So fundamental are the phenomena involved that, were he right, culture and society themselves might well be enchanted and quite inexplicable by empirical means. Thus, far more than with Sacks's investigation of experiential meaning among neuropaths, our referential competence is being challenged, for if the intersubjective realm is fundamental, and is governed by mechanisms at once Spenglerian and unpredictable, then we shall clearly be in the sway of powers whose workings we can glimpse, but whose nature will ultimately remain obscure to us. Indeed, since we become aware of these powers only through their impact on the body social, and find their sources occulted, we face here a quite rigorous analogue, albeit applied to the collectivity, of the Blows Invisible Aubrey chronicled in *Miscellanies*. Just as some of his unfortunate contemporaries were subject to beatings by invisible agents, the investigation of which required special powers, we are prey to unpredictable social injury at the hands of invisible processes investigable only by hermeneutic insight, and then only after the fact. Both the formal and the substantive similarities here are quite striking, as is the equanimity with which the phenomena are recounted. (Though readers may instinctively view the comparison as damaging to Taylor, they might better see it as diminishing the distance between ourselves and Aubrey.)

Thus enchanted events perhaps occur no less frequently today than in Aubrey's time, even though they are occasionally reported upon by individuals who do not recognize them as such and who would view Aubrey's own investigations as suspect. The inquiries of Sacks and Taylor illustrate this well, and give us a preliminary sense of where enchantment today resides. Though by no means sharing common ground, the niches they have chosen show intriguing formal similarities, some of which they share with Aubrey's much more distant terrain. One thing distinguishes between the two investigators, however: whereas Sacks recognizes and celebrates enchantment in the exotic experiences that attract his regard, Taylor does not. In a sense this is odd, because by any criterion Taylor would appear to have encountered as bizarre and certainly more consequential phenomena. On the other hand, Sacks's concerns are highlighted against a successfully naturalized backdrop, while Taylor's are not. Thus just as Aubrey could report one oddity after another without cause for exclamation, having become nonchalant, Taylor's equanimity appears undisturbed under what one must consider extreme provocation. We should wonder whether this is not itself symptomatic, for despite his complaints about the hegemony of "verificationist" social sciences, there appears to be not only space for his inquiry, but an interpretive community that finds little startling about it.[23] Moreover, the generic attraction of such research has been felt not

23. There is significant (though by no means general) acceptance in the social sciences of the sort of "critical theory" represented in Taylor's essay—as in the work of (among others) Habermas and Foucault. (For a recent compendium of such "antiverifi-

just broadly but, as later chapters will show, by the most influential students of culture writing today. All have been similarly fascinated by an investigative milieu defined by the very evasiveness and irregularity of the phenomena that constitute it. We can grant that these do not appear quite as magical as Aubrey's Apparition or his Blows Invisible—yet the difference is simply that whereas his favored niche is now very widely thought outré, those of Sacks, Taylor, and the others we shall take up are not.

Of course this still requires a heavy burden of demonstration. Yet if we surveyed interpretive studies of culture, we could assemble a catalog of phenomena surely as curious as Aubrey's. Once again, this will be thought dismissive, but the point is simply that both may be understood to have tackled difficult referential niches, of which Aubrey's has become disreputable. Our analysis cannot escape the similarity and indeed will constantly underline it by playing naturalistic devil's advocate, drawing wonder books and contemporary studies of culture closer together than some readers will find fair: yet a certain skepticism and dogged literalness are unavoidable if we are to create the background against which contemporary enchantment, defamiliarized, can be made to appear. But at the same time a respect for all investigators, whether of the seventeenth century or our own, and a provisional agnosticism about their findings, would seem the best policy.[24]

Our aim, however, is not just to uncover the enchantment in studies of culture, but to show why this is both sociologically and epistemically predictable. As suggested earlier, we need to understand the relation between the referential ecology of culture on the one hand and the way inquiry into it is organized on the other. The ecology depicted in Aubrey's *Miscellanies*, it seems in retrospect, was singularly unpromising—at least if one's aim was scientific explanation. Similarly, it may be that culture is unpromising terrain for disenchantment. But we need note as well that nature in Aubrey's day was the studied by largely autonomous and "undisciplined" investigators—as is culture today. Over the in-

---

cationist" strategies in the social sciences, see Skinner 1985, and for a skeptical review of them, see Crews 1986:159–178.) Taylor's latest work, *Sources of the Self* (1989), has received an unusual welcome in sociology through an appreciation by Craig Calhoun (1991). We join Calhoun in viewing Taylor's ideas as stimulating guides to naturalistic research problems, and second him in hoping Taylor will master his instinctive hostility to such inquiry.

24. Indeed, dogged literalness and skepticism are often taken as marks of respect for the arguments to which they are applied, at least in mature sciences. That they will, in less mature disciplines, often be seen as a manifestation of closed-mindedness is one of the phenomena we would like to explain.

tervening time, as natural philosophy was gradually transformed into today's sciences, it grew to be a more cooperative endeavor very narrowly focused on relatively tractable niches—and employed new mechanisms of social control to guarantee that focus. If it was through increasingly organized and coordinated investigation that the maturing sciences developed a boundary between enchanted and disenchanted domains, it is on the basis of autonomous inquiry that the study of culture today not only remains enchanted but is often unable to recognize itself as such.

There is, then, a sociological component to our topic. We need to understand how the organization of inquiry (and resulting norms) affects ecology—how it favors certain niches at the expense of others. But we need to know how various niches affect organization as well. Aubrey's has not disappeared; it simply is not studied today by mainstream scientists. Neither will Sacks's nor Taylor's, though how and under what organizational conditions they are to be studied has long been a subject of controversy. After all, a sense that culture was somehow distinct from nature caused the *Geisteswissenschaften*—systematic inquiries into the meaning of human activity and cultural products—to develop along methodological and organizational lines different from the natural sciences. Perhaps what links the neo-Kantian architects of these inquiries with contemporary virtuosi like Sacks and Taylor is a continued interest in phenomena that prove inherently resistent to disenchantment. If so, it is clear that the subject of *meaning* will be crucial here, for though they investigate quite different forms of this, Sacks and Taylor join the neo-Kantians in finding it essential to the study of personality, society, and culture.

This conviction has a strong intuitive basis and is broadly shared. The philosopher Thomas Nagel, for instance, has argued in "What Is It Like to Be a Bat?" (1979) that a knowledge of what it means or feels like to be a certain creature would be essential for a full understanding (and thus an adequate explanation) of its activity. This is, in fact, the rationale behind Sacks's phenomenological neurology. Yet from another point of view, argued across a spectrum that links newfangled literary theorists with old-fashioned behaviorists, the desire to unearth *a* meaning (however complex) for a person or a period, *a* sense of what it meant or felt like to be alive in that body or at that time, rests upon a questionable "essentialist" assumption: that what these "meant" could be delimited and described to general satisfaction. This seems plausible, it is argued, only until we try it. Then we find that what appeared to have traceable contours and a determinate content turns out in practice to be variously and unendingly interpretable. So, perhaps, would Taylor's intersubjective meanings, which is why dispute over them, as he confesses, ultimately results in a contest as to whose insight is of greatest interpretive depth. In practice such subjects prove indefinitely figurable, behaving in the end rather like an ignis fatuus. Thus they might be fascinating subjects for edification, but can have only a questionable place in *explaining* a person's actions, not to speak of the transitions between historical eras.

The quandary this leaves us in was referred to earlier: how can one get the physical substrate of personality or culture—*this* body, *these* particular events or artifacts—to link up in any stable way with their meaning? The former, upon sustained interpretation, always turn out to signify *too much*, so that their ability to be construed always exceeds their carrying capacity for meaning. Indeed, this awkward result will be familiar to anyone who has inquired into the interpretive history of any significantly complex personality, event, or artifact. Yet this cannot entirely dislodge the intuition that if I do not know exactly who I am—what it "means" to be me—I am normally in no danger of confusing myself with someone else; or that if I do not know exactly what discriminates one era from another, I rarely mistake the seventeenth century for the present. Thus the impression of limits on interpretation is as strong as the sense that in practice these tend rarely to be found.

Both intuitions are certainly plausible and respond to features of meaning that are equally "real." Yet they involve us in a conundrum, for there is simply no way that meaning could be bounded on the one hand and endlessly figurable on the other—something determinate that is nevertheless always subject to further construal. If determinate and bounded, it should be a thing about which we can gain referential competence. Indeed, if we did not already possess enormous amounts of this, it is hard to imagine how we could function as highly verbal, social animals. On the other hand, if our competence were entirely adequate, or could be imagined so in principle, then it would be hard to understand why we have so much trouble agreeing about the meanings of reasonably complex events or artifacts. Thus it seems that meaning is sometimes the most inhospitable of referential terrains and sometimes not.

Not before chapter 6 will we be able to deploy all the tools necessary to resolve this conundrum, but readers will by now probably have intuited that our subject bears upon contemporary disputes in literary theory. We have dealt with experiential and intersubjective meaning, but could just as easily have entered our subject through reflections on the "textual" variety. Different attitudes toward this have of late separated certain, primarily poststructuralist, literary theorists from traditional critics and historians. The former have argued with great ingenuity (albeit in an edifying register) that textual meaning is *ontologically* enchanted, a conclusion which, if mistaken as empirical rather than metaphysical, has the effect, as M. H. Abrams (1977:425) put it, of "making impossible anything that we would account as literary and cultural history." Just as important, theorists of social constructivist stripe, such as Stanley Fish, have argued that literary texts, and by extension culture itself, cannot usefully be thought of as a referential ecology, since our perceptions of their character in this regard will always be relative to the particular strategies we use to interpret them. By way of contrast, "conservative" theorists like E. D. Hirsch have perhaps gone furthest in articulating (though in quite different terminology) the grounds for viewing culture in just this light.

We will return to these matters in chapter 6, and need note here only that none of these positions has quite carried the day, and that the issues involved remain alive across a spectrum of disciplines. As we will see in later chapters, they have consistently forced themselves upon anthropology, where the question of whether culture can be understood by naturalistic means—and thus disenchanted—or proves forever beyond them has been struggled with most centrally and consistently. Yet the problem of meaning and its relation to enchantment can be shown to have more or less the same character across disciplines, in each of which scholars ambitious for consensus about their descriptions or explanations of cultural phenomena have been pitted against others who celebrate the diversity resulting from the "free" play of interpretation.

It may seem by now, however, that we have strayed some distance from our original concerns, since the issue of culture's status as referential ecology appears quite tame by comparison with apparitions, "Martian" states of being, and cultural Blows Invisible. It is possible, after all, that culture could escape explanation, never becoming a fitting subject for naturalistic inquiry, without possessing the uncanny qualities required to evoke wonder. Yet, as we shall see in the next three chapters, the *mechanisms* thought responsible for culture's capacity to elude explanation, for its ability always to exceed our grasp, are indeed most strange—even when, as is sometimes the case, their output is banal. To put the matter differently, culture's ability always to mean *more* is often accounted for by discovering *new* (and generally quite exotic) generators of meaning. Suitably defamiliarized, they can easily be brought within the ambit of our argument.

We leave on hold for several chapters, however, the issue of how the organization of inquiry affects such discoveries. We need first a much better sense of the relationship between explanation, interpretation, and meaning—which have thus far been introduced only casually. As we shall argue, though explanation is itself a kind of interpretation, the goals of these practices are often different. By understanding their contrast and interplay we can get a better sense of how and where enchanted phenomena are encountered and why they excite virtuoso interest. And we should better be able to see why they prove difficult to explain.

2 Explanation, Interpretation, and Referential Ecology

As intellectualism suppresses belief in magic, the world's processes become disenchanted, lose their magical significance, and henceforth simply "are" and "happen" but no longer signify anything.

Max Weber, *Economy and Society*

From Plato's *Timaeus* through Renaissance Neoplatonism and on into such scattered outposts as Romantic *Naturphilosophie,* Western thinkers sustained a conviction that the world's processes signified something beyond themselves. In fact modern science itself was to no small degree the handiwork of investigators who expected to read the Book of Nature through it (Westfall [1958] 1973). Studying natural processes, it was assumed, would expose a still occult message, an unfathomed design, to be deciphered through interpretation. By the time Weber wrote, however, the sense that nature possessed an obscure signifying power had been driven to the margins of intellectual respectability. Science and technology had joined since the seventeenth century to circumscribe the play of those "mysterious incalculable forces" (Weber 1946:139) given voice to through the world. To explain nature, it was assumed, was to obviate any need for further interpretation.

In chapter 1 we saw Sacks and Taylor resisting a similar conclusion with regard to culture. The former's phenomenological neurology and the latter's hermeneutic science both make explanation subservient to an enterprise of deeper insight that probes the underlying meaning hidden within and yet still expressed by culture—and in pursuing this they have, wittingly or not, discovered mysterious incalculable forces. Our preliminary reconnaissance suggests, then, that the relation between enchantment and disenchantment is bound up in the interplay between specific forms of interpretation and explanation. We now need to examine this in greater depth, and as a way of getting at it we will explore further the notion of referential ecology.

This notion obviously presumes that we can talk speculatively about properties of the world as they exist prior to and quite apart from our knowledge of them. While this is perhaps epistemologically dubious, an argument that the world varies in its hospitality to consensual designation, investigation, and eventual explanation is certainly useful when we try to account, for instance, for why we have achieved broad-ranging competence in classical mechanics but not in the social sciences. Of course this *might* be an accident—the laws of social behavior might eventually prove even simpler than those of falling bodies, though we have perhaps failed to see this due to the dull-wittedness of sociologists—yet no one would be advised to stake money on it. Suppose, then, we adopt the notion of referential ecology as a heuristic device and see what mileage can be gotten from it.[1]

If we thought of referential ecology on analogy to physical terrain, what would it look like? In speculating about this we will start out somewhat abstractly and indirectly, drawing examples from nature so as to illustrate the generality of the principles involved. To begin with, all phenomena we might like to understand, whether objects or processes, are "structured." Structure is the manner of articulation of a phenomenon across space and time, and variation in it should affect the facility with which it can be explained. As a quality, structure varies along numerous dimensions, two general categories of which will be of interest to us. Using a distinction occasionally hard to draw in practice, we can say that the difficulty of understanding a given structure is due either to its intrinsic properties or to the problems these pose for investigators like ourselves—saddled as we are with a limited sensorium, only certain technologies with which to enhance it, and minds of just such powers. Some properties of structures are thus observer neutral, whereas others are not. We can take these up in turn.

One observer-neutral dimension of structures is constituted by their complexity. They may have more or less of this, and we might preliminarily measure it simply in terms of the number of links between component parts. We can leave the notion of "links" quite vague, remarking only that gravity and rhyme, for instance, both are links. A second feature of structures is that they have more or less variety. While variety probably cannot be collapsed into a single measure (though information theory perhaps comes closest to doing so), we can intuitively conceive of it as the sum of differences in a structure. If we suppose that each class of link therein has a specific character, then variety is simply the number of different links. The more links but the lesser their differ-

---

1. That the structure of the world exerts some constraint on the "flow" of explanation—analogous to the constraint of topography on the flow of water—is not something that can itself be warranted naturalistically. Yet though the "structure of the world" here remains something of an occult force, the justification for recourse to it is simply that it is less occult than the alternatives. Still, readers uncomfortable with realism in this regard will find that Robert Ackermann (1985) has developed a nonrealist analogue of referential ecology in his notion of "data domains." We stick with referential ecology simply for its appeal to common sense, and note that a spirited defense of realism will be found in Giere (1988).

ence, the more monotonous an object; the more links and the greater
their difference, the more diverse. Obviously, then, the dimensions of
complexity and diversity are related, since links must be present before
they can be different. Finally, structures have degrees of entailment. This
is the property that subtends organization (or connectedness) and its
degree of determination. Essentially, it refers to the strength of links,
though there are so many varieties of entailment that this notion is itself
vague. In any event, a structure that is weakly entailed is likely to be
indistinctly bounded, sensitive to external disturbance, and apt to de-
compose (perhaps spontaneously), whereas one that is strongly entailed
will be firmly bounded, insensitive to disturbance, and self-maintaining.
The so-called strong force in physics represents the most powerful entailment of which we know, whereas the bonds that knit the elements
of a work of art into an aesthetic whole seem less strong, at least in the
sense that we can imagine many changes to incidental details that would
have little bearing on overall impact. Clearly, then, some structures are
less entailed than others (a body of gas, for instance, less than an organ-
ism), while cross-cutting entailments may allow us to judge the centrality of substructures within larger units (as the appendix, though
thoroughly entailed in humans by genetic articulation, is less thoroughly entailed functionally—as indeed are the appendixes of most
texts). Strongly entailed structures we will simply call "strong," and
weakly, "weak."

We can easily imagine a property space defined by our three dimensions, aligned so structures that are maximally simple, monotonous, and
strong are grouped together near a hypothetical zero point, from which
those that are increasingly complex, diverse, and weak recede along a
diagonal. We will identify this direction in a moment, but for now simply think of a process whose structure places it relatively near our zero
point—say the fall of a body through a medium that offers no resistance. Its acceleration is simple, regular, and strongly entailed, forming
a closed system whose states are easily predictable from one another.
When we noted in chapter 1 that classical mechanics was a discipline
concerned with a particular referential niche, we meant that many of the
structures of concern to it had a location in our property space near that
of a falling body. We can compare this with the location of a more complex structure formed, say, by the behavior of molecules in a cloud of
gas. While a gas is monotonous, it is also complex and weak—to the
point where the movement of a particular molecule within it seems
nearly random. Faced with such phenomena—at once suffocatingly
complex and thoroughly monotonous—we normally retreat to a level
of analysis where simplicity is regained through statistical summary.

Our capacity to refer competently to phenomena (and perhaps eventually to explain them) is partly a function of their distance from the hypothetical zero point in our property space. If we allow the diagonal receding from this point to define the relative "wealth" of a structure, those near our zero point are maximally "poor," whereas those most distant from it are maximally "rich." Explicability is thus related to the poverty of the phenomenon with which we are concerned. Admittedly our terms here may seem arbitrary, since it could as readily be said that "rich" structures are "impoverished." In fact they are sometimes so structurally "thin" that it is almost impossible to see them, at least in their fine detail. Yet they are rich in resources that allow them to elude understanding, with the consequence that they occasionally prove both difficult and fascinating.

Our property space is meant only heuristically (we have in mind no metric for any of our dimensions), so it makes little sense to wonder exactly how the ecological terrain within it would appear. We could imagine wealth as a regular gradient whose increasing altitude makes certain structures difficult to encounter and observe. Or we might think of the terrain as much more irregular, with rivers or swamps punctuating areas that are otherwise quite accessible. Recent discoveries indicate, for instance, that even seemingly "poor" structures can behave quite unpredictably—an eventuality that would be like finding our path across easy terrain blocked by an unfordable river. Study of these structures has been grouped together under the rubric of "chaos" (see Crutchfield et al. 1986; Gleick 1987), part of which concerns itself with "simple" phenomena that behave deterministically but are in principle unpredictable. For instance, the structure formed by water dripping from a faucet is occasionally so irregular as to appear random, though it can be shown to map onto a geometrical form, known as a "chaotic attractor," which reveals a pattern to it without permitting us to make predictions. (In this regard it resembles what Taylor called an "open system" in the last chapter.) Chaotic behavior often occurs in simple systems when unmeasurably small differences in initial states give rise to exponentially divergent later ones. In the study of history an appreciation of something like chaos is reflected in hypothetical causal models of the "for want of a nail the shoe was lost, for want of a shoe the horse was lost" kind. In such models, presumably insignificant initial conditions are viewed as generating critical large-scale outcomes, such as the winning or losing of wars.[2] More generally, the capacity of simple structures to produce

2. Events of this sort, critically governed as they are by "accidents," have structures that are weakly entailed. In these circumstances, explanation is reduced to the narration

chaotic behavior underscores the variability of our referential terrain: to us, it often appears that poor phenomena exist "next to" rich ones, so that the march of our understanding is occasionally halted by an unexpected swamp.

Turning our attention to properties of structures that are observer dependent, some are as straightforward as complexity, diversity, and entailment, whereas others will on first acquaintance appear odd. Among the former we would certainly include such spatiotemporal features as make a structure conveniently observable. Rather like Goldilocks, we prefer phenomena that are neither too small nor too large, too quick nor too slow for our faculties or instruments to encounter. Thus the "beds" in which reference and explanation feel most comfortable are of a certain size and temporal dimension, though advances in instrumentation over the past several centuries have vastly increased the margins within which inquiry is comfortable. Were our sensorium differently constituted or the time scale of our lives radically altered, the margins of our preferred referential bed would change as well. We don't have a convenient name for this quality of structures, though it clearly has something to do with their "obviousness"—to us at any rate.

Other qualities of structures that contribute to obviousness have "foregrounding" potential. Some phenomena "stand out" readily before our sensorium or instruments, whereas others do not. A stroke of lightening, for instance, stands out nicely, whereas the odor of an individual does not. The latter can be appreciated by a dog, though for us it is generally beneath our threshold or lost in a background of olfactory noise. We do not need to catalog all foregrounding qualities, though among them would certainly be boundedness, frequency of movement against a fixed backdrop, and striking coloration. Such features cause the opposite of camouflage, and would be desirable in objects used for the translational bridge referred to in the last chapter. Again we lack a common term for them, though the dimension they define has to do with the "isolability" of phenomena. The more isolable, the easier to point to and achieve referential consensus about.

The notion of obviousness is itself rather obvious, and by and large makes phenomena easier to understand. To proceed through a catalog of such features would invite boredom, but with the general idea clear we can move on to ones that are less obvious and more controversial.

---

of events that cannot be encompassed within a single system or subsumed under higher-level causal patterns.

These are best thought of as contributing to the "mercuriality" of phenomena. Thinking back to our dripping faucet, for instance, the irregularity of the drops makes us wonder whether there is any "structure" to them at all, and the fact that there *is* can only be revealed through sophisticated mapping procedures. Structures that are either constant or periodic prove relatively easy to see, while aperiodic ones give a mercurial impression. This is true as well of phenomena that suffer attenuation or fade-out upon scrutiny (the more we look, in other words, the less we see). This awkward quality is often encountered by parapsychological investigators, and their willingness to put up with it is thought daft by more conventional scientists, who make failure to attenuate more or less a prerequisite for phenomenal status. But, understandable as this criterion is, it has failed to impress many researchers who find that the potential payoff in such phenomena outweighs the inconvenience of their fading out in the course of research.[3]

Attenuation, then, is a strange and controversial property that is not just observer but observation dependent, and it has come to serve as a borderline where investigators cease to agree over whether they are confronting *phenomena* in the first place. An even stronger borderline of this sort is established by the property of "equipresence"—which is to say the intersubjective availability of a phenomenon. Lacking equipresence, a phenomenon will be scorned by mainstream empirical disciplines, a gesture enshrined in the Royal Society's motto *Nullius in verba*. The practical rationale for this is strong, constantly buttressed by exposures of the "Clever Hans" variety,[4] and yet not universally accepted. Just in the last chapter, for example, we found Charles Taylor rejecting it when he suggested that "intersubjective meaning" was not intersubjectively available, but instead could be understood only by those of developed sensibility. Throughout history many disciplines, alchemy perhaps foremost among them, have assumed that the really important phenomena fail to show themselves to just anybody, and in this

3. In general, the willingness of investigators to put up with mercurial phenomena depends upon how well the latter can be integrated with existing knowledge. In contemporary physics, for instance, so-called dark matter has proven quite elusive, yet continues to be sought and written about because it would fit so nicely with our current sense of how the world works. (In fact without it this would have to be revised.) ESP, on the other hand, would not fit well.

4. Hans was a supposedly enumerate German horse whose skill in calculation excited great public interest and admiration. Only upon painstaking investigation did it become evident that Hans was unable to solve the problems addressed him, but instead was quite astonishingly adept at picking up subtle and perhaps unconscious somatic cues from his owner (see Pfungst [1911] 1965).

regard the prejudice of modern empirical disciplines for equipresence, understandable though it may be, is quite possibly in the minority.

In much empirical investigation equipresence is less a matter of the bald "thereness" of phenomena than it is of confidence in the instruments and procedures that extend our senses so as to isolate nonobvious phenomena. In fact, we find that at the forefront of study, where procedures have not yet been broadly agreed upon and thus "sedimented" in scientific practice—to use Bruno Latour's (1987) term—numerous phenomena are encountered that do not immediately show equipresence. (They are identified by one test, for instance, but not by another, or only by certain experimenters using the "same" test, posing difficulties for the ideal of replication: see H. M. Collins 1985.) When these turn up, considerable effort may be expended to reveal the superior pragmatic benefits of one or another of the test procedures and to school others in its use: if this can be done, the phenomenon can be made to "behave." Consequently, equipresence is often symmetric with sedimentation of procedures, which is to say the routinization of inquiry and its spread as a craft skill.

We will return to this in chapter 7 when we discuss so-called mature sciences; for now it is sufficient to take the dimensions we have discussed and imagine them defining a second property space. Thus obviousness, isolability, and the factors of stability (periodicity or regularity, constancy versus attenuation, and equipresence) can be aligned with a zero point of maximum perspicuousness—away from which a diagonal extends toward maximum occultness. (We might think of this as defining the relative "visibility" of phenomena.) In occult environs we meet phenomena so infinitesimal or grand, brief or slow, so camouflaged, irregular, coy, or choosy about presenting themselves for our inspection, that they often evanesce, perhaps with a curious perfume and melodious twang. Whether good spirits or bad, they are the devil to investigate.

Once again we are thinking only in a very rough and heuristic way: clearly, more properties than we have mentioned contribute to the visibility of phenomena, and all of them interact in complex ways. At some risk, we have permitted our terrain to be defined by several properties that will meet with skepticism; yet it seems best to remain agnostic and note simply that they contribute only at the margins to what is otherwise an entirely straightforward quality of structures. Looking on these in observer-neutral terms, we have found they vary from extreme poverty to great richness, while looking on them in observer-dependent terms, we have found they vary from being thoroughly perspicuous to quite occult. In fact, it is possible to superimpose our two property spaces so that the gradients of wealth and visibility line up with one another. At our new zero point we have phenomena that are both poor and perspicuous, whereas extending away from us they are increasingly rich and occult. Obviously, the further from our zero point we go, the more apt we are to encounter phenomena that excite wonder, that is, phenomena we can account for only by assuming them governed by principles not just presently obscure, but potentially of a different order, familiarity with which would radically alter our sense of how the world works. Alternatively, we might say that it is along the line defined by wealth and visibility that the advance of disenchantment, beginning with the poorest and most perspicuous structures, has for the most part occurred. It does so by providing good explanations for phenomena that were poorly explained or not explained at all before. It is time, then, to address explanation directly.

Throughout the previous discussion we have taken our examples from nature rather than culture simply for convenience. Yet cultural phenomena are structured and exist in our terrain just as much as natural ones: some are poor and perspicuous, while others are rich and occult.[5] We noted earlier, for instance, that gestures like simple facial expressions seem to be interpreted universally in more or less the same fashion, suggesting that their meaning is simple and perspicuous, while on the other hand gestures like Leonardo's in painting a smile on the Mona Lisa are considerably more complex and obscure. In the same way, action governed by rational calculation is normally simple and perspicuous, while a poem by Mallarmé is not.

For the moment, however, simply consider explanations themselves: as semantic structures they are generally rather low on wealth and high on visibility. In fact, we strive to get them as near the zero point in this regard as the phenomena they purport to explain will permit. Or at least we can say that this is a desideratum in the sciences: if we look at explanation anthropologically we will often run across ways of accounting for things that appeal to rich or occult phenomena (see TenHouten and Kaplan 1973). For instance, to say of some occurrence that it was "fated" is to give it a cause that is weakly structured and mercurial—and thus enchanted. From the perspective we are adopting here, however, this simply avoids explaining anything. Thus our concept of explanation is prescriptive. Furthermore, it is very narrow. We are interested

5. We defer until chapter 6 the objections certain relativists might raise to this. For them, the properties of cultural objects are always and only social constructions dependent upon the interpretive practices of a given community, and are thus not analyzable in terms of referential ecology.

here primarily in "genetic" accounts, that is, in attempts to explain phenomena through their development or etiology. While this is only one form of explanation, it seems both psychologically and pragmatically the most satisfying.[6] (We additionally assume these accounts will be presented in a naturalistic register rather than an edifying one.)

Genetic accounts can be thought of as having three components: first, something that is to be explained (an "explanandum"); second, a description of the conditions out of which it developed; and, third, a set of transformations (or causes) that produce it from these conditions. (The conditions and causes constitute our "explanans.") The more complete and necessary the set of transformations, the more strictly entailed the phenomenon—which is both a psychological and pragmatic desideratum of explanations, though not one that is easy to achieve in practice (see Humphreys 1989). In essence, then, the most satisfying explanations are "strong" structures in the sense outlined above. Their links are constituted by the laws or rules that are the basis of our theories about phenomena. Empirical sciences essentially provide us with strong links we can insert between phenomena and their initial conditions to explain how and why they came to be.[7] In what we might call the "Laplacean dream," it was imagined the entirety of phenomena might be understood in this way, and though this now appears quite implausible, it still holds a psychological attraction for us. Einstein's discomfort with the Copenhagen interpretation of quantum mechanics both underscores this attraction and suggests that on occasion we find ourselves unable to satisfy it by identifying strict entailments. Sometimes the reasons for our impasse are theoretical (Heisenberg's principle and so on) and sometimes practical. We have already discussed the unpredictability of chaotic phenomena, but biological evolution presents us with much the same problem. We are only rarely able to uncover the specific historical causes of whatever mutation or genetic recombination led to some novel structure, which means we are without a complete explanans for the event—which remains, in practice if not in principle, unentailed. Furthermore, some such events are "random" in that they result from accidents—which is to say from "rich" antecedent structures. In fact,

6. In addition to genetic explanations, "compositional" ones explain a phenomenon in terms of the properties of its constituent parts, "structural" ones by its place in an ordered sequence, and "functional" ones by the needs it serves in some broader system. We borrow here from Levine (1986).

7. Probabilistic links are of course less strong than deterministic ones, but are still able to function in explanations (Humphreys 1989). It is possible, of course, that the criteria by which we estimate entailment are culturally relative, but there seems little doubt that they "work."

the explanation of evolution is constantly forced to appeal to such rich structures, which perhaps accounts for our residual dissatisfaction with it. The same may be true of all historical disciplines, as noted before. But as with the example of "fate," allowing too rich or occult a structure into an explanation has the effect of short-circuiting it. In other words, unless explanations are relatively poor and perspicuous, they don't work very well.

As cultural phenomena, then, explanations constitute a particular region of our terrain, where they are joined by other artifacts of "instrumental" character. (By and large, we have less difficulty understanding specific uses of a knife, say, than of an orchestra.) While items in this region may of course have a certain complexity and diversity, they are always strongly entailed and perspicuous, and in this they characteristically differ from "expressive" phenomena—which are often valued precisely for their richness and lack of visibility. More of this in a moment.

Of course scientific knowledge goes beyond providing isolated explanations of phenomena, being anxious to relate these to one another systematically. The quality of "theoreticity" allows us to view phenomena that are on their surface quite different as instances of the same laws or processes. Our sense that we possess a "deep" explanation for something, in fact, depends upon being able to trace its causes back to quite abstract (and thus "fundamental") principles. As Finn Collin (1985:60) suggests: "The layman may know about the tides, about the way heavy things fall to the ground, and he may know the position of the moon on the firmament throughout the seasons. But this falls far short, both in scope and abstractness, of the physicist's grasp of the very same phenomena." It is not that the layman's understanding lacks theoreticity, but simply that the physicist's possesses so much more of it. A feature of all knowledge that is even remotely systematic, it builds new levels of relatedness into our understanding of phenomena.

With all this established (however sketchily), the relation between explanation and enchantment should be obvious. So poor and perspicuous are explanations—satisfying ones, at any rate—that they simply have little place in them for mystery. They make the behavior of the world so predictable that our pragmatic competence is rarely called into question.[8] Thus to have explanations is to comfortably occupy referential terrain, and to have more of them is to expand the territory in which

---

8. Strictly speaking, we should say they make it explicable rather than predictable, since probabilistic theories need not be symmetric in this regard: clearly it is explanatorily satisfying and of enormous pragmatic benefit to know that administering an antibiotic will reduce deaths from a given disease significantly, even though we are unable to predict which persons it will save.

we feel at ease. One might think this an unalloyed blessing (as the Enlightenment apparently did), but the more common attitude toward it is ambivalence. Weber (1968:506) suggested that disenchantment led to "a growing demand that the world and the total pattern of life be subject to an order that is significant and meaningful"—a demand often made today by hermeneutic inquirers (see Bernstein 1983). To this "spiritual" concern, one might add an aesthetic argument that people are not unambiguously attracted to explanations, since their essence is in the end a sort of poverty. Clearly we enjoy the beauty of their purer, more mathematical forms, just as we enjoy the detective work that goes into forging and tightening them up. And ordinarily we appreciate the technological benefits that spin off from them. But in themselves they are rather straitened things. They have a Spartan quality that is unforgiving of spontaneity and insensitive to the foggy or the strange. It is understandable, then, that we are torn between the attraction of rigor, of poverty and perspicuity, that resides in explanation, and the fascination of the rich and hidden domains that resist it. The latter are, in fact, among the most potent of cognitive intoxicants, and attract the regard not just of virtuosi but of the broader public, especially when they are incorporated into what it "means" or "feels like" to be us.

Not unexpectedly, then, much of culture (particularly in its "expressive" domain, where we articulate our experiences and feelings) is given over to structures considerably richer and less perspicuous than explanations. Religion and art, for instance, exploit "logical scandals" so as to provoke sublime and uncanny experiences. Music, rather like chess, plays off a certain clarity of structure against an infinitude of possibilities to achieve a compellingness perhaps greater than any available in the medium of language, though how it does this remains obscure. As Paulson (1988) has noted with regard to literature, expressive phenomena contain a great deal of "noise" which, as it prevents conceiving of them as determinate structures, opens the opportunity for rich and varied interpretations. Even small expressive units, such as particularly rich individual symbols, sometimes allow us to perceive "the world in a grain of sand." Clearly, phenomena of this sort beckon us just as strongly as explanations, yet have precisely the opposite character and allure. The signifying power of cultural phenomena, as we argued at the end of chapter 1, always seems excessive, producing more than can comfortably be linked to its material substrate in behavior or artifact. But this would mean that many cultural phenomena are too rich and mercurial, too unstable, ever to be viable as explananda. Like their more traditional occult brethren, they do not sit still long enough to have their picture taken.

Thus the existence of ineffably rich expressive phenomena creates what we might think of as a structural mismatch for explanation. No doubt intuitions of this fueled the conviction that the *Geisteswissenschaften* had aims and required methods quite different from the study of nature. But note that the problem here arises only when we take the *meaning* of cultural phenomena to be our proper explanandum. This normally seems obvious, but on the other hand all of culture is carried in physical media—modulations of sound, marks on paper, nerve impulses in brains, and so on—whose behavior is, we presume, systematically entailed from antecedent phenomena that are also physical: culture, in other words, is always instantiated in or conveyed through structures that, however complex, *will* sit still long enough (in principle at any rate) to have their picture taken. About these we could hope to acquire as much referential competence and theoretical understanding as of anything natural—though, granted how idiosyncratic most cultural phenomena are, it is unlikely we will progress very far along this avenue. Yet our point for the moment is simply that we have here a potential way out of our problem, a way of understanding culture even while standing quite resolutely "outside" it. The result would be somewhat odd, however, for we would have acquired a satisfactory explanation of cultural phenomena without understanding what the latter *meant,* having approached them *beneath* their capacity to signify.

Whether this would prove feasible or not is still a matter of debate among philosophers of social science (e.g. Winch [1958] 1963; Harris 1964; Headland et al. 1990). From one side, exemplified already by Thomas Nagel and by Sacks's concern with phenomenological neurology, an understanding of meaning is crucial to explanation, while from another, most intriguingly worked out at a practical level by anthropologist Marvin Harris (1964), it isn't. We return to the topic in chapter 6, but might note here that our intuitions about it are apt to be conditioned by the specific examples of cultural phenomena we have in mind. Thus we would presumably see the simple facial gestures studied by Darwin as more easily explicable without reference to meaning than we would one of Mallarmé's poems. On the assumption that facial gestures are "hard-wired" into us by evolution, we might study them just as "externally" as we study the behavior of insects. Unique poetic gestures, on the other hand, could not easily be approached in this way. However this may be, we are more or less stuck, for the present at least, with "meaning" as our avenue to understanding culture, and since the term is notoriously vague, it would perhaps help to become somewhat more precise about it.

As many as four distinct types of meaning are commonly involved in discussions of culture: symptomatic, experiential or existential, conventional, and—denominated in its own right—"significance." (The difficult case of "symbolic" meaning we reserve for the next chapter.) In examining these for the part they might play in explanation we want to speculate about the degree of referential competence we might anticipate with regard to them.

Consider, then, symptomatic meaning. It is always established through (or dependent for warrant upon) the principle of concomitant variations. As underlying conditions change, so do their symptoms—which thus stand as indexes for or clues to them, as when smoke is said to *mean* fire. Though in practice the direction of causation sometimes remains to be established, we can think of the symptom as part of our explanandum and the underlying condition as part of our explanans. In empirical disciplines (as in everyday life) it is assumed that a symptom must be strictly entailed by its underlying conditions, but looking on the matter more broadly, this is perhaps an unusual quality. Heterodox disciplines like astrology, folk psychology, and psychoanalysis rarely find symptomatic meaning so clear-cut. As a result they might be deemed to explain very little, while giving the appearance of doing more. In any event, where meaning of this sort can be shown to vary regularly with underlying conditions, it is referentially accessible; otherwise, it behaves much more problematically. We have already encountered an example of this in Taylor's estimate of the symptomatic meaning of certain events in the sixties.

Experiential or existential meaning—what it "means" to have undergone, or to exist as, something—is sometimes thought, as we saw in the last chapter, essential to explanation. This would clearly be true when it could be used to predict behavior. For instance, knowing what it "means" to be the calculating twins might afford us not just empathy but the ability to anticipate their reactions. In such a case it would serve, in other words, as our explanans. Yet it seems that criteria of predictive adequacy are infrequently applied to descriptions of experiential or existential meaning. Instead, the latter are taken to be valuable in themselves as entrée into the life worlds of other beings, and here they prove very difficult referential terrain, failing badly of equipresence—as we have seen with Sacks.

Conventional meanings, our third type, are possessed both by language and by nonverbal gestures that have assigned interpretations. To have an accurate sense of what a gesture, statement, or text means would obviously be crucial to viewing it as an explanandum. For instance, to know that plucking the upper teeth with one's thumbnail is a gesture of contempt would be helpful to understanding the occasions of its use, and this proves true as long as the gesture, statement, or text in question is not too rich or occult. When acts or utterances are ambiguous, vague, profound, or nonsensical, however, we have entered difficult referential terrain. Conventional meaning can then behave in ways that force us to wonder whether culture is perhaps inexplicable. As a practical matter, conventional meaning here lacks equipresence and thus behaves mercurially (or proves subject to deconstructive attenuation). Or at least so it appears: it has been suggested that some of our problems could be cleared up by allowing the "intended meaning" or "authorial intention" of a semantic object to select among possible construals. Obviously, this cannot eliminate whatever vagueness or ambiguity an author *intended* (this would simply be turned into a nonproblem), but it would obviate all those construals that were *not* intended—which would be a help (see Hirsch 1967). General agreement on this constraint would thus enhance equipresence if not make it absolute; yet, as we shall argue in a moment, intentions often do not get us as far as we would like.

Finally, significance: in the broadest sense, phenomena acquire this by standing out against a backdrop of other phenomena. For instance, when Breton (cited by Golding 1988) said of *Les Demoiselles d'Avignon* that it "goes beyond painting, is the theater of everything that has happened over the last fifty years . . . is the wall before which have passed Rimbaud, Lautréamont, Jarry, Apollinaire and all those whom we continue to love," he was carving out a special position for it vis-à-vis other cultural phenomena. Picasso's painting is apparently being singled out as exceptionally meritorious, though we would be hard-pressed to articulate just what it "means" in result, since Breton has characterized it in a peculiar, metaphorical way. But through such means, phenomena seem to "speak" as if they had their own voices. The more we see bound up in them, the profounder the message they carry, so that in the end they approach the status of symbols, becoming both rich and mercurial. Yet this poses no problem for explanation, since knowledge of significance would not be needed for a genetic account of a phenomenon: knowing that *Les Demoiselles d'Avignon* is "the theater of everything that happened in the last fifty years" gives us no clue to how Picasso came to paint it. Normally, estimates of this kind refer less to properties of the object than to its impact upon us, the history of its reception, and so on. While this might be interesting to explain as a separate phenomenon—and might be crucial to appreciating or understanding the relevance of the item—it is still incidental to our concern.[9]

9. If this is not immediately apparent, it is presumably because we normally allow "significance" to cover much broader territory, including symptomatic meaning. For in-

We can ignore estimates of significance henceforward, then: though clearly interpretations, they have no place in the genetic explanation of the phenomena they make meaningful. All the remaining forms of meaning, however, become involved in explanations, and all of them vary in richness and visibility. We have seen that symptomatic and experiential-existential meaning are poor and perspicuous just to the degree that they can function successfully in explanations, whether as explananda or as explanans. Where they don't do very well in this regard, alternatively, they may be sources of enchantment attracting the regard of virtuosi—as we have seen with Turner and Sacks. With conventional meaning, further, the same sort of variation is found: semantic phenomena may be obvious as to their meaning or obscure, and it is in the mists of obscurity that enchantment is most often experienced. We can begin to understand *why* by considering certain characteristics of interpretation as a practice.

This is both a more general and a more varied activity than explanation (at least in the restricted sense we are giving the latter). It would equally be instanced, for example, not just in Sacks's and Taylor's work, but in Heidegger's treatment of Being in *Sein und Zeit* or in a paranoid's reading of people's motives. What these diverse activities have in common is that they utilize what Frank Kermode (1967) calls "fictions of relation." When we encounter some anomalous or peculiar event, practice, locution, or whatever, we attempt to give it a sense by integrating it into a broader structure of phenomena that makes it intelligible. Thus the paranoid makes sense of the stranger's casual glance by relating it to previous impressions of being spied upon. What might appear an accident can then take on symptomatic meaning: it falls into line with other events that collectively have coherence and intelligibility. Phenomena are thus made less perplexing if we contextualize them, showing how they are linked, intrinsically or by analogy, to things with which we are more familiar. Interpretations thus are structures through which intelli-

---

stance, were we to suggest that the popularity of punk rock reflects the malaise of youth facing permanent unemployment in modern service economies, we would certainly be giving the phenomenon significance as commonly understood—though by seeing it as a symptom. This is rather different from the form of import discussed above, for we are not commenting on how *well* a particular cultural vehicle expresses the circumstances of a group—which is generally an aesthetic judgment—but seeing it as *caused by* these circumstances. (Strictly speaking, the term "reflect" above allows both aesthetic and causal interpretations, which would be disambiguated by reference to epistemic register. Were this edifying, we would be talking about significance; were it naturalistic, about symptomatic meaning. In practice, however, registers tend to be left vague, with considerable mischief in result.)

gibility can be discovered where previously none was to be had—or where it could be only dimly perceived.

If giving sense to things provides a sort of "explanation" for them, explanations (in our restricted sense) employ fictions of relation just as do interpretations. ("Fiction" in this context is neither pejorative nor congratulatory, but simply refers to the fact that interpretations and explanations, like any other human artifacts, have to be made.) In fact, explanations are only that subset of interpretations that happen to be poor, perspicuous, causal, and warranted by naturalistic evidence. It follows that when we seek to provide explanations of cultural phenomena that are of obscure meaning, we first have to interpret them in a way that removes this obscurity, finding in them clearer and more perspicuous structure.[10] This is one possible aim of interpretation, and yet it is not always as normatively drawn to poverty and perspicuousness as explanation is. For instance, the notion that the "best" interpretation of a poem, painting, or piece of music is another of its kind underscores the possibility that reducing obscurity entails, as does translation, a sort of treason. Indeed, interpretation need not make things more comprehensible in the first place. If we think of Heidegger's treatment of Being as an interpretation, for instance, we could see it (controversially perhaps) as a process that destroys existing clarity. Which way interpretation will be used (whether for clarification or not) is a matter of the norms followed by a given interpretive community.

Moreover, obscure cultural phenomena can be incorporated into fictions of relation that reveal their enchantment, their capacity to behave in unexpected and apparently inexplicable ways. This is what Taylor does in linking certain events of the sixties to intersubjective meanings that behave at once capriciously and according to a Spenglerian dynamic. Indeed, to demonstrate conclusively that such fictions were somehow inappropriate, that they produced a factitious enchantment, we would really have to *explain* the events in question—a desideratum not easily achieved, however much scientific students of culture might lust after it. As we shall illustrate at length later, however, this has been the goal not just of the "scientists" among us, but of many literary scholars, and by briefly examining their arguments and some of the problems these encounter, we should better understand why culture is so frequently experienced as enchanted.

The goal of discovering a univocal meaning for cultural phenomena like texts—as a result of which they necessarily achieve a certain stability

---

10. Note again that this would not mean the removal of ambiguity but merely its stabilization, so that we are confident of the parameters in which it operates.

and perspicuousness of structure—has been most strongly advanced by interpreters of "intentionalist" persuasion (e.g. Hirsch 1967, 1976; Juhl 1980). Intentionalists view the meaning of an act or a text as determined by the intention of the actor or author. (In the phenomenological tradition, indeed, intentionality discriminates between "action" and "mere behavior"—reflexes and so on—and thereby marks the borderline between nature and culture.) As we shall argue in chapter 6, however, while intention is often advanced to discriminate between "valid" and "invalid" construals, it might also be said to *explain* what is being construed, standing as a potential *cause* of meaning in a naturalistic framework (see Toulmin 1970; cf. Collin 1985:57–103). Certainly if we assume (as it seems we must) that intentions exist in some final sense as neurophysiological processes in our brains, with which we correlate "meaningful" verbal descriptions, they would seem both the causes of our actions and the ground of their meaning. Intentions are the agency behind activity, "motivating" it both by accounting for it and by giving it intelligibility. For these reasons, they seem to offer a royal road both to explaining cultural phenomena and to discovering perspicuous structure (or determinacy) for their meanings. In fact, one might argue that both aspects are arrived at simultaneously, since the same fiction of relation that will decide between alternative ways of construing an expressive phenomenon will have discovered its cause—an intention. From this point of view, valid interpretation and explanation entail one another—and necessarily prove disenchanting.

Yet there are some problems with this eminently reasonable argument, two of which we should look into now. First, it will work only where intentions themselves turn out to be poor and perspicuous, whereas one might suggest they often don't. And second, it will work only where we exclude, commonsensically but more or less by fiat, the possibility of "strange" intenders, that is, of intentional agents that work in peculiar and mysterious ways. These might seem unusual or marginal entities, but twentieth-century inquiry into culture, at least from Freud onward, has aggressively sought out strange intenders—and consistently discovered them. Let us look briefly, then, at each of these problems, starting with obscure intentions and moving on to strange intenders and strange texts.

The problem of rich and occult intentions can best be understood if we look first at the contrasting case of poor and perspicuous ones. Suppose, for instance, that someone purchased a desired item when it was on sale—and then was asked why it was preferred cheap above dear. No answer would suggest itself here because the intention behind this is so impressively poor and perspicuous that it is inconceivable to be puzzled by it, at least barring some mitigating circumstance like obscene wealth. In other words, the intentional structure of economizing, granted desire for the item in the first place, entails the purchase just as much as one billiard ball smacking into another entails its subsequent motion. There simply seems no room here for questions, for doubt about motivations. Postulated desire plus discounted price fully explain the act in question.

Consider now quite different terrain. A poet—let us say Mallarmé—is composing a poem. His objective, based upon a well-worked-out aesthetic, is to lower its "semantic" entailment (its sense making, operationalized as ease of paraphrase) while heightening its "aesthetic" entailment (the impression that the words "belong together" above and beyond their "sense"). This involves "ceding initiative to the words" so that the latter somehow govern lexical selection.[11] In practice this requires, say, weakening the syntactical entailment of the "sentences" in the poem (by, for instance, introducing irregularities in the embedding of phrase structure); transforming the lexical field so as to deliberately violate semantic expectations; and then allowing diction to be governed by an intuitive sense of the local "harmonics" between words. This last is perhaps the key: words are chosen not for their semantic prospects, nor perhaps even for their sound, but rather for their "fittingness" in the company of the words already selected. This can be established by trial and error: elements of the lexicon are inserted until one is found that "works"—as established by its "feeling right".[12] Just how this occurs is obscure: all one knows is that some words feel right whereas others don't. (In the end it thus seems as if the words are choosing themselves, so little is it a matter of conscious control.)[13] Yet in spite of the apparent haphazardness in this, the finished product is quite striking. Mallarmé and his admirers find the poem has an uncanny aesthetic integrity that is maintained across the widely varying meanings one might find in it.

Suppose now we ask him to explain how he came to write *that* poem

11. As Mallarmé (1945:366) expressed it, "L'oeuvre pure implique la disparition elocutoire du poète, qui cede l'initiative aux mots."

12. Mallarmé believed the *body* had a role in composition just as crucial as the intellect, and his sense of the fittingks of a particular poetic locution was gained through a sort of corporeal consultation, an interrogation by consciousness of his "disposition" toward it, which he found announced deep within him as if it welled up out of his body.

13. In discussing an early version of "*Ses pures ongles*," Mallarmé once said "the meaning, if it has one (but I would console myself with the contrary thanks to the amount of poetry it contains, it seems to me), is evoked by an internal mirage of the words themselves. In letting oneself go while murmuring it several times one experiences a rather cabalistic sensation." Letter to Cazalis of July 1868, cited by St. Aubyn (1969:22).

rather than some other, thinking the problem similar to explaining the economizing behavior above. His reasons would prove difficult to articulate. He could respond by outlining his general aesthetic principles (which will "make sense" of the lexical selection process, perhaps) and then offer a *narrative* of the trials and errors by which the specific words came to be chosen. But narratives of this sort are weak structures. They do not entail the poem in the way economizing entails a purchase. Figuratively speaking, the structure of the poem *is* the aesthetic relations between the words, and though some such relations are poor and perspicuous (rhyme, for instance, or "poetic justice" on occasion), these are not. The difficulty is not that the words were "randomly" selected: if we trust our shared intuitions about the aesthetic integrity of the poem, we have to presume it results from some process we are tuned into along with Mallarmé. We can't say what this is, however, because it is "subconscious"—as captured figuratively by Mallarmé in his notion of the participation of the "body" in composition. His intentions thus lie somewhere within him, obnubilated.

Put somewhat differently, we can say that the articulable intentions behind the poem don't constitute a very good explanation of it. Just as we don't allow children to explain their misbehavior by saying they "just felt like it," so we can't explain the genesis of cultural products by saying they "felt good." Like fate, feeling good is a capricious phenomenon: it explains nothing. Yet whatever makes Mallarmé "feel good" also produces an uncanny aesthetic order. Thus it cannot be *entirely* capricious: better to say it produces structure, but in ways we cannot fathom. Of course we have the option of calling the poem largely unintended, but this will have awkward consequences as well. A good deal of our expressive behavior may more nearly approximate poetic composition than it does economizing, and to have all this removed from the sphere of intentions would in one sense be to return a large part of culture to the status of nature. Yet our other option, to see culture as significantly a product of unconscious intentions, is not very helpful either, at least with regard to explanation.

If we conceive of intuitive aesthetic decision making as intentional, it will be apparent that intentions vary in wealth and visibility just like everything else we have been talking about. Aesthetic decision making can have a strong and lucid structure, similar to economizing activity, or it can have a weak and occult one, as in the case before us.[14] Perhaps

14. Or at least this is how it *appears* to us in the domain of meaning, though as we noted before it might at the neurophysiological level have reasonably poor and perspicuous structure. We will return to this issue several chapters hence.

we might say that a certain portion of culture results from perspicuous reasons with the same entailment we often find in nature: at least it seems as difficult to argue against this as against the regularities of physics. But as we depart hospitable referential terrain, analysis becomes increasingly benighted, so that we find ourselves, whether actors or analysts, strapped to comprehend culture in terms of its motivations or intentions. When Mallarmé handed a proof of *Un coup de dés* to Valéry, he wondered whether the text might not represent "un acte de demence," and much of our expressive life, in escaping rational constraint, invites this query.[15]

Thinking back to our earlier arguments, we see that culture—or at least its rich and occult aspects—is not a particularly fertile site for explanation and thus for naturalistic inquiry. Or perhaps we should say that what most interests us about culture proves least amenable to analysis. It is not just that we can't easily settle upon what it means, but that we have no algorithms or generative matrices that might give rise to it. Unlike economizing, rich and occult cultural phenomena do not have an easily graspable "logic" that entails them. We might summarize this by saying that the intentions underlying culture often seem strange. But this is only one part of the problem, since strange intentions seem to open a space for "strange intenders"—peculiar entities found to account for cultural phenomena—which take the place of more perspicuous algorithms or matrices.

Perhaps it is easiest to get at the notion of strange intenders through the subject of dreams. On the assumption that dreams have meaning, interpreters throughout history have speculated about the agents that might express intentions through them. For dreams to have divinatory utility, for instance, they must transmit the intentions of spirits or of the cosmos as a whole.[16] Or for them to have psychoanalytic utility, they must inscribe the expressive agenda of the Id without our being aware of it. Further, because strange intenders are rarely found to express themselves straightforwardly, it has been customary to assume they

15. A phrase like "rational constraint" is intuitively useful but hard to pin down outside the simplest instances. A helpful discussion of rationality as a concept, particularly as used in the social sciences, will be found in Lukes (1977). For Mallarmé's comment to Valéry see Fowlie (1953:219).

16. Though "spirits" or "the cosmos" are generally dismissed by naturalistic inquiry, many of their attributes are maintained, as we shall see, by entities like "myth," "language," or "power"—at least according to recent and influential investigations. To the extent that such phenomena are seen as somehow controlling individual expression, its intentions necessarily flow from a supraindividual agent—and one not obviously different from a spirit or cosmic force.

communicate in ciphers. In order to find out what a dream "really" means, for instance, analysts must crack the code through which this has been hidden in surface images or actions. In doing so, they find meaning conveyed by elements of the "text" not ordinarily presumed semantic, discovering in the process a "strange" text within or parallel to the obvious one. Further, when the manifest content of dreams has little bearing on matters of interest to us, heroic strategies of decryption may be needed to discover their latent message. Among these, for instance, are numerological mechanisms that break down words or images into their components, assign numerical equivalents, translate the latter into semantic units, and then read the result according to the rules in a translation manual. Thus by motivating what to the unprivileged observer might seem "meaningless" components of the text, a new one is found within the old.

Dream divination might seem a bit off our track, but similar practices have been fundamental to extremely sophisticated interpretive traditions, both antique and modern. Rabbinic interpretation of the Haggadah,[17] for instance, employed *gematria* and *notarikon* in order to penetrate beneath the surface of the Torah. *Gematria*, a largely numerological strategy of interpretation, usually assigns, as above, numbers to each letter of the Hebrew alphabet, which are then summed so as to generate another level of meaning. For example: "R. Judah inferred from the verse, "From the fowl of the heavens until the beasts are fled and gone" (Jer. 9:9), that for 52 years no traveler passed through Judea, since the numerical value of *behemah* ("beast") is 52" (Scholem 1974:337). Of the seven forms of *gematria*, not all are numerological: one transforms the letters in words according to *atbash*, substituting the first letter of the alphabet for the last, the second for the penultimate, and so on, so that a new word may be produced. *Notarikon*, on the other hand, is an interpretive rule that views each letter in a word as the initial letter of another, with all the "primary" biblical words thus being seen as acronyms.

17. The Haggadah is that narrative portion of the Bible which, in having primarily historical or moral bearing, may be differentiated from the Halakah, or legal-regulatory component. By and large, the interpretive practices we discuss in the text are confined to the Haggadah, presumably because the latitude they allow would threaten the stability of the law, correct observation of which was crucial to the well-being of the Jewish community. However, one can find *gematria* and *notarikon* used in close proximity to legal interpretation—as for instance in the *Shulhan Arukh* of Joseph Karo (1488–1575), which was the major early-modern codification of Jewish law—though always in a supportive rather than an innovative role. On Karo, see Werblowsky (1962); on *gematria* in halakic interpretation, see also Scholem (1974:339).

What are we to make of this? Such interpretive practices, as Lieberman (1962) has shown, had their origins in dream divination and were widespread throughout the Hellenic world. *Gematria* had been used since the fifth century B.C.E. by Greek interpreters of the *Iliad* in order to explain away eccentricities and paradoxes in the text. Yet the flowering of numerological interpretation was in sixteenth-century kabbalistic inquiry, where *gematria* was used so profligately as to constitute, at least for Harold Bloom (1983:46), an "interpretive freedom gone mad, in which any text can be made to say anything." For Moshe Idel (1989), however, this was a very methodical "madness" serving ends that have a strangely contemporary ring. The kabbalist Abraham Abulafia, for instance, used *gematria* as a means of "deconstructing language as a communicative instrument, into meaningless combinations of letters which, following strictly mathematical rules, would lead the mystic beyond the normal state of consciousness. . . . [This] phenomenon of deestablishing the biblical text is to be understood as part of a feeling that the divine spirit is present and active again" (1989:xi). More importantly, it is not just the spiritual aims of Renaissance kabbalism that sound modern, but the tools it used as well. Though today's deconstructors do not employ numerology, their interpretive strategies show certain parallels. When the late Paul de Man, for instance, found the tropological character (or "rhetorical structure") of a document put in question any "literal and thematic reading that takes the value assertions of the text at their word" (1979:67), he was discovering a new level of meaning where none had been identified before. (Here initiative is ceded less to "words," as with Mallarmé, than to categories of rhetorical figures.) The resultant "code"—perhaps less immediately peculiar though certainly no less "artificial" than the kabbalistic one—unlocked a second level of meaning alongside (and contradicting) the one more conventionally conveyed by the text. In similar fashion, though taking a different tack, J. Hillis Miller (e.g. 1976) finds the etymological histories of specific words to be presently operative in the constitution of textual meaning. Thus in his case, as in de Man's, features of the communicative apparatus not previously thought to possess signifying power are found to have acquired it, with the consequence that texts appear "strange" or "uncanny," displaying the same elusive and mysterious qualities as the kabbalistic Scripture. Were the aims of deconstructive inquiry naturalistic rather than edifying, we would be thrown back in accounting for this on strange intenders (like "language") that are only somewhat less occult than the cosmic powers of old.

Thus the impulses that produced *gematria* as an interpretive tool are by no means as exotic or as farfetched as they might initially seem: clearly, similar tools are widely esteemed today and integrated into the work of interpretive communities no less vital than early modern kabbalism. Frequently these communities are built up around the discovery of a new realm of intentions in texts, conveyed by means the unsuspecting had hitherto ignored. We often unreflectingly assume that certain components of texts are unmotivated and certain phenomena thus nontextual—indeed, it would probably be hard to get communication started otherwise—but at the same time unreflectingly exclude strange intenders. Innovations in interpretive methods are often brought about by questioning just what and who is signifying, and when findings are conveyed in a naturalistic or ambiguous register—compare Freudian to deconstructive ambitions—they have the power to enchant. With each newly discovered strange source of intentions, the referential terrain of culture thus comes more and more to resemble the one in which Aubrey operated.

In this chapter we have been at pains to point out similarities in the behavior of natural and cultural phenomena—and in our response to them. Some things—both natural and cultural—have rich and occult structure. They do not behave in systematic ways, and sometimes seem to violate criteria of phenomenality developed over the last several centuries in the sciences. These criteria have been marvelously useful in identifying tractable terrain, but at the cost of dismissing certain other niches. In the seventeenth century virtuosi still mined this general terrain with great enthusiasm, though in the course of time we have come to think them naive. In particular, their sense that unusual phenomena might express the intentions of another realm of agents has come to be stigmatized by the sciences, just as have their referential niches. Yet the interests of virtuosi have not died out: they live on wherever rich and occult niches have not yet been stigmatized, which is to say in the least mature fields of investigation.

In interpretive inquiry today, enchantment results from encounters with strange intenders just as it did from Aubrey's encounters with apparitions—provided they are discussed in the proper epistemic register. Most interpretive practices can be employed either for edifying or naturalistic ends, and only in the latter case do they become enchanting. As we have seen, interpreters find that some aspect of phenomena (which others might assume nonsemantic) carries meaning, a meaning that flows from intentional agents whose character and behavior we can apprehend only dimly. Yet this is not the consequence, we suggest, of "interpretive freedom gone mad," but, originally at least, of the difficulties rich and occult cultural phenomena present as referential terrain. It is not that factitious means have been developed to fantasticate "texts" that could be read clearly and plainly by commonsensical effort, but rather that commonsensical effort seems ill-equipped to engage certain texts in the first place (see Kermode 1979). Still, the collective effect of exotic interpretive strategies is to paint a panorama of mysterious goings-on quite as striking as the one offered by Aubrey at the birth of the Scientific Revolution. And like Aubrey, present-day virtuosi are content to catalog and display their discoveries instead of using enchantment as a spur to explanation—should this prove feasible in the first place.

Of course we have illustrated this thus far only in the most haphazard fashion. A brief look at Sacks and Turner, some references to Freud, and a look at certain (occasionally edifying) paths to strange intenders hardly indicate that enchantment is pervasive enough to merit interest. In the next two chapters, then, we want to take up figures central to a discipline with (arguably) naturalistic ambitions. We shall look at the two most broadly influential anthropologists of the last quarter-century—Clifford Geertz and Claude Lévi-Strauss. As social scientists, they normally subscribe to norms—as to accuracy of description, naturalistic warrant for assertions, and so on—that give their reports the power to enchant. We shall assume, then, that if our investigators discover strange phenomena, the latter pose practical difficulties for us of the sort necessary to generate enchantment. That this occurs in particular with Geertz and Lévi-Strauss seems significant for our argument. Surely few anthropologists—indeed, few scholars—have had greater influence outside their discipline, generating widespread interest as to their methods, so that through them we could, if we wished, trace the spread of specific forms of enchantment across many disciplines that study culture. Indeed, their popularity perhaps says something important about the place of enchantment in modern thought.

Since our evidence resides substantially in these two cases, we need to examine them in some detail. (Readers anxious to continue with our argument should skip directly to chapter 5.) As before, we aim to highlight the enchantment in what might otherwise appear business as usual, defamiliarizing it. In doing so, we consistently appear insensitive to the ambiguous register in which Geertz and Lévi-Strauss confess to write. Yet without querying their findings from an unambiguously naturalistic (and thus rather pedestrian) vantage point, we cannot fully appreciate the oddities they discover, or their tendency to overlook paths to the naturalistic warrant their findings seem to require. When we see them on analogy to seventeenth-century virtuosi, however, their habit

3 Culture as a Text?

It has been the office of others to reassure; ours to unsettle. . . . We hawk the anomalous, peddle the strange. Merchants of astonishment.

Clifford Geertz (1984:275)

In the previous chapter we reviewed various features of culture that cause it occasionally to prove difficult referential terrain. It is not just that the conventional meaning of verbal culture is itself frequently obscure, or that the same might be said of symptomatic or experiential-existential varieties: in addition, it is unclear which aspects of culture have the power to signify in the first place. Interpretive communities, it turns out, differ markedly in the range of phenomena—even linguistic phenomena—they see as communicative. Indeed, as twentieth-century thought has more and more been shaped by linguistic models and metaphors, this range has probably grown. Forms of semiotic analysis, for instance, in being applied more widely, reveal more of our world—from what we eat to what we wear—as message laden. Exactly what is being communicated, on the other hand, remains subject to controversy, as does the precise nature of the entities that communicate and the means by which they do so. It is little wonder, then, that culture is an occasion of enchantment.

Prominent among "peddlers of the strange" in this vein has been Clifford Geertz, whose semiotic anthropology encourages us to look upon culture as a text.[1] Those inclined to smile at Mallarmé's conviction that the world existed to wind up in a book will find it harder to dismiss Geertz's idea that culture, at least, has always been a text to begin with. It is this book, or culture-as-text, that he sets out to interpret:

The concept of culture I espouse . . . is essentially a semiotic one. Believing, with Max Weber, that man is an animal suspended in webs of significance he himself has spun, I take culture to be those webs, and the analysis of it to be

---

1. For the time being we will ignore the somewhat technical distinction drawn by some hermeneuticians between "texts" and other uses of language. On this view (see below), texts are seen as separated from their authors and historical contexts—thus becoming autonomous sources of meaning—whereas other uses of language are not. Though the meaning of the latter may be constrained by authorial intention, "texts," in having been given an atemporal existence through inscription, may not. While this distinction has quite probably influenced Geertz, it plays little part either in his programmatic statements or in his ethnography—and thus can be reserved for later discussion.

therefore not an experimental science in search of law but an interpretive one in search of meanings. It is explication I am after, construing social expressions on their surface enigmatical. (1973:5)

On this view the sphere of social expression, of text, is largely coextensive with culture, since all our artifacts and actions, whether linguistic or not, are capable of being involved in webs of significance whose enigmatic surface it becomes the goal of the anthropologist to decipher and explicate. A Balinese cockfight, for instance, is potentially as much a text as one of Mallarmé's poems. And since both, as texts, fail of perspicuousness, understanding them requires an interpretive act, a construal that renders them more accessible to us. A successful reading reduces the enigma, appropriating the foreign by connecting it, through a fiction of relation, to more familiar categories of our experience.

Yet in Geertz's hands this preliminary familiarization often eventuates in its opposite: an encounter with the strange. If culture is found to be a text, its message often turns out to be sublime—which is to say quite rich. More central to our concern, however, is that the mechanics by which this message is conveyed remain mysterious, since they operate extralinguistically and, it appears, beneath awareness. Thus precisely what is being conveyed, by what means, by whom (or what), and with what effect is in Geertz's work left occult, while a conviction that *something* is going on is very effectively generated—a combination that evokes enchantment and may well add to the widespread appeal of his work. To demonstrate this, we need to sketch some methodological background and introduce distinctions that would commonly be made in naturalistic inquiry, recognizing the while that Geertz holds himself somewhat apart from the latter. Nevertheless, it is because naturalistic canons are presupposed in his work (while at the same time held at a distance) that his results have the potential to enchant.

His first collection of essays, *The Interpretation of Cultures,* is introduced by one on "thick description," a term he borrows from Gilbert Ryle to distinguish between the behavioral surface of action, which could be "thinly" described in terms of mere physical gestures, and the public signification of those gestures—something that depends both on established codes of meaning and on the actors' intentions to bring these into play. Though a twitch of the eye might resemble a wink physically, for example, the twitch is not a wink, nor is a burlesqued or ironic wink the same as one meant straightforwardly. Any purely external or behaviorist investigation would initially be frustrated by an inability to recognize these distinctions, which shows that understanding symbolic action involves knowing the conventions according to which it signifies and determining whether these are being brought into play. As Geertz (1973:10) says, "Once behavior is seen as . . . symbolic action—action which, like phonation in speech, pigment in painting, line in writing, or sonance in music, signifies . . . the thing to ask is what its import is: what it is, ridicule or challenge, irony or anger, snobbery or pride, that . . . is getting said." Here it seems to be the *message*—whatever gets *said* by action—that Geertz's semiotic anthropology sets out to describe as thickly as possible. In the statement quoted earlier, on the other hand, Geertz wanted to explicate Weberian "webs of significance." Referring back to our discussion in the previous chapter, however, it would appear these two are different things. Messages of necessity employ conventional meanings, based in public codes, to convey information,[2] whereas significance results from probing the "import" of things—which we identified as an activity aimed primarily at edification. Significance, we saw, is not conveyed through a linguistic medium, but rather is investigated through reflection upon the "bearing" things have for us. Granted that it may be rhetorically useful to imply that the significance of some phenomenon is what it in fact *signifies,* one would not want to take this literally. Thus conventional meaning, being conveyed through a public code, requires one type of reading, whereas significance, not being encoded at all, requires another.

Consequently, if it is messages ("what . . . is getting said") that are at issue rather than webs of significance, the textual metaphor is prima facie appropriate. Further, if we are not to confront strange intenders, the senders of these messages must be standard persons and their code a "native" one. To understand what is getting said thus requires knowledge of the code and, if it is encrypted, the ability to crack it. Note again, however, that expressive behavior that does not take advantage of a code cannot really get anything said—at least *sensu strictu.*[3] (It may, of course, evoke feelings in us, but there is no reason to view this on analogy to language, since roughly analogous feelings are evoked by

2. An exception to the rule that messages can be conveyed only through conventional signs is discussed by Sperber and Wilson (1986; see also Collin 1985:39–42), who draw upon Grice's analysis of language. They show that when sender and receiver are in visual contact and perceiving the same circumstances, quite rich messages can be conveyed by novel nonverbal gestures. Despite the importance of this, however, it has no bearing on the sort of communication presupposed in viewing culture as a text. Thus we will ignore it henceforward.

3. As Collin (1985:335) suggests, "semantic notions do not apply to action outside of language. . . . [Their metaphorical] use is not founded upon deep-seated affinities which would warrant the hopes for successful theorizing in social science modelled upon linguistic structures."

natural phenomena.) Thus though Geertz refers to the message or import of "pigment in painting, line in writing, or sonance in music," these media are not normally conventionalized so as to convey messages. Though our metaphorical usage tends to ignore it, they actually *say* no more than do the glades, the brooks, or majestic Niagara. Of course their significance might be pondered, just as Breton pondered *Les Demoiselles d'Avignon,* but this is a different matter. At any rate, Geertz emphasizes (in principle if not always in practice) that cultural texts must employ native codes: certainly if the "ridicule or challenge, irony or anger" referred to above are not getting said by and to concrete individuals, by means of some code they find intelligible, they are getting said in highly unusual ways.[4]

A caveat is necessary here, though, for it is possible that cultural texts could be inscribed and communicated beneath awareness. In fact (as is presumably the case with our own "body language" on occasion) it is possible that people could be quite unaware both of the messages they send and the codes they employ. Perhaps cockfights, to cite a case we will look at momentarily in greater detail, "say" something to people by means of resonances below a conscious level, so that they are unable to articulate either the message or the code employed. To demonstrate such a phenomenon would be a signal achievement, since the burden of evidence is quite onerous, at least if we adopt naturalistic standards. Consider by way of analogy the example of symptomatic "meaning" as read through medicine: there the most elaborate methodological precautions must be taken to establish a diagnostic reading, the eventual verification of which becomes a long-term community project. Though students of culture cannot be expected to employ such exacting verificational standards, the basic principles by which we would gain confidence in the decoding of any supposedly unconscious communication are the same as those used to discern symptomatic meanings in medicine: we need to show how some information has been encoded, identify the specific means by which it is conveyed, and then show that its reception has some discernable effect. In the absence of such evidence, we will worry that the mysterious messages in question are being received only by the investigator.

Though tedious to make in the abstract, distinctions between significance and signification, expression (in the sense of "artistic expres-

4. See also Geertz's comment (1983:22, emphasis added) that "Interpretive explanation—and it is a form of explanation, not just glossography—trains its attention on what institutions, actions, images, utterances, events, customs, all the usual objects of social-scientific interest, *mean to those whose institutions, actions, customs, and so on they are.*"

sion") and communication, and conscious or unconscious use of codes are all crucial if we are to understand where to view culture as a text and how to develop evidence to substantiate any interpretation of particulars. Geertz's interpretive practice, by way of contrast, is equivocal across all three distinctions, while his notion of a text remains largely intuitive, so that we must puzzle it out from the individual analyses. In some of these he introduces us to exotic native codes, familiarity with which allows us to understand foreign happenings for the gestural dialogues they are, and on these occasions viewing culture textually seems not only apposite but mandatory. Fascinating as these cases may be, however, they don't evoke enchantment. Other interpretations find messages communicated in the absence of native codes and beneath native awareness, and it is these that share in mystery.

Before turning to an example, we should remark Geertz's concern with symbols and "symbolic action," since in the last chapter we neglected to touch on the methodological difficulties of symbolism. Though symbols often seem richly meaningful to us, Geertz's anthropological colleague Dan Sperber (1975) has argued that they are, strictly speaking, meaning*less*.[5] Rather than being bearers of messages, they serve as culturally designated prompts to *supply* meaning. Just as a taste or smell from our past can, when reencountered, evoke a flood of memories, so a symbol, when encountered, can bring on a flood of associations. It is a dubious move, however, to consider these *conveyed by* the symbol in the same way that a message is conveyed in language. Symbols are meaningful only because they have received public (and often inconsistent) exegesis, which we are apt to recall under their stimulus. Inserted in a message, a symbol serves as a hiatus recipients are expected to fill, partly with this public lore and partly with idiosyncratic resonances the symbol may have acquired for them. Were public exegesis able to *fix* the interpretation of the symbol once and for all, we could indeed see it as having a conventional meaning similar to publicly coded gestures. A symbol would then convey something specific, in the sense that plucking your teeth with your thumbnail conveys contempt. Yet then it would become a sign, eliminating one of its primary functions, which is to cause us to contemplate, actively, some weakly structured and occult terrain, extracting from it a series of images or meanings we then impute to the symbol itself. Because this function of symbols is so important, their exegesis is generally recognized to be open-ended. As

5. Sperber (1975:13) argues, for instance, that "it is . . . impossible to circumscribe the notion of meaning in such a way that it may still apply to the relationship between symbols and their interpretation."

Sperber (1975:144) has written: "[The] absence of stable interpretation . . . is characteristic of cultural symbolism. The presence of exegetical commentary only determines the first of a series of [interpretive] cycles which end only when the attention is turned elsewhere. Moreover, the repetitive side of cultural symbolism is there to set the endless evocation periodically in motion again." The evocative potential in symbols is similar to what Blake found in his grain of sand: contemplated long enough, whole worlds of significance can be organized around them. In fact, what makes the experience so profound is that this "whole world" often becomes instantaneously present in the face of the symbol, rather than being encountered sequentially as in language. This happens when we are so well acquainted with the existing exegesis that a good deal of it can be summoned up to resonate in intuitive ways with our own idiosyncratic associations.

There is a question, then, as to whether a symbol is properly thought of as *textual*. It is semantically vacant and lacks the features of a language: as Sperber points out, there is no "symbolic competence" comparable to linguistic competence such as would allow us to understand a novel symbol. Unlike a novel sentence, each new symbol is blank until made meaningful through public commentary and private contemplation. In providing this we are manufacturing significance rather than reading what it signifies. That we do so is of course of immense importance, especially to anthropology, where the study of symbolism is a crucial field. Yet it is not clear that it would benefit from linguistic metaphors or semiotic models. The experience of symbols is similar to that of works of art: in fact when Breton "saw" so much of the twentieth century in Picasso's painting, he was looking on it largely *as* a symbol.

With Geertz, on the other hand, symbols and other objects of significance (like painting and music) are taken to be semantic phenomena, and thus can get something said. Given his acute eye for the symbolic potential in culture, it proves thoroughly message laden, as can be seen most clearly in his celebrated analysis of the Balinese cockfight, a brilliant work that has achieved exemplary status among recent interpretive documents in the social sciences.[6] The cockfight, which might appear to untutored eyes only a questionable amusement, is there found to be a text—and the Balinese to be its readers. Once deciphered, further-

6. "Deep Play: Notes on the Balinese Cockfight" was originally published in *Daedalus* 101 (Winter 1972) and has been extensively reprinted—nine times, for instance, since 1985, the year *Daedalus* began keeping records. (Thanks to Margaret Menninger, permissions manager at *Daedalus*, for this information.) It was one of the charter documents in Rabinow and Sullivan's *Interpretive Social Science* (1979), and continues to be reprinted despite increasingly vigorous criticism (see below).

more, its message turns out to be sublime, and in understanding this the Balinese fascination with it becomes somewhat less perplexing. Yet just how this not-evidently-linguistic phenomenon actually conveys its message in turn becomes a mystery—if one Geertz chooses not to probe. To see why, we need to look at the cockfight in some detail, exploring the ethnographic setting in which it occurs.

In the first place, that cockfights are important in Balinese life seems beyond question: they are proscribed by law, and the Balinese often risk prosecution to put them on; they introduce most major religious festivals, and occur legally only before the more important of these; and they require preparations that take up an inordinate amount of male labor, an amount termed "crazy" by aficionados themselves. Further, elements of cockfighting are so antithetical to the customary pattern of Balinese culture that this centrality is perplexing: the Balinese are civil, polite, well-mannered in the extreme, formal, order loving, not easily given to violence—and yet the cockfight is chaotic and violent; the Balinese abhor animals and animality in general—yet treat their cocks with such meticulous care (at least until they lose a fight) as almost to privilege them over humans. In short, something hardly rational seems to be going on here. Though the fights afford much simple pleasure of gambling and because of this act as a draw for the circulating markets of the countryside, we remain puzzled by this choice of an activity that smacks of cultural schizophrenia. Cockfights are on their surface certainly enigmatical, in need of an interpretation that would make them, and the Balinese, less so.

To provide this Geertz first defines a category of behavior, "deep play," and suggests why the Balinese cockfight should belong to it. The concept of deep play is taken from Jeremy Bentham, who meant by it:

play in which the stakes are so high that it is, from his utilitarian standpoint, irrational for men to engage in it at all. If a man whose fortune is a thousand pounds . . . wages five hundred of it on an even bet, the marginal utility of the pound he stands to win is clearly less than the marginal disutility of the one he stands to lose. In genuine deep play, this is the case for both parties. They are both in over their heads. Having come together in search of pleasure they have entered into a relationship which will bring the participants, considered collectively, net pain rather than net pleasure. Bentham's conclusion was, therefore, that deep play was immoral from first principles and, a typical step for him, should be prevented legally. (Geertz 1973:432–33)

The depth of play varies in cockfights, but the ones attracting the most attention and spectator betting are precisely the deepest, where the cocks are evenly matched and the "central" bets placed by owners and their kin are high in relation to net worth. It was in part the "irrational-ity" of this that brought on its proscription by the government.

Now though Geertz uses the notion of deep play to inaugurate his reading and pull Bentham's nose a bit, a subsequent comment suggests it is not quite apposite: as he notes (1973:434), cockfight betting is only *momentarily* deep because though wagers are indeed high in relation to net worth, they are also so frequent and the cocks so evenly matched that one can expect to recoup one's losses quickly. The system thus re-sembles what Lévi-Strauss has called "generalized exchange," where one gives readily to generalized others in the expectation of getting back from them. Over a longer span of time, then, cockfight gambling does not meet Bentham's criterion of net pain—at least apart from the occa-sional tragic case. Before admitting this, however, Geertz uses the no-tion to establish a preliminary, if somewhat obscure, rationale for fasci-nation with fights:

It is in large part *because* the marginal disutility of loss is so great at the higher levels of betting that to engage in such betting is to lay one's public self, allu-sively and metaphorically, through the medium of one's cock, on the line. And though to a Benthamite this might seem merely to increase the irrationality of the enterprise that much further, to the Balinese what it mainly increases is the meaningfulness of it all. And as (to follow Weber rather than Bentham) the imposition of meaning on life is the major end and primary condition of human existence, that access of significance more than compensates for the economic costs involved. (1973:434)

Further, the fights are watched in a state of kinesthetic rapture by parti-cipants and bettors, whose intoxication ebbs and flows with the signifi-cance of the struggles as social dramas.

In these the cocks stand for human actors. Balinese society, Geertz argues, is ascriptive, hierarchical, clan-and-caste structured, and freighted with implicit and explicit social tensions between groups. Pres-tige is partly fixed by birth but to some degree collectively enjoyed, be-ing focused, in the village Geertz visited, in four major endogamous descent groups, among whom antagonisms arise without this resulting in violence. In part, cockfights dramatize these antagonisms. Further-more, when fights are between cocks representing different villages, in-ternal divisions are suppressed so that one village presents a united bet-ting front against the other. In view of this, especially those fights between prestigious owners or groups take on the aura of symbolic bat-tles, fictitiously loading the cocks with prestige which is then fictitiously won or lost according to the outcome. Against the civility of Balinese life and its abhorrence of direct aggression, a competitive side can be displayed without real consequence, since no prestige is actually at issue in the combat. Its redness of claw (or spur) could be permitted into social life only suicidally.

Thus far, Geertz's interpretation seems headed toward functionalist conclusions and carries with it an implicit explanation. If fictitious prestige contests have import beyond the minor dramas played out in them, it might seem that they allow the expression of tensions in an innocuous form, with fowl taking the drubbing that would await people were the dramas removed from the stage and played out in community life. Yet though it seems clear that the Balinese sometimes place bets in ways that signal allegiance to or defection from kin groupings, and likewise clear that men are through their cocks placing reputations metaphorically on the line, and clear, finally, that the Balinese themselves interpret the outcomes as events within an economy of group or personal status (rather as in America football or baseball teams carry the prestige of local supporters and either fumble or advance it), Geertz is not suggesting we look on cockfights as some moral equivalent of war. Nor does he rest content with viewing them as vehicles whereby the framework of affiliation and hostility constitutive in part of Balinese social structure is put on public display and read as such. Rather, the "function" of cockfighting is gradually cast into a quite different and more numinous arena where Balinese sensibility is being materialized for purposes of contemplation, edification, and cultural instruction. On this view:

Attending cockfights and participating in them is . . . a kind of sentimental education. What [a man] learns there is what his culture's ethos and his private sensibility (or, anyway, certain aspects of them) look like when spelled out externally in a collective text; that the two are near enough alike to be articulated in the symbolics of a single such text; and—the disquieting part—that the text . . . consists of a chicken hacking another mindlessly to bits. (1973:449)

Here what looked on the surface to be only a cockfight takes on the dimensions of an *éducation sentimentale*—with the allusion to Flaubert's novel quite clearly intended. Contests for rank and survival among poultry are found equivalent to the higher realms of literature, as texts to be read just as we might read or attend *Macbeth* (as Geertz goes on to note). But what is it these *say*, granted they are about ethos and sensibility?

Geertz's answer exploits material we cannot fully review here, but the result shifts us further in the direction of the sublime:

Drawing on almost every level of Balinese experience, [the fight] brings to-gether themes—animal savagery, male narcissism, opponent gambling, status rivalry, mass excitement, blood sacrifice—whose main connection is their involvement with rage and the fear of rage, and binding them into a set of rules which at once contains them and allows them play, builds a symbolic structure in which, over and over again, the reality of their inner affiliation can be intelligibly felt. . . . Enacted and re-enacted, so far without end, the cockfight enables the Balinese, as, read and reread, *Macbeth* enables us, to see a dimension of his own subjectivity. As he watches fight after fight . . . he grows familiar with it and what it has to say to him, much as the attentive listener to string quartets . . . grows slowly more familiar with them in a way which opens his subjectivity to himself. (1973:449–451)[7]

Seen in this light, the cockfight-as-text integrates diverse themes around a central ambivalence toward rage, opening a door to the Balinese psyche by externalizing its core emotional structure, and doing so "theatrically" before a people whose fascination with the theater is well known. The addictiveness of cockfights is thus explained by their capacity to mirror the Balinese soul, and they are attended as a form of tutelage through which profound truths of a personal and cultural nature are slowly encountered and appropriated. Cockfights are canonical texts for the Balinese just because they are, when interpreted, so very Balinese, as *Faust,* for instance, is thought so very Occidental. As we understand this, the enigmatical surface of the expression disappears and the Balinese are revealed not as "crazy" or culturally schizophrenic, but quite like ourselves. The anthropological appropriation of the foreign is accomplished by making it appropriate.

This interpretation is indeed compelling: cockfights, we find, convey rich and powerful messages. As we have indicated, however, a considerable mystery arises as to just how this occurs. Have the Balinese established a code through which information about sensibility can be read off cockfights? If not, is it nevertheless there and somehow received subconsciously? In pursuing these questions, let us first be clear that Geertz hopes to *explain* attendance at fights as an exercise in textual interpretation: at one point in the essay, for instance, he writes that the Balinese *"go to cockfights* to find out what a man . . . feels like when, attacked

---

7. As Jeffrey Alexander (1987:325) has pointed out, Geertz describes what the cockfight says differently at different points in the essay. We have cited only the fullest of these, but alternative thematic complexes are introduced (1973: 420, 443). Joined together, his list of the cockfight's themes would include, as Alexander has it, "man and beast, good and evil, ego and id, the creative power of loosened animality . . . hatred, cruelty, violence . . . death . . . masculinity, rage, pride, loss, benevolence, chance . . . animal savagery, male narcissism, opponent gambling, status rivalry, mass excitement, [and] blood sacrifice."

. . . and driven in result to the extreme of fury, he has totally triumphed or been brought totally low" (1973:450, emphasis added), while at another he claims the cockfights are "a Balinese reading of Balinese experience, a story they tell themselves about themselves" (1973:448). It seems, then, that tuition in culture and sensibility is what Geertz believes the Balinese seek in their pastime. But by what means do they receive it? He does not uncover a code for cockfights linking them to sensibility, nor does he provide evidence the Balinese are much aware of their bearing in this regard, so we must assume that extralinguistic messages are somehow being received subconsciously. Presumably men who attend the fights unwittingly absorb what they say and thus grow more proficient at seeing "a dimension of [their] own subjectivity." But if so, we are clearly confronted with a "text" of quite occult powers.

Like Charles Taylor, Geertz is nonchalant about just how strange a text he has discovered. Though cockfights appear to communicate quite peculiarly, he fails to explore their workings further. Again like Taylor, his concern seems more with the depth of the interpretation (or the thickness of description) than with its empirical warrant. Following a methodological tradition displaced by modern science, Geertz presents and then re-presents the phenomena of concern to him, illustrating them in different locations and aspects, as we shall see momentarily. Like Goethe in his scientific investigations (see Schneider 1979), he appears more interested in *Darstellung* (presentation) than *Erklärung* (explanation) as a road to understanding—a feature both he and Goethe share with virtuosi like Aubrey. Of course we are perhaps taking Geertz's talk about texts too literally here, yet though he admits to using phrases like "what the cockfight says" metaphorically,[8] the rationale of his semiotic treatment must rest on this being more than a *façon de parler*. Otherwise the question before us simply boils down to one of whether the cockfights are somehow in tune with Balinese sensibility, and though this might be the case, claims of this sort are overwhelmingly tautologous and very difficult to warrant. Consider that cockfighting as a species of blood sport is quite broadly distributed across cultures and is pursued in many of these with a zeal over which the Balinese have no monopoly.[9] A cursory review of the literature suggests the pastime is currently en-

8. He suggests (1973:449) that his "extension of the notion of a text beyond written material, and even beyond verbal, is, though metaphorical, not of course, all that novel." He mentions the tradition of reading Nature as a text and refers casually to Nietzsche, Marx, and Freud as exemplars of textualizing culture, concluding that the practice is "theoretically undeveloped . . . and has yet to be systematically exploited."

9. For European examples, see Thomas (1983:144) and Marvin (1984); for the North American example, Hawley (1989); and for a Caribbean case, Affergan (1986).

demic throughout much of Southeast Asia and certainly proves to be as addictive in the Philippines as it does in Bali, though the cultural differences between these two sites are enormous.[10] Granted that fascination with cockfights is very general, it is difficult to understand how they could express something specifically Balinese.[11] The wide distribution of the pastime further suggests how awkward it would be to explain the Balinese case by subconscious resonances between "text" and public, since the former seems to "resonate" successfully across different cultures and personality types.

Considering the matter commonsensically, furthermore, a problem results from the frequency with which the cockfight-as-text is repeated in Bali. In our own experience of theater, for instance, we simply cannot bear this sort of redundancy and monotony, however sublime the message. Thus on the surface of it Geertz's allusions to Shakespeare, Flaubert, and string quartets are problematic, since whatever insights into our subjectivity we gain through such works, these do not cause us to read or attend them over and over again. Perhaps, however, we could salvage the textual metaphor by scaling the allusions down, calling now on Punch and Judy shows, mystery plays, or the *arlecchinos* of commedia dell'arte, all of which are enjoyed for their formulaic qualities. Yet the redundancy of the cockfights still seems excessive in comparison.[12] To generalize with abandon, no dramatic text bears the frequency of repetition we find here unless supported by externalities of one sort or

10. To our knowledge there is no comparative ethnography of cockfighting. It certainly appears to be popular in the Philippines, where a periodical entitled *Sabong* caters to it and a promotional literature has developed (see below in text). We have seen references to cockfighting in northern Malaysia, while in Sarawak (Malaysian Borneo) it seems to be as popular as in Bali. James Barclay (1980:18) noted that cockfights highlight the lengthy parties given by the Iban, and are in that circumstance "undertaken with fanatical zest by birds and men alike." A serious review of the literature would probably find addiction to cockfighting (and governmental perception of it as a vice) general throughout the area, though the cultures vary quite dramatically. Certainly there is no evidence that Iban sensibility bears any particular resemblance to Balinese.

11. Of course they might do so if they were "coded" differently in each culture, thus telling a different "story" about sensibility to each local clientele, but this possibility merely underscores our inability to show they are coded anywhere in the first place.

12. Compare, however, Janice Radway's interesting *Reading the Romance* (1984), where formulaic fiction is shown to be consumed in quite astonishing quantities. Her research is a model of the patient attention to ethnointerpretation required if we are to understand why people are attracted to a particular genre of cultural product. Precisely how one might draw an analogy between Harlequin romances and cockfighting is unclear, but even were one to see individual cockfights as enjoyably varied instances of a constant theme or plot, as the romances clearly are, we would be left with the problem of explaining what is specifically Balinese in them.

another, perhaps religious or obsessive. Yet Geertz's ethnography gives us no reason to view them this way. Whichever way we go with the cockfight-as-text, it seems to entail consequences, at least on the basis of our own experience, that it does not have in his reporting. Read naturalistically, it turns the Balinese into "redundancy freaks," mesmerized by a single document and addicted to its repetition. Thus our confrontation with the enigmatical winds up with the Balinese as foreign to us as they began, or perhaps more so.

That this result is not more commonly experienced by readers of the essay is itself an interesting datum. It is discouraged in part by our lust for thick description, in part by Geertz's particularistic focus on a single culture, and in part by our nonchalance in the face of strange goings-on. The sense that we are gaining access to the murky depths of the Balinese through the cockfight is of course seductive, and would have been difficult to sustain had Geertz taken a comparative perspective. In the latter, the problem of explaining Balinese fascination with fights disappears, since it is by no means culture specific. For instance, the Filipino enthusiast Angel Lansang (1966:17) writes:

Our national sport . . . is not only an institution, it is a way of life. In fact the sport is . . . closely bound up with our sensibilities and is patently considered an integral part of our cultural evolution . . . [because in it] our passionate nature really finds expression. . . . In a very real sense, cockfighting reflects our true culture as a people. It is here that our real selves come to the surface.[13]

Of course in each culture where they prove popular, their capacity to "reflect" sensibility might deepen their attraction, particularly among contemplative segments of the population. A visitor might then be taken to them in the same way foreigners are taken to baseball games or Thanksgiving dinners—so as to illustrate, albeit mysteriously, what it is to be "American." Yet though we may speak loosely of how "the Ameri-

---

13. We should note here that among educated elites, for whom sport is frequently an object of contemplation, the "symbolic" attractions of games may often supersede more ordinary ones. Similarly, occult or divinatory practices often have quite different popular and elite rationales. In the former a practice is seen as having some capacity to act on the world, as alchemy turns lead into gold or the I Ching advises about appropriate courses of action. In the elite view, however, such an interpretation is vulgar: the occult practice instead aims at the development and exploration of subjectivity or spirituality. The I Ching has had this elite reading in China at least since the thirteenth century, just as have, at various times and places, alchemy, tarot, horoscopy, and the rest. In fact in such cases real "codes" that allow events to be "read" are frequently produced. There is, however, no evidence that this has happened for cockfights; and if it had, there would still be a question of whether their "symbolic" attraction for elites would account for their quite general popularity.

can story" is told every day on the diamond or yearly in the giblet gravy, our foreign friends would certainly be baffled if we suggested these were texts they could read for themselves, quite apart from our commentary.[14] To do so is to venture into occult terrain, and while there is charm to this it proves no more forthcoming that Aubrey's apparition.

Thus if we insist that culture is a text, it turns out to be a most peculiar one, able to communicate in occult ways. On the other hand, if one's aim is to "hawk the anomalous, [and] peddle the strange," Geertz has succeeded admirably, if not exactly as he had in mind. But rather than rest our case on this single example, however influential, let us look briefly at another. Cockfighting is not the only cultural practice found to communicate rich messages in occult ways: another is taken up in the essay "Art as a Cultural System" (1983). At one point the discussion concerns the place of "line" in Yoruba sculpture and sensibility. Relying on the analysis of Robert Farris Thompson (1973), Geertz first notes (1983:98) that:

the vocabulary of linear qualities, which the Yoruba use colloquially and across a range of concerns far broader than sculpture, is nuanced and extensive. It is not just their statues, pots, and so on that the Yoruba incise with lines: they do the same with their faces [cicatricially]. . . . But there is more to it than this. The Yoruba associate line with civilization: "This country has become civilized," literally means, in Yoruba, "this earth has lines upon its face."

He then quotes Thompson's article, where etymological and homonymic relations between various Yoruba terms are given: "civilization" is "the face lined with marks"; one word for incising facial scars also means "to clear the bush"; others have to do with cutting roads, marking boundaries, and plowing fields. Finally, as Thompson (1973:36, cited by Geertz [1983:99]) notes, "the basic verb to cicatrize (*là*) has multiple associations of imposing human pattern upon the disorder of nature . . . allowing the inner quality of [its] substance to shine forth." With this in mind, Geertz comments that "the intense concern of the Yoruba carver with line, and with the particular forms of line, stems therefore from rather more than a detached pleasure in its intrinsic properties, the problems of sculptural technique, or even some generalized cultural notion one could isolate as a native aesthetic. It grows out

14. Though Jacques Barzun is supposed to have argued that "whoever wants to know the heart and mind of America had better learn baseball," it is difficult to make much of this in a naturalistic framework. Admittedly, the *differences* between American and Japanese brands of baseball perhaps result from real cultural differences—but see Griswold (1981) for generalized caution about excesses here—yet these do not necessarily take us to the "heart and mind" of either society (assuming it makes sense to talk about this in the first place).

of a distinctive sensibility the whole of life participates in forming—one in which the meanings of things are the scars men leave on them." Thus a consequence of line in Yoruba carving, he goes on to note, is to "materialize a way of experiencing, bring a particular cast of mind out into the world of objects, where men can look at it."

The strategy here is similar to the analysis of cockfighting. "Line" spreads out associatively to signify a distinctive sensibility and indeed much of Yoruba life, though the device by which it does this is etymological and homonymic. In making lines on carvings and faces, as potentially in bordering properties, cutting paths in the bush or furrows in their fields, the Yoruba do not just *that*, but something characteristically Yoruba, alluding with each stroke to all others and thus to a modality of experience both sublime and uniquely theirs. The marks of scarification, path making, or agriculture constitute, as Geertz (1983:99) has it, "primary documents . . . conceptions themselves that seek—or for which people seek—a meaningful place in a repertoire of other documents, equally primary." These inscriptions or microtexts are linguistically interrelated, with any line potentially registering its meaningful place in a network of allusions, not just fecundating it with significance, with "something rather more than . . . its intrinsic properties," but with signifying agency.

Let us again play the pedestrian critic. In his analysis, Geertz is not particularly clear about what viewing "line" linguistically entails, though we can distinguish a variety of claims of varying strength. For convenience, let us confine ourselves to the case of sculpture, which in any event seems to offer the richest possibilities. Here a minimal claim would simply be that these carvings (or some of their properties) commonly have extra-aesthetic significance for the Yoruba, though perhaps of an indeterminate sort such that connoisseurs, much like our own art critics, would find quite varied meanings in them. In this case they would be expressive objects serving as foci for speculative construal as to significance. A somewhat stronger claim would be that specific qualities of sculptures are linked through a code to other realms of Yoruba experience in such a way that relatively determinate information can be read off the figurines. Here certain of their properties could be said to have conventional meaning in addition to significance. Still more strongly—and more nearly approximating the apparent thrust of Geertz's discussion[15]—the full complex of sculptural qualities, perhaps

15. See particularly his argument (1983:99, emphasis added) that "the signs or sign elements [of Yoruba as of Western art] make up a *semiotic system* . . . ideationally connected to the society in which they are found."

aided by resonance with other "inscriptive" media, might be able to signify some unique global experience or "cast of mind" we would expect to be commented upon in sculptural appreciation. In such a case figurines might be judged better or worse in terms of their relative success in bringing all this "out into the world of objects, where men can look at it." Finally, and here going somewhat beyond what Geertz directly suggests, Yoruba carving might have both lexical and grammatical properties in result of which sculptors could communicate varied messages about their cast of mind to connoisseurs—in which case the medium would be fully linguistic by any standard.

Granted the aesthetic eloquence of Yoruba sculpture and the longevity of the tradition of which it is a part, to find evidence for even the strongest of these claims would not astonish us. Yet if information about sensibility is being conveyed by the sculptures, it appears to happen without being much noticed: on consulting Thompson's essay, we find that the Yoruba comment on sculptural line in rather banal terms that give but minor indication of interests extending beyond a formal aesthetic. Thompson solicited evaluations of sculpture from various Yoruba carvers and connoisseurs, isolating the major criteria utilized in judgment. One of these was "visibility," a quality partly expressed through "linear precision"—meaning the clarity of definition in the knife work by which the eyes, mouths, fingers, or coiffure of the figurines were rendered. Appraisals of this quality were quite straightforward and unembellished. The sculptor Bandele, for instance, commented in criticizing a piece simply that "The mouth remains [unfinished?]; they have not lined it. They have not incised the sash. They have grooved it" (1973:34). Yoruba, whether sculptors, connoisseurs, or men in the street, recognize detailing and precision as properties that distinguish good work from bad, and Thompson (1973:35) indeed suggests that "the notion of linear connoisseurship is highly developed among traditional Yoruba." It is in expanding on this that he draws on the terminology of scarification and notes the etymological relations between this and various words for civilization, the carving lexicon, marking borders, and so on. Yet these associations do not enter into the commentary he elicited, which did not go beyond suggesting that in certain instances lines were "too faint" or perhaps "more visible" on one statue than another.[16] Thus it would seem that if information about Yoruba sensibility

---

16. Thompson's original assessment (1973:36) was merely that the linear terminology, particularly in its relation to scarification, "sharpens the eye of the Yoruba critic and gives the sensitive non-carver the knack of talking about clarity of line with conviction." Thus they are able to "defend their tastes when judging sculpture which does or does not satisfy local feelings about linear visibility."

or the sculptor's cast of mind is being conveyed to connoisseurs, it must be in ways that do not cause them to take notice.

As we shall see in a moment, there is more to Yoruba sculpture than Bandele's commentary would suggest, but in light of the expectations Geertz has raised, the framework in which it is commonly discussed seems quite prosaic. To hazard an analogy, it resembles the one in which certain connoisseurs among us appraise horseflesh. Elaborate if somewhat intuitive conventions have been established in this domain and are taught to neophytes so as to make their estimations approximate those of experts. Thus judgments as to beauty of conformation can be broadly shared without this leading to suspicions of extra-aesthetic significance. More often than not, this is true of Yoruba sculpture as well: the quest for ulterior significance or encoded messages is missing—at least to outward appearances. What, then, is going on? How does the sculpture-as-text, through which information about Yoruban sensibility is conveyed, work?

Thompson has made it clear in personal communication that sculpture can have nonaesthetic import for the Yoruba, while certain of its properties have been codified so as to signify something for particular connoisseurs, though not necessarily about casts of mind. He writes (1987), for instance, that

a priest of divination spontaneously talked about the criterion of visibility and linked it to the discretion of spirit possession and dreams—if the spirits "come down" or pass through a dream they have *fi ara hon,* made their body visible, meaning, they want the issue they represent or carry made patent. *Ko fi ara hon,* the opposite, means the god of fate does not want to show himself, and we will in dreams or divination "see another side which will not be relevant to the question." Visibility to them is more than mere craftsmanship; it has to do with discretion and the very privilege of being told pure truths as opposed to necessary euphemisms.

Thus we can see that behind the criticisms of a sculptor like Bandele may lie realms of significance by which specific conventions acquire extra-aesthetic import. For at least some informants, furthermore, visibility in sculpture is linked to a dimension of spiritual experience characterized by degrees of revelation or, more accurately, by variable privilege in exposure to truth. In fact, the sense of a dimension of expressive potential beneath or beyond surface verisimilitude is, Thompson suggests, widespread among connoisseurs, for whom figurines are able to address "larger social issues, coded by stance and so forth." The vocabulary through which this is done is shared by Yoruba at least within the precincts of the divination cult.

Rather as we would expect, then, Yoruba sculpture shows itself capable of serving as a focus for speculative inquiry into significance, and capable as well of conveying some extra-aesthetic information. Yet exactly how widespread this is or how it connects with the aesthetic and craftsmanly considerations which appear to dominate Yoruba artistic production and criticism is unclear. In any event the evidence supports in certain contexts the weaker claims we have outlined with regard to Yoruba sculpture. As yet, however, we have encountered nothing that would support the stronger claim that carving materializes and makes public some global Yoruba experience or cast of mind. Indigenous commentary, as we have seen, ignores this matter, and how it is to be conceived of other than tautologically is problematic: of course in their carving the Yoruba express a distinctive sensibility or cast of mind; but then they could hardly do otherwise, since to an external observer the conventions of sculpture are one of the things that make this sensibility distinctive in the first place. For a strong textual claim to have weight, then, we must be able to conceive of a specifically Yoruban cast of mind independent of and yet materializable through techniques that prove specifiable in practice. Sensibility could then be communicated by sculpture in a format meriting textual metaphors. Yet though one can imagine referring to specific achievements in sculpture as "characteristically Yoruban"—in the same sense that we sometimes refer to films like *Jules et Jim* as characteristically French—neither Geertz's discussion nor the ethnographic information on which it is based give us any sense of how to go further, how to "read" the information presumably conveyed. But if we cannot do this, and still wish to consider sculptures as "texts," then they must radiate messages in some as yet unexplicated manner.

Once again readers may have difficulty appreciating the peculiarity in this, grounded as it is within interpretive customs that are more or less routine in humanistic discourse. Perhaps Geertz does no more than exploit these conventions—but in that case his semiotic anthropology becomes an edifying enterprise and his view of Yoruba sculpture analogous to Breton's view of *Les Demoiselles d'Avignon*. This might be interesting and worthwhile, though it is unclear what it has to do with anthropology, where empirical features of Yoruba sculptural production and consumption would presumably be at issue. Indeed, though the claims Geertz makes for semiotic anthropology and the widespread influence of his work seem based on its ties with empirical anthropology, when we read him this way, we are inevitably involved in mysteries, since then Yoruba sculpture must convey large amounts of information (a "sublime" view of the Yoruba) in ways about which neither we nor they seem very clear. Pragmatically, the purely quantitative issue of how so much can get into so little would be troubling.[17]

It seems, then, that when we read Geertz's analyses in a naturalistic framework they prove enchanting. What would be unremarkable as an edifying claim that cockfights and sculptures are suitable vehicles through which to reflect on sensibilities becomes remarkable when they are taken as texts somehow communicating these sensibilities. Yet that Geertz entirely ignores the comparative or quasi-experimental investigation that would warrant such a view[18] suggests it is foreign to his epistemic ambitions for semiotic anthropology. But what *are* his ambitions, then? Here we should note that at least one strand of hermeneutic practice, drawing on Continental traditions, sees the explication of human action on a textual model to be less an empirical than a "spiritual" matter. Before turning to Geertz's own discussion of his epistemic register, it might be an idea to examine this position.

In a 1971 article, Paul Ricoeur encouraged us to think of all meaningful action as having a textual character.[19] Action that was not perspicuous would thus be "read" more or less as one interprets a difficult literary document. In Ricoeur's project, however, the term "text" takes on a special and restricted reference which distances it both from its author and its historical situatedness as the product of specific events. He sees a text as characterized by four qualities differentiating it from standard uses of language: "(1) the fixation of the meaning, (2) its dissociation from the mental intention of the author, (3) the display of non-ostensive references, and (4) the universal range of its addressees" (1971:546). To take these characteristics up in order, texts are of course *written,* giving them permanence at the cost of those effects that are *voiced* in spoken discourse. Using Austin's distinctions, Ricoeur suggests that texts cannot convey most of the illocutionary and perlocutionary effects available vocally. What remains when these are subtracted is the propositional content of language, what it *says* as opposed to what it

17. See, however, Paulson (1988) and our discussion in chapter 6.

18. As we have suggested, comparative evidence would reveal the cockfight to be a non-problem. The Yoruba case, being singular, would require a (somewhat farfetched) quasi-experimental inquiry. Warrant for a strong correspondence between sculpture and sensibility, for instance, would be revealed if blind adult individuals were given sight and then presented with a variety of sculptural styles. Should they recognize Yoruba sculptures as "theirs," we would be convinced. (Though farfetched, this experiment illustrates the length that must be gone to in such circumstances to escape tautology.)

19. "The Model of the Text: Meaningful Action Considered as a Text" was originally published in *Social Research,* but is reprinted in Rabinow and Sullivan (1979), where it joins Taylor's and Geertz's work as a programmatic document for interpretive social science.

does in dialogic circumstances. This first difference between spoken and written language is accompanied by a second: in acquiring permanence through writing, a text "escapes the finite horizon lived by its author" with the consequence that "the author's intention and the meaning of the text cease to coincide" (1971:534). Ricoeur is not clear about just why this occurs: it is not a matter of the impracticality of discovering authors' intentions (posthumously, say), but of a public and transhistorical appropriation whereby "what the text says now matters more than what the author meant to say, and every exegesis unfolds its procedures within the circumference of a meaning that has broken its moorings to the psychology of the author." This result is paralleled in the third quality of texts, their nonostensive reference. Whereas in dialogical uses of language reference is normally to the immediate *situation* of speakers, elements of which can be pointed to, the reference of a text according to Ricoeur is to the *world* in which we conceive it to have been written. A "world" is a "possible mode of being" constituted on the basis of documents, as we might infer the lineaments of "the world of the Greeks" from certain texts or the "world of the Yoruba" from their sculpture. The terms of texts thus refer not to actual historical things or events but to their representations in the "world" we have constructed. Finally, while spoken language is addressed to particular individuals, a text is addressed to anyone capable of reading. Ricoeur draws no particular lesson from this universality of address, however, and we may presume that it simply reinforces the effects of the first three characteristics, by which texts are freed from the direct circumstances of their creation.

It is this model that Ricoeur proposes extending to meaningful action in general. In viewing Weber's *sinnhaft orientiertes Verhalten* as textual, he reconceptualizes the social sciences as hermeneutic disciplines probing the spirituality of action, which is to say its meaning independent of its specific situatedness. The four properties that distinguish texts from other uses of language Ricoeur finds characteristic of action as well.[20] Action, for instance, is "fixed" just as language is "fixed" by inscription: as he suggests, "meaningful action is an object for science only under the condition of a kind of objectification which is equivalent to the fixation of a discourse by writing" (1971:537). He is not clear about the precise nature of this objectification, however, suggesting

20. He does not address the logical difficulty that results. If nontextual uses of language are themselves "meaningful action"—as of course they must be—then as action is taken to be a text the basis for his original distinction between the texts and other uses of language is lost. Though Ricoeur wants to avoid the obvious "deconstructive" conclusion—that language is in all circumstances "always already textual"—his argument drives us directly to it.

only that through it "action is no longer a transaction to which the discourse of action would still belong. It constitutes a delineated pattern which has to be interpreted according to its inner connections"—these latter being explicated in terms of the "propositional content" of action or its "noematic structure." Whatever this is, it presumably can be abstracted from the circumstances under which actions occur as historical events. But how is it "fixated"? Ricoeur notes that we can speak metaphorically of an event having "left its mark on time" rather as a pen marks paper, but defers consideration until the bearing on action of the remaining features of texts has been discussed.

Action is detached from actors, Ricoeur suggests, in the same way a text is detached from its author. Just as texts have meanings not intended by authors, so acts have consequences not intended by actors. Furthermore, actors are drawn into "courses of events" in ways that make isolating the contributions of specific historical individuals extremely problematic. Ricoeur here suggests that the notion of a "course of events" is analogous to the inscription which fixes discourse. Thus actions are objectified by being situated in "patterns which become the *documents* of human action" (1971:542). Actors involved in such patterns are often unable to discern them and thus recognize their own contributions, but the patterns may be evident to the interpreter, for whom they have an objective character similar to an inscription.[21] Furthermore, once seen in the context of courses of events, acts have an importance that extends beyond their immediate situation. Thus just as the reference of texts is wider and less immediate than that of spoken discourse, aiming at the "world" in which they are written, so courses of events are understood in terms of their relevance to the "world" in which they occur. "To say the same thing in different words, the meaning of an important event exceeds, overcomes, transcends, the social conditions of its production and may be reenacted in new social contexts" (1971:543). Finally, in such circumstances, actions must be considered "*addressed* to an indefinite range of possible 'readers'" (1971:544), thus meeting the last criterion distinguishing texts from other uses of discourse. Seen in this framework, actions can be interpreted in terms of their transcendental bearing.

Whether or not one finds Ricoeur's argument convincing, its effect is to secure the epistemic register for a particular brand of discourse.

21. Recognizing the "Whiggish" character of his argument, Ricoeur writes (1971:542–543) that "this hypostasis of history may be denounced as a fallacy, but this fallacy is well entrenched in the process by which human action becomes social action when written down in the archives of history."

Not unexpectedly, the subject matter of this discourse is difficult to characterize in terms of our previous discussions. On the one hand it sometimes seems Ricoeur is interested in the significance of action: he wants to know what is important about a specific event from a generalized perspective—what we could perhaps call its human significance anent the "course of events" or "world" in which it exists. This would seem clearly an edifying concern were Ricoeur not insistent that significance is somehow "objectively" present in the action itself, as its propositional content or noematic structure. Yet as this is quite distinct from the actors' intentions, it fits into none of the categories of meaning we have previously discussed.[22] Perhaps what he seeks in action is most similar to what Taylor sought in "intersubjective meaning," though this notion is itself too vague to be of much help.

As we saw with Taylor, such meaning is most comfortably discussed in an ambiguous register. The data that are to be made sense of are of course empirical, but are abstracted from so as to expose their inner connections and then integrated into historical patterns or cultural surrounds. These latter are fictions of relation which bind the abstractions together into intelligible wholes, as in "the world of the Greeks." Such constructions can be "validated" in terms of their relative probability, Ricoeur argues, by using an argumentative process "comparable to the juridical procedures of legal interpretation" (1971:549). This gives us, he suggests, "a scientific knowledge" of our subject matter. By invoking science in this way, he apparently seeks to insulate himself from relativist conclusions. Yet exactly how these are to be escaped is not clear, since the sorts of meaning of interest to him are normally used precisely to make the case for relativism. So mercurial are they that they are commonly assumed to have no purchase outside the interpretive process, being appropriately contemplated for their edifying potential rather than for their pragmatic or explanatory application. But Ricoeur wants to resist this conclusion as strongly as he wants to sustain the transcendental character of texts by abstracting from their historical situatedness. Consequently, "action as a text" winds up being spoken of in a register left ambiguous between edification and naturalism, perhaps so that interpretive latitude can be had within the framework of a "scientific" procedure.[23]

22. Elsewhere, Ricoeur approvingly explores Freudian interpretation, which produces the non-naturalistic equivalent of symptomatic meaning. But though the present essay clearly opens the epistemic space in which Freudian interpretation could reside, Ricoeur does not seem to have it in mind.

23. Looked at more broadly, the suggestion that nonlinguistic elements of culture (or history, or society) be looked on as texts is rarely made with a view to increasing our

Is this what Geertz seeks for semiotic anthropology as well? We should note first that any simple appropriation of Ricoeur's notion of action as a text would be prohibited by Geertz's professed concern with what "institutions, actions, images, utterances, events, customs, all the usual objects of social-scientific interest, mean to those whose institutions, actions, customs, and so on they are" (1983:22). Though this is a canonical (and presumably empirical) concern of descriptive anthropology, such meanings would be tangential to Ricoeur's project since they do not yield the human significance of things, their meaning beyond authorial intentions. (Clearly, Ricoeur is not after what Geertz calls "local knowledge.") On the other hand, the results of Geertz's interpretations generally have more in common with Ricoeur's objectives than they do with descriptive anthropology as commonly conceived. Thus it is not surprising that his methodological statements seem consistently to vacillate between naturalism and edification (and between realism and relativism: see 1984) until the epistemic status of his discourse is thoroughly blurred. In *The Interpretation of Cultures*, for instance, he argues that his explications are fictional, but only "in the sense that they are 'something made,' 'something fashioned' . . . not that they are false, unfactual, or merely 'as if' thought experiments" (1973:15). Exactly how we are to evaluate such "factual fictions" is left unclear however, since doubt is cast on their epistemic register by a later passage (1973:29) where he argues that

to commit oneself to a semiotic concept of culture and an interpretive approach to the study of it is to commit oneself to a view of ethnographic assertion as, to borrow W. B. Gallie's by now famous phrase, "essentially contestable." Anthropology, or at least interpretive anthropology, is a science whose progress is marked less by a perfection of consensus than by a refinement of debate. What gets better is the precision with which we vex each other.

Vexing one's colleagues is of course a great academic pleasure, but it is odd in this context to find it being elevated over the "perfection of consensus" at which empirical disciplines generally aim. Odd also is how we are to conceive of Geertz's thick descriptions as being "essentially contestable," since they do not directly meet the criteria Gallie lays

explanatory power as judged by naturalistic standards. In Richard Harvey Brown's *Society as Text* (1987), for instance, the rationale for the analogy of the title is largely moral or political: viewing people as "authors" of their circumstances and society as a dialogic phenomenon would be empowering, whereas a naturalistic view is reifying. Similarly, when Geertz (1988:147) argues that the goal of contemporary ethnography should be "to enlarge the possibility of intelligible discourse between people quite different from one another," he need not subscribe to explanatory aims.

down.[24] Whether the Balinese attend fights to learn about their sensibility is not the same order of question as whether Lenin's mantle should be seen as falling on Stalin or perhaps on Trotsky. The latter is essentially contested because we cannot develop consensus over the criteria for being a proper inheritor. We will be similarly stymied with regard to Balinese motives only if we conceive of them as beyond empirical discovery—as Taylor or Ricoeur might encourage us to do. But in that case they will prove mercurial, belonging to a sector of our referential ecology where objects present themselves sporadically and in different guises to each person who investigates them. We might think them products of our imagination, but Geertz wants to avoid this option since it would diminish their claim upon our attention, the reality of their enchantment. Thus they must be conceived as "out there" but nevertheless in a location that prevents us from achieving "perfection of consensus" as to their character.

There is considerable logic, then, to the amphibolous register Geertz adopts. It is designed for a particular subject matter—culture as a text—whose mysterious powers and occult behavior have fascinated many interpretive social scientists. In "reading" culture, it is argued, we may understand what it means to be other than we are: what it is, for instance, to be Balinese. Inscribed in blood sport, Balinese otherness becomes almost palpable—though it undoubtedly will be "felt" differently by each reader of the text. Such phenomena cannot easily be talked about in either a naturalistic or an edifying register since the former does not let them get off the ground, so to speak, while the latter lets them fly too high, detaching them from the ambit of empirical phenomena and thus from specific form of authority naturalistic inquiry is able to confer.

Hence Geertz, like Ricoeur and Taylor, blurs the distinction between naturalistic and edifying registers, making room for a mode of discourse between the empirical and the imaginative. Assertions in this mode are grounded in empirical phenomena, but needn't answer to naturalistic standards of warrant. Far from being exotic, this register is common to everyday life, where we all use it in casual discussions of the significance of things. As an illustration, consider a passage from the essay "Blurred Genres" (1983), where Geertz celebrates attempts to erode disciplinary

24. Graham Watson (1989) arrives at the same judgment independently, though from the "reflexive" side of anthropology. He argues that, programmatic statements to the contrary, Geertz consistently adopts a realist rhetoric whose aim is to forfend claims of essential contestability. On the latter, see W. B. Gallie (1964), where the matter is taken up in chapter 8, of which Wayne Booth (1977) has provided a useful précis.

boundaries. He cites an unusual array of instances, provided by thinkers as disparate as Sartre and Castaneda, where a "jumbling of varieties of discourse" has taken place. Over the recent past, he suggests, such jumbling has occurred at an increasing rate, so that now "one waits only for quantum theory in verse or biography in algebra." Though recognizing that genre boundaries have never been absolute, Geertz concludes (1983:20) that their supposed collapse represents "a phenomenon general enough and distinctive enough to suggest that what we are seeing is not just another redrawing of the cultural map . . . but an alteration of the principles of mapping. Something is happening to the way we think about the way we think." Though he is somewhat vague about just what is happening to "the way we think about the way we think," such an assertion is of a very respectable genre we might style "quasi-referential." In the above passage Geertz is offering a fiction of relation that may cause us to "see" certain phenomena in a new way, as having significance anent a change in habits of thought. To appreciate this, however, requires that we assume a "real" transformation is occurring in the way we think. Unless we do—and some caution is advised[25]—the web of examples Geertz has woven frays a bit and ceases to make sense. Yet the rules governing this sort of discourse prevent us from calling on him to *demonstrate* what he presumably intends we consider only casually. To hold him to exacting standards, calling on him to create some empirical measure of genre blurring, apply it to a representative sample of thinkers across time, analyze the results, and so on, would simply be tactless, mistaking his genre.[26] Significance of the sort he is after here is always quasi-referential and thrives on modal ambiguity: it seems clear that we are not to hector it with demands for empirical warrant, and yet its raison d'être would be weakened if its "fictive" nature were fully and publicly underscored. Significance, once spun, must appear not to have been spun at all, but rather *discovered*. Without this mimetic or referential caste its persuasiveness would be diminished. On

25. Whether something is afoot now in thought presumably depends on how one evaluates "postmodernism" as an intellectual development. Though it has rather aggressively promoted genre blurring, one might question (see Dogan and Pahre 1990) whether the empirical frequency of the latter has actually increased, as well as whether, if so, the effect will prove permanent enough to merit much notice. Perhaps, for instance, it has simply been taken up by that segment of scholars (of a size difficult to gauge) who characteristically champion novelty. If so, it presumably constitutes but one in a lengthy series of intellectual ripples, to be followed shortly by another.

26. However far genre blurring has advanced, it has not gotten to the point where the inappropriateness of such a response wouldn't be recognized—even by Geertz, who would correctly accuse us of a *bêtise*.

the other hand, it cannot highlight its empirical pretensions if the consequence is to arouse strong demands for warrant. Thus it is stuck in an ambiguous register.

Our point is not that there is something amiss with such talk, its quasi-referential tone, or its epistemic ambiguity: that is simply the way significance is discussed. But it should be clear that when we blur the distinction between this and anthropological investigation, we will often wind up in enchanted terrain. Explaining how the significance we discern actually exists—as, say, a text—will entail postulating, explicitly or not, entities that behave in mercurial and ultimately mysterious ways. Virtuosi may welcome this, but other investigators may not.

Have we, however, perhaps focused on a tangential aspect of Geertz's work, rather than on a central one? It seems not: in a general review of developments in anthropological theory, for instance, Sherry Ortner (1984:129) addresses precisely the matters we have singled out: "Geertz's most radical theoretical move . . . was to argue that culture is not something locked inside people's heads, but rather is embodied in public symbols, symbols through which the members of a society communicate their world-view, value-orientations, ethos, and all the rest to one another, to future generations—and to anthropologists." It is the enchantment in this radical theoretical move, exemplified in the cock-fight-as-text, that we have sought to foreground. And Ortner is not alone in her estimate of Geertz's contribution: Marcus and Fischer (1986:26), in reviewing the development of interpretive anthropology, note that

The metaphor of cultures as texts, popularized by Clifford Geertz . . . served to mark vividly the difference between the behavioral scientist and the cultural interpreter. According to this view, social activities can be "read" for their meanings by the observer just as written and spoken materials more conventionally are. What's more, not only the ethnographer reads symbols in action, but so do the observed, the actors in relation to one another.

Along with the practice of "thick description," then, the textual view of nonlinguistic phenomena has probably been Geertz's most influential contribution, both inside anthropology and out.

As to his more general impact, we might note that it was relatively strong both in anthropology and history (see Walters 1980) during the seventies. During the eighties, while perhaps waning somewhat in anthropology, it carried over into literary studies, to be linked up with Foucault via the "new historicism" (see Veeser 1989:xi; Pecora 1989:247). Interestingly, the possible decline of his influence in anthropology cannot be explained by criticism of his work in empirical terms, however much this grew in the course of the decade (see Roseberry 1982; Shankman 1984; Lieberson 1984; Hirschfeld 1986; Crapanzano 1986; Schneider 1987). Indeed, these criticisms seem to have had no impact at all.[27] Instead, as the "interpretive turn" in anthropology spiraled inward to concentrate on epistemological and political concerns (see Clifford 1988; Clifford and Marcus 1986; Marcus and Fischer 1986), Geertz's work lost its vanguard character.[28] By contrast, the concurrent rise of his fortunes in literary studies seemed somehow fated, and not only because he has always acknowledged his debt to literary theorists and worked to break down distinctions between anthropological and literary analysis.[29] Rather, as the "new historicism" in literary studies (perhaps reacting to the edifying aims of deconstruction) sought to mold an ambiguous, quasi-referential epistemic register for its own discourse, Geertz was already on the scene as a particularly appealing exemplar. Furthermore, though his attitude toward Foucault can only be characterized as reserved (see 1988:7), that they should together have stimulated New Historicist work seems somehow fitting, since it is in its Foucaultian aspect that this movement has itself become a scene of enchantment, discovering occult "economies" in the symbolic order and grappling with the ultimately mysterious dynamics of "power."[30]

Of course we have foregrounded in this chapter only one aspect of a

27. Rabinow and Sullivan ignore it, for instance, in the new introduction to the second edition of *Interpretive Social Science* (1987), which again includes "Deep Play." A novel illustration of how impervious the essay is to criticism is its reprinting by Jeffrey Alexander (Alexander and Seidman 1990), who elsewhere (Alexander 1987) criticizes it (see n. 7 above). The capacity of "exemplary" interpretive documents to survive what might appear to be rigorous empirical critique is a datum for the sociology of enchantment we outline in chapters 5 and 7.

28. For Geertz's reflections on this development, which he has both criticized and contributed to, see *Works and Lives* (1988). His offering has been neither epistemological nor political, however, but concentrates on the rhetorical strategies deployed in classic anthropological texts.

29. The call for papers (see Geertz [1971] 1974:ix–xi) for the *Daedalus* volume on Myth, Symbol, and Culture—a call jointly authored by Geertz and Paul de Man—explicitly sought to link literature and the social sciences. Geertz's fullest discussion of the relationship will be found in *Works and Lives*.

30. Judith Butler (1990), for instance, while generally appreciative, has noted the degree to which Foucault's concept of power took on vitalist characteristics. Similarly, Paisley Livingston (1988:150–151 n. 2) suggests that "Foucault's sweeping historical theses are oriented and supported by an unbridled metaphysical speculation whereby they are linked to an inordinate proliferation of mythical entities, such as the "forces," "diagrams," "regimes," and "strata" that are posited as the unseen conditions behind the realities of human history."

The Mysteries of Myth

*The Ancients . . . were Authors of Fables . . . but sure enough their
meanings were of more high nature, and more difficult to find
out . . . else they had not writ them so obscurely.*

Reynolds, *Mythomystes* (1632)

If Geertz's work sometimes seems to slide out of our focus by blending
into the genre of edifying reflections on significance, this is a problem
we do not face with Lévi-Strauss's: a unique creation, his work cannot
easily disappear into a neighboring genre. Structural anthropology can
be seen as at once more orthodox and more radical than Geertz's semi-
ology. It is more orthodox in that the vehicles of meaning it studies are
themselves by and large linguistic, but more radical in that their messages are conveyed by entirely novel mechanisms whose workings are
not just unconscious but quite possibly self-regulating across individuals
as well as across time and space. On the basis of studies of primitive
myths, Lévi-Strauss suggested that native peoples were unknowing ar-
ticulators of a mythopoetic metalanguage that maintained itself in the
face of historical accidents and spatial dispersal.[1] Not since Freud had
such terra incognita been traversed, nor since Freud had it been recon-
noitered with such brilliance. Both further shared a virtuoso commitment to prolong enchantment rather than dispel it, and thus eschewed
naturalistic strategies that might have warranted their findings and
probed the mechanisms behind them.

While psychoanalysis endures with some success outside scientific
circles, however, structuralism, after exerting enormous influence over
cultural studies for more than a decade, went the way of many Continental intellectual enthusiasms. In fact it became passé so rapidly that
one might well wonder why it is being dealt with here: both appreciative

---

1. Dan Sperber (1975:72) offers a similar image: "We might be tempted to see in
Mythologiques the description of a language of which each Indian society knows only bits
which have finally been reassembled by Lévi-Strauss. A splendid metaphor which some
accept to the letter: since myths arise from the human mind and form this language that
no one speaks, then this human mind is the mind of no one, a metaphysical entity, similar
to the Hegelian universal Mind." He adds, however, "I do not know how this interpretation could have been arrived at. In my view, Lévi-Strauss's purpose has less grandeur but
more import." Be this as it may, it is precisely the *suggestion* of "grandeur" here that is
enchanting, and it occurs in occasional programmatic statements (e.g. Lévi-Strauss
1969:12) of the "myths think themselves in men" variety scattered about the Lévi-
Straussian corpus.

and critical commentary are widely available, after all, and so much has been said about the subject that there seems little prospect of novelty.[2] Despite being well-worked terrain, however, structuralism can hardly be ignored in this context since it offers perhaps the most striking example of enchantment since Freud. Flowing from an analytic paradigm that had in Troubetzkoy's and Jakobson's hands turned phonology dramatically in the direction of a systematic science, Lévi-Strauss's insights originally promised to transform our understanding of how culture was produced, as well as of the messages that were encoded within it. As his researches probed more deeply into the system of Amerindian myth, the mechanisms required to explain its functioning grew more and more exotic. Yet a willingness to see unusual processes occurring beneath the surface of culture was evident early in Lévi-Strauss's career and accounts in part for the excitement with which his work was received.

We will look in a moment at several examples, two from early works and one from the more imposing *Mythologiques*. It might help to preface them, however, with some reflections on the relation between structuralism and psychoanalysis. Until very late works like *The Jealous Potter* (1988), Freud is mentioned only incidentally in Lévi-Strauss's work, and yet one feels his presence everywhere, just as one feels Marx behind Weber's *Protestant Ethic*. Perhaps it can be argued that the aim of structuralism was to preserve a role in culture for unconscious agents while relieving them of the exclusively sexual concerns Freud worked so hard to establish. Having suffered as the scene of scandalous emotional drives, the unconscious was to be rehabilitated: for Lévi-Strauss, its energies were not sexual but intellectual, and it functioned to produce order in the cultural domain, continually working against the entropy of "history," taken here as inevitable but unpredictable dislocations that disturb the harmony of culture and social structure. The result could best be seen in "primitive" circumstances, where in the absence of exogenous aids to order such as writing (allowed by "civilization"), the unconscious revealed itself as naturally self-disciplined rather than chaotic.[3] Lévi-Strauss's appreciation for the "undomesticated" but spontaneously well-ordered products of primitive thought and social organization

---

2. Foremost among the methodological critiques are Pettit (1975) and Seung (1982). More empirically or ethnographically oriented are Harris (1979:165–215) and Thomas et al. (1976). Thoughtful appraisals that salvage something of structuralism are Kirk (1975) and Sperber (1975; 1985:64–93). A useful survey of Lévi-Strauss's work that concentrates on its political agenda is Pace (1986).

3. Particularly interesting in this regard is John M. Cuddihy's *The Ordeal of Civility* (1974), where Lévi-Strauss's concern with taming impulsivity is analyzed and compared with Freud's.

combined with his jaundiced view of contemporary society to produce a further challenge to Freud: the latter's anthropological fables, in which civilization restrained destructive natural impulses and allowed for social order, were replaced by a story drawing on Rousseau, in which natural restraint was displaced and corrupted by civilized manners (see Pace 1986). Other similarly Romantic themes (to which we will return) contributed to Lévi-Strauss's view of the world and guided his inquiries into the working of primitive culture.

Turning, then, to our cases: perhaps the most intriguing example of structural analysis in *Tristes Tropiques* (1974), Lévi-Strauss's popular mixture of autobiography, travel narrative, and anthropological speculation, involves Caduveo face painting. In its simplest form, facial decoration among this Brazilian tribe resembles bilaterally symmetrical ornamental grillwork: tendrils ending in bulbs or arrowheads grace curvi- or rectilinear hatched areas arrayed symmetrically across the centerline of the face, with the focus generally on the mouth. More complex forms, of greater interest to Lévi-Strauss, introduce higher orders of symmetry such as an inverted bilateral pattern, while diagonal sectioning produces effects that resemble modern playing cards. Asymmetries may also be introduced so that the decorations either hint at irregularity or embrace it to a point that strict symmetry survives only locally.[4] The patterns that result are complex enough that Lévi-Strauss calls on the terminology of heraldry to describe them.

What most strikes him in contemplating this art form is how its basic dualities—curvilinear as against rectilinear forms, bilateral symmetry, diagonal division, and symmetry itself as against asymmetry—are played off against the stability and unity of its final effects.[5] Searching for an analogy for this tension between dividedness and unity, Lévi-Strauss returns to the subject of playing cards. Somewhat opaque reflections upon them (1974:194) suggest that their specific form, with each card differentiated from others (i.e. asymmetrical) so as to perform a specific "role" in a game, but symmetrical across its oblique axis so as to "function" in two directions, stands as a compromise between "two contradictory forms of duality"—complete asymmetry or complete symmetry—suggested respectively by role and function. Similarly, he suggests, the unity of face paintings might best be seen as achieving a compromise between various contradictory forms of duality.

4. Compare 1974:194, figure 26, "A facial painting," and plate 2 (plate 6 in French edition), "A Caduveo belle in 1895."
5. In fact, his impressions in this regard also involve dynamic qualities of the process of composition which for ease of exposition we are ignoring.

Thus far Lévi-Strauss's analysis has been largely immanent, first isolating the formal aspects of face painting and then seeking a way to summarize their compositional effect, just as one might look at the elements and patterns in, say, Islamic decorative art with the aim of succinctly describing their impact. Rather than leave the matter there, however, he suggests an explanation for them, arguing that the particular form Caduveo facial decoration takes is not an arbitrary convention, but instead is directly determined by the sociopsychological function it serves.

To get at this, he first notes a problem posed for this tribe by its caste system:

For the nobles, and to a certain extent for the warriors too, the main problem was one of prestige. The early accounts show that they were paralysed by the fear of losing face, of not living up to their rank and, most important of all, of marrying below their station. The danger present in a society of this kind was therefore segregation. Either through choice or necessity, each caste tended to shut itself in upon itself, thus impairing the cohesion of the social body as a whole. (1974:195)

In neighboring tribes this disintegrative strain was "offset" by moiety exogamy, the practice of drawing a marital partner from outside one's "half" of the group. Though, for instance, the Guana and the Bororo still married strictly within their social class, the fact that their moieties crossed class boundaries provided a form of affiliation whereby these societies were knit more strongly together than the Caduveo: as Lévi-Strauss concludes (1974:196), "the asymmetry of the classes was, in a sense, counterbalanced by the symmetry of the moieties." Interestingly, this relation between asymmetry and symmetry is just what one finds in Caduveo facial decoration, which raises the possibility that it substitutes in some sense for moiety exogamy. Lévi-Strauss argues that the Caduveo were too obsessed with caste purity ever to countenance the fiction of cross-caste association implied by moieties, and yet

the remedy they failed to use on the social level, or which they refused to consider, could not elude them completely; it continued to haunt them in an insidious way. And since they could not become conscious of it and live it out in reality, they began to dream about it. Not in a direct form, which would have clashed with their prejudices, but in a transposed, and seemingly innocuous, form: in their art. . . [which] is to be interpreted . . . as the phantasm of a society ardently and insatiably seeking a means of expressing symbolically the institutions it might have, if its interests and superstitions did not stand in the way. (1974:196–197)

Thus the Delphic squiggles on Caduveo faces can be explained as compensating unconsciously for the disintegrative strains imposed by the caste system, filling a need other tribes satisfy by the concrete institution of moieties.

Unconscious intentions thus both give meaning to and account for the play between symmetry and asymmetry in face painting that Lévi-Strauss's interpretation has highlighted. For Fredric Jameson (1981:77–80), the result stands as a model for the investigation of the "political unconscious" as it governs the formal and aesthetic contours of symbolic acts.[6] Indeed, as we shall see, the assumption that expressive culture responds, beneath awareness, to social or socio-ideological quandaries continues to animate Lévi-Strauss's investigations. In the present instance, the causal process (though by no means the substantive content) is distinctly Freudian: the Caduveo have a problem the remedy for which they repress from consciousness because it conflicts with their sense of caste propriety. What is repressed cannot be dismissed, however: it continues to trouble them until it finally works its way, in a disguised and abstracted form, into the symbolic content of face painting, just as desire worms its way clandestinely into dreams. Without this odd means of release, which is sought "avec une passion inassouvie" (1955:203), the Caduveo would presumably be less able to cope with their social tensions than they already are.

If enchantment begins in the impression that we are under the sway of as-yet-unimagined powers, this analysis of facial decoration will certainly evoke it. While many details are left vague, the image that forms is of an unconscious mechanism—certainly a bizarre intender—that registers certain disintegrative strains in Caduveo society, identifies moieties as a putative solution to them, and then, in the face of "conscious" opposition from the ideal of caste purity, abstracts and encodes this so as to smuggle it into Caduveo expressive life beneath awareness. Such a possibility, as Jameson (1981:80) notes, "deserves serious exploration and systematic experimental verification."

Conforming to virtuoso habits, however, Lévi-Strauss neglects empirical warrant in the interest of moving on to further occasions of enchantment. In defense of this, one might point out that the Caduveo case is unique, and it is not clear how one would go about "verifying" the hypothesis in the first place: certainly the variables involved are not readily amenable to manipulation. Accordingly, Lévi-Strauss's best case

6. While in the Marxist tradition expressive culture is normally assumed to unconsciously *reflect* important—and generally *antagonistic*—features of social organization (see in this regard the works of Lucien Goldmann), Lévi-Strauss's functionalism causes him to see it as compensatory and meliorative. Jameson thus seems at his most whimsical in advancing Lévi-Strauss's Caduveo example—and especially, given his own sour view of empirical verification, in recommending that it be experimentally verified.

for his strange intender—here he again follows Freud—might be to pile up instances that are suggestive rather than to pursue the present one definitively. On the other hand—as we assume once again our role of critic—certain conceptual and methodological problems crop up that suggest why close attention to the Caduveo case might be misspent. For the sake of brevity we note only two of these. To begin with, Caduveo face painting is done by women and not by men: "Caduveo art is characterized by a male/female dualism—the men are sculptors, the women painters; the art of the former is figurative and naturalistic, in spite of its stylizations, whereas the latter practice a non-figurative art" (1974:190).[7] That men sculpt figuratively and naturalistically, however, means they lack the mechanism that produces the particular style of face painting among women. Though the putative goal of this painting—counterbalancing disintegrative strains produced by caste—would be met regardless of who produced it, it is striking that only women should do so. Thus a puzzle arises that Lévi-Strauss does not address: granted that all Caduveo are exposed to the same social strains, what accounts for the gender specificity of the response? Why should like causes in this instance not have like effects?

This conceptual problem is accompanied by a methodological one that will continue to trouble Lévi-Strauss's analyses. As will have been evident from our description, he characterizes Caduveo face painting at a very high level of abstraction: in the end he reduces its complexities to a balance of symmetry and asymmetry. An analogy is then noted between this and the balance of symmetry and asymmetry to which caste and moiety systems among the Guana and Bororo might also be reduced. While the match in this case may seem quite good, the problem is that many elements of culture or social structure, subjected to similar abstraction and reduction, might be shown to play off symmetry against asymmetry. The somewhat loose fashion in which Lévi-Strauss interprets playing cards and heraldic emblems from Western societies underscores the problem: it seems that in any society there will always be arti-

7. Lévi-Strauss leaves it unclear whether this has always been, or has only recently become, the case. He does not suggest that men were ever painters, but makes it clear they used to have themselves adorned. Women are said to continue the custom today because of the erotic allure of the painted face. (Though the text implies that women were always and only the painters, one must wonder, granted the degree of gender segregation common among South American native peoples, whether men would entrust work with such impact on their presentation of self to women, especially as it sometimes involved tattooing.) In any event, gender differentiation in artistic style is built into Lévi-Strauss's model, since "men and women, painting and sculpture" are two of the "dualisms" said to be captured in the abstract by the facial decorations (1974:191).

facts suitable for so abstract a characterization, with the consequence that it will always be possible to show a relation between social structure and *some* cultural product.[8] In other words, this method of cracking the Caduveo code is too flexible to generate confidence. Perhaps it is such a difficulty that causes him to venture onward in search of new ones.

While the fieldwork upon which parts of *Tristes Tropiques* were based was done in the thirties, the book itself was not published until 1955. By then Lévi-Strauss had already formulated his first program for the structural study of myth, which in all likelihood influenced his analysis of Caduveo face painting. In terms of the Romantic biases to which we have referred, myth posed a particular challenge for Lévi-Strauss because in its aboriginal forms it seemed such good evidence for imaginative chaos, for the *disorder* of *pensée sauvage* as opposed to its natural restraint. Because our own mythic texts come down to us in a format that has undergone the domestication of literacy, whether we look to Hesiod, Pausanias, or Ovid (or to the tales of Norse, Celtic, and Germanic mythology), we find for the most part stories which, however they may indulge in the odd metamorphoses that so dominate preliterate narrative, are motivated by a psychosocial logic not significantly foreign to us (see Goody 1977).[9]

Though primitive myths are not always devoid of a familiar logic, we are apt to be struck by the consistency with which highly dramatic acts simply *occur*, quite lacking a context, and then disappear from concern without any moral being drawn. The effect is vertiginous. Details are left to dangle, characters are dropped without comment, and consequences are made to flow from antecedents not evidently germane, so that when the tale concludes, the "accounting" that has been done is itself unaccountable (for an illustration, see the Tukuna myth discussed

8. For instance, Lévi-Strauss, unaware of or unconcerned with the damage this does his case, suggests that Bororo villages themselves are organized according to a plan similar to Caduveo face painting, though this would *reflect* their social organization whereas the Caduveo *compensate* for theirs.

9. For instance, when in Ovid's *Metamorphoses* Phaëthon rashly asks Jupiter for the reins to the chariot of the sun, we anticipate trouble because a specific personality and a specific quality of youth that *leads to* trouble are being developed. The pandemonium that ensues, and the obligation Jupiter accepts in slaying his son to save the world from conflagration, have expected places in a cautionary tale, while the use of Phaëthon's misadventure to account for the burned, black skins of his fellow Ethiopians or the similarly burned deserts of Libya are standard conventions in myths of origin and "just so" stories. Thus the surface of Ovid's text has little enigmatical about it, with its "mythic" quality deriving largely from the supernatural grandeur and the originary accountings. In effect, the familiarity or modernity of the narrative motivation that typifies Greek myth makes it rather banal in comparison with the stories of so-called primitive peoples (see Kirk 1975).

below). Such violations of narrative logic give myth the appearance of being weakly structured, as Lévi-Strauss noted in his first programmatic statement: "It would seem that in the course of a myth anything is likely to happen. There is no logic, no continuity. Any characteristic can be attributed to any subject; every conceivable relation can be found. With myth everything becomes possible" (1963a:208). The phenomenon has, as the allusion suggests, somewhat Dostoevskian overtones of a failed regulating principle, of bewildering narrative entropy often squeezed into several hundred words. But at the same time, as Lévi-Strauss went on to argue (1963a:208), the "apparent arbitrariness" of myth "is belied by the astounding similarity of myths collected in widely different regions." After all, the myths of most cultures tell of the origins of things, of gods and men, of the sources of common practices, of human blights, of customs and artifacts, and so forth. This thematic regularity is matched by certain genre qualities differentiating myths from stories or poems and accounting for the fact that "the mythical value of the myth is preserved even through the worst translation" (1963a:210). In one sense, the messages of myths are linguistically impoverished, being independent of the connotative aura of any particular embedding in words—the opposite of poetry—while their narrative weakness sets them in opposition to stories as commonly conceived.

The task Lévi-Strauss set himself was to show how a message could be carried by a myth beneath its linguistic surface and independent of its narrative logic (or lack thereof). The weakness of mythic structure would thus be in one sense real, in that the stories don't make use of customary narrative form as a source of structural strength, and illusory in that an entirely different, achronological modality of organization operates in its place. Myths were enigmatical because we approached them in terms of the wrong conventions of reading. Replacing these with structural ones would penetrate the barrier that had made myth appear such compelling evidence for the primitiveness of savage thought. Newly read, the tales would finally speak not "badly" but simply in a different language—though one whose mechanisms ultimately remained obscure.

Modeled on Prague School phonology, the structural approach to myth began with a decidedly formalist emphasis. It was not the semantic *elements* of myths that conveyed a message, building up a grammatical sequence out of independently signifying positive terms, but rather the contrastive *relations* between these terms, their difference itself. With regard to these differences and their mediations, the "positive" qualities of particular events, persons, or things were largely incidental, since the same contrast could be produced by any of a variety of elements that fit the oppositional "slot" in a formal structure. The latter might be likened to an algebraic equation with more than one numeric solution, with the individual letter terms standing for a spectrum of potential numerical values. More than anything else, Lévi-Strauss seemed to suggest, myth *was* this sort of formula, a cognitive structure that could be filled out with various elements (the latter differing from society to society according to accidents of history and ecology) but nevertheless revelatory of universal intellectual functions, an ordering system perhaps expressing the structure of the brain itself. Formalism was thus fundamental to structuralism; yet if Lévi-Strauss sometimes encourages this supposition, showing little interest in what myths consciously communicate and concentrating on how they "think themselves in men" so as to express a structure in relation to which their surface meaning is incidental, at other times a clearly hermeneutic aim predominates and the issue of what myths mean activates the decoding of their encrypted forms.[10] Furthermore, despite claims to the effect that myths are "disinterested" intellectual fabrications, aimed only at bringing pleasing order to the world, his readings almost always presume a social function, giving the myth some moral or psychological value in a primitive community, just as face painting had for the Caduveo. Often, in fact, the purported social role of the message is the only means of authorizing the reading, of showing why it should be preferred to some other. Consequently, formalist, hermeneutic, and sociological moments, though sometimes advanced independently by Lévi-Strauss, are subtly fused in his practice. Looking at the treatment given the Oedipus myth in "The Structural Study of Myth" (1963a), we can illustrate this and explore its enchantment.

To introduce his method, Lévi-Strauss offered a revolutionary interpretation of the locus classicus of Freudian theory. To show that beneath the surface of Oedipus's tale there lurked not the incestuous and parricidal wishes Freud had seen, but instead an aesthetic resolution to a conceptual dilemma faced by the Greeks, would neatly make the case for the primacy of social and cognitive considerations over sexual ones in the unconscious. Before we look at the interpretation, however, we should summarize the method used to arrive at it. Lévi-Strauss

10. In the CBC Massey Lectures published as *Myth and Meaning*, Lévi-Strauss links this to his own experience of writing: "You may remember that I have written that myths get thought in man unbeknownst to him. This has been much discussed and even criticized by my English-speaking colleagues, because their feeling is that, from an empirical point of view, it is an utterly meaningless sentence. But for me it describes a lived experience, because it says exactly how I perceive my own relationship to my work. That is, my work gets thought in me unbeknown to me" (1979:3).

(1963a:211) calls for a preliminary division of a myth into its "gross constituent units." Loosely following a paradigm from phonology, he argues that these units should consist of "a certain function . . . linked to a given object" that would more or less spontaneously appear when the myth was written out sentence by sentence on index cards. The gross constituent units would then be organized into sets in terms of surface similarities, rather as chemical elements might be distributed according to the periodic table. If one ignores the sequential or diachronic position of the units in the myth, "bundles" would thus be formed whose units express the same relation between object and function. Finally, one would bring these bundles into relation with one another, discerning at the same time the formal architecture of the myth and the message it was expressing.

Applying this procedure to the story of Oedipus, Lévi-Strauss isolates eleven gross constitutive units whose surface similarities suggest they should be grouped into four columns (see the right side of figure 1). Twice, for instance, monsters are killed by protagonists, while relatives are murdered on three separate occasions. There are also three incidents in which relatives find themselves bound by emotional, sexual, or ritual dependency (as Europa must depend on Cadmos to rescue her, and the dead Polynices on Antigone to bury him, while Oedipus and Jocasta are linked in marriage and filiation). Finally, Lévi-Strauss infers a similarity in the names of Oedipus and his paternal kin (Laius and Labdacos) which, when thrown into a broader anthropological context, suggests they all bear marks of autochthonous origins, of having grown asexually from the earth rather than from congress between man and woman.

It is this latter supposition that provides the key to organizing the columns and then interpreting them. If we assume the monsters in the story are chthonic creatures, then their violent deaths might be seen as rejecting the chthonic order, by inference denying the autochthonous origin of men exemplified in the agricultural birth of the Spartoi. In this light the "object" of monster killing becomes autochthony and its "function" a denial, while the patrilineal names have the same object but a different function, since they suggest the impossibility of escaping marks of earthly generation. Similarly, the columns that evidence dependency on cognates (blood relatives) and antagonisms between them might contrast an "overrating" of blood relations with an "underrating" that permits murder. All four columns can then be related in terms of a comparison or proportionality: the underrating of blood relations is to their overrating as the attempt to deny autochthonous origins is to the impossibility of escaping them. This startling account of the myth's

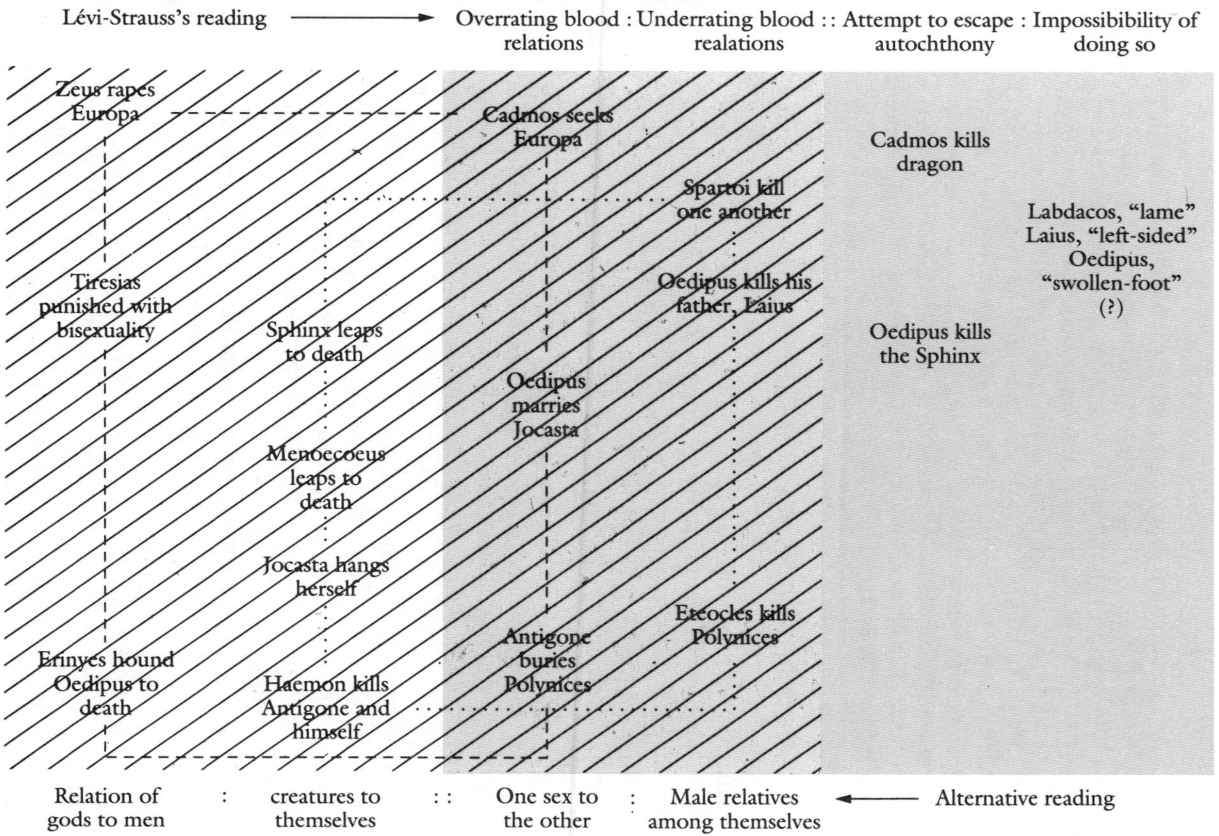

Lévi-Strauss's reading ⟶

Overrating blood : Underrating blood :: Attempt to escape : Impossibility of
relations   realations   autochthony   doing so

Zeus rapes Europa

Tiresias punished with bisexuality

Erinyes bound Oedipus to death

Sphinx leaps to death

Menoeceus leaps to death

Jocasta hangs herself

Haemon kills Antigone and himself

Cadmos seeks Europa

Oedipus marries Jocasta

Antigone buries Polynices

Spartoi kill one another

Oedipus kills his father, Laius

Eteocles kills Polynices

Cadmos kills dragon

Oedipus kills the Sphinx

Labdacos, "lame"
Laius, "left-sided"
Oedipus, "swollen-foot" (?)

Relation of gods to men : creatures to themselves :: One sex to the other : Male relatives among themselves

⟵ Alternative reading ⟶

Figure 1: Schematic of Oedipus myth. Adapted from Claude Lévi-Strauss, *Structural Anthropology*, vol. 1. © Basic Books Inc., 1963. By permission of Penguin Books and of Basic Books, a division of HarperCollins. Shaded area identifies events in original interpretations, hatched area events in alternative reading; dashes connect changing relations of dominance in dual orders; dots connect fatal outcomes among single orders.

message is then thrown into a sociocosmological framework to demonstrate its relevance:

> The myth has to do with the inability, for a culture which holds the belief that mankind is autochthonous . . . to find a satisfactory transition between this theory and the knowledge that human beings are actually born from the union of man and woman. Although the problem obviously cannot be solved, the Oedipus myth provides a kind of logical tool which relates the original problem— born from one or born from two?—to the derivative problem: born from different or born from same? By a correlation of this type, the overrating of blood relations is to the underrating of blood relations as the attempt to escape autochthony is to the impossibility to succeed in it. Although experience contradicts theory, social life validates cosmology by its similarity of structure. Hence cosmology is true. (1963a:216)

Thus a myth that on straightforward reading we might assume to be about the impossibility of escaping one's fate by a devious stratagem, dramatizing this by having it lead to parricide and incest, or that on a psychoanalytic reading would be disguised evidence of the emotional drives that produce the family romance, turns out to solve a cognitive inconsistency between the facts of human generation and fictions of origin. Furthermore, upon subsequent rumination, the formal pattern by which one opposition is compared with the other allows Lévi-Strauss (1963a:228) to hazard a generic structure for myths:

> It seems that every myth (considered as the aggregate of all its variants) corresponds to a formula of the following type:

$$F_x(a):F_y(b) \simeq F_x(b):F_{a-1}(y).$$

This particular architectonic, put forward here tentatively (and without strict correspondence to myth just analyzed), is dropped in later discussions, but served at the time as a rallying point for the possibility of formal analysis, a way of broadcasting the prospect that myth was about something of entirely novel character.[11]

Before wondering about the warrant for so revolutionary an analysis, we should reflect for a moment on why the avenue it opened seemed so

---

11. As Sperber (1985:65) notes, the formula is mentioned again in *From Honey to Ashes*, where Lévi-Strauss (1973:249) comments, "it was necessary to quote it at least once more as proof of the fact that I have never ceased to be guided by it." Showing some exasperation, Sperber suggests that "Should a chemist or a linguist make a similar claim, he would be expected to elaborate upon his formula beyond any risk of vagueness or ambiguity. Lévi-Strauss does nothing of the kind. He does not give a single step-by-step example. He does not even mention his formula anywhere else in his work. Most commentators have wisely pretended the formula did not exist."

promising. Myths are often cluttered with details previous interpretive strategies found no way to motivate. In the psychoanalytic reading of Oedipus, for instance, the Sphinx is without a clear role, while in the fatalist interpretation her demise simply earns Oedipus the Theban kingship and thus Jocasta's bed. On a structural reading, however, the Sphinx not only becomes an integral part of the story as a chthonic symbol, but the question she asks Oedipus, which might seem an incidental if quite good riddle, acquires new meaning. Though Lévi-Strauss does not note the parallel himself, once we know that the names in Oedipus's patrilineage "all refer to difficulties in walking or standing upright" and that this marks autochthony, it is hard not to see the Sphinx pointing in the same direction when she queries men about the animal that walks first on four legs, then on two, and finally on three in the course of a day. Thus the riddle, previously outside the thrust of the story's meaning, is brought close to its center. Structuralism, turning its back on the most powerful convention of reading, the logic of development we expect in plot, found meaning off the beaten path, bringing the apparently marginal, and *all* of it, to the center of what myths said.[12] And this aspect of the strategy, which here produces a remarkably nonobvious interpretation, would increase in importance as it was applied not to domesticated, plot-full tales such as the Greek myths, but to the savage variety whose innocence of development left no apparent path at all. Assembling details into columnar bundles would give intelligible structure to the text; collapsing these downward, synchronically, into an underlying algebraic equation, would disclose an ultimately simple formula beneath the apparent disorder of the text. With this latter movement, so much in contrast to Geertz's pursuit of the sublime, structuralism gestured in the direction of science and its reductive urge. Myths flowed from an unconscious structuring mechanism, presumably "hard-wired" into the brain, as it worked on pressing social and conceptual problems in such a way as to reduce their urgency. Thus myths were not just "good to think": in addition to offering the purely aesthetic pleasure of order, they reduced the tensions that might arise from unresolved conceptual problems. By these various means, culture could be explained both thoroughly and in previously unimagined ways, being the product of a very strange intender. In the hands of a brilliant thinker like Lévi-Strauss, the enchantment that resulted was substantial.

Yet naturalistic warrant for it was weak, and the interpretation with

---

12. Compare Freud (1966:186 n. 17) on dream analysis: "It is always a strict law of dream-interpretation that an explanation must be found for every detail" (cited by Fish 1989a:535).

which it was launched (admittedly only for purposes of illustration) plagued with problems, of which for the sake of brevity we consider only one.[13] Lévi-Strauss has left out, without explaining why, some of the gross constituent units of the myth. In figure 1 we reproduce, to the right-hand side, Lévi-Strauss's original units in their columns, while to the left adding some of those left out, also in columns. A little speculation about what these new columns might mean (arbitrarily ignoring the autochthony bundles) allows interpretations of similar subtlety but no greater conviction. For instance, the myth perhaps suggests a contrast between the relations of dual orders (gods-men, men-women), which are those of subordination and dependency, and those of single orders (creatures by themselves, men-men), which are annihilative. Once we start down this route it becomes difficult to stop, and further formal patterns, which might also convey messages, can be discerned in the diachronic structure of the columns. For instance, men have dominant familial and sexual roles at the outset of the myth (Zeus rapes Europa, who must then depend on Cadmos for rescue), while dominance seems scrambled toward the middle (Tiresias's peculiar bisexuality, or the reversal between Jocasta and Oedipus), leading to the assumption of dominance and responsibility by women toward the end (Antigone and the Erinyes). Ignoring the diachronic dimension of course eliminates this pattern, but it is nevertheless "there" for a structural reading should we wish. Similarly, there is a curious symmetry between the columns for suicide and for underrating blood relations—a symmetry in which violence across generations seems to be interlarded between vio-

---

13. Among the others, for instance, the etymologies for the names Lévi-Strauss views as marking autochthonous origins are admittedly hypothetical (see 1963a:215). Robert Graves (1955:397), in contrast, proposes "help of torches" for Labdacos and "having cattle" for Laius—not evident marks of autochthony. Next, though Lévi-Strauss asserts (1963a:215) that "in mythology it is a universal characteristic of men born from the Earth that at the moment they emerge . . . they either cannot walk or they walk clumsily," this is contradicted by the myth in question: the Spartoi emerge in full military mettle and find no impediment to immediate fratricidal slaughter. These same Spartoi raise further difficulties. Lévi-Strauss uses the dragon from whose teeth they grow to symbolize the chthonic, so that its dispatch by Cadmos represents a negation of autochthonous origins; yet he notes (1963a:215 emphasis added) that the beast "has to be killed *in order that* mankind be born from the Earth," which would seem to cast the event in an affirmative, productive light. Killing the dragon does not negate autochthony; rather, it establishes it. Cadmos's previous companions, eaten by this dragon, were normal sexual progeny, and their replacement by the Earth-born Spartoi, or at least those who survive fratricide, gives Thebes an autochthonous charter. Thus if any event signifies the denial of Earthly generation, it would have to be this fratricide, though Lévi-Strauss places it in the column about underrating blood relations. More could be said here, and none of it would inspire confidence.

lence within a generation. Alerted to such patterns by the tenets of structural reading, we find them appearing almost spontaneously: the main difficulty becomes to choose among them.

Lévi-Strauss restricts his choices by adopting certain conventions before analysis, such as that the diachronic dimension will be ignored and that the final formalism will be a four-term analogy, though in doing so he raises the specter of a procrustean interpretive bed. Consequently, the warrant for his interpretation must be sociological, that is, must derive its relevance from the social context in which the myth supposedly played a part. In this vein, however, things go awry, since we lack evidence the Greeks were troubled by the "conundrum" of mythic autochthony versus sexual reproduction. Lévi-Strauss assumes that the motif of earthly generation represents a Greek *belief* as opposed to a *façon de parler*, an article of faith as opposed to a conventional image. Yet this seems questionable: Malinowski, for instance, not only found little that resembled a belief system in Trobriand myths (which contradict themselves from moment to moment: see [1935] 1965:69 n. 1), but found the Trobrianders, perhaps the paradigmatically autochthonous people, unruffled by the "contradiction" between their earthly provenance and their current habits of reproduction. Ancestral emergence seems an imaginative trope by which they lay claim, clan by clan, to specific plots of land: indeed, the myths have status in Trobriand law and enter into disputes over land tenure (see [1935] 1965:chap.12). True, Trobrianders are not Greeks, but they do make us wonder why the latter should be prey to what is, after all, a rather silly sociocosmological perplexity. The irony of Lévi-Strauss's reading of Oedipus is thus that while it lifts myth out of the Freudian swamp into higher cognitive realms, it does so by turning the Greeks into muddled creatures, caught in webs they have unconsciously spun and inexorably magnifying nonproblems in an effort to escape.

Thus there are both methodological and comparative reasons for worrying about Lévi-Strauss's interpretation, though they are perhaps ill-applied to an example that claims merely illustrative ambitions.[14] Nevertheless, through it we are introduced to a quite astonishing possibility—a weird source of intentions—that we certainly would not otherwise have imagined. The question is what to make of it, and this grows more pressing as we read through *Mythologiques*. Warrant for the interpretations offered there does not rise much above the standards encoun-

14. In offering it, he likens himself (1963a:213) to a "street peddler, whose aim is . . . to explain, as succinctly as possible, the functioning of the mechanical toy he is trying to sell to onlookers."

tered thus far, though in producing them Lévi-Strauss points out certain properties of mythic thought that we may find ourselves unable to account for without slipping into a structuralist mood. A feeling that he may be "onto something" with regard to myth is thus reinforced, even while disabling doubts remain: as traditional strategies of reading become less suitable, structural options grow more attractive. By way of illustration, we want first to characterize the strategies of *Mythologiques* and then consider one instance in detail.

Recall that the problem myth poses for the interpreter is that "anything can happen." The sheer absence of sequential motivation casts us adrift and encourages groping for some way to provide coherence. Lacking this, the obvious attraction of the genre for preliterate peoples remains deeply enigmatic. The approach to this problem taken in *Mythologiques,* while bearing some resemblance to that of "The Structural Study of Myth," is more nuanced, relying on three general means of accounting for the text that are normally integrated but can be viewed independently for analytical purposes.

In the first place, a specific element or motif of a myth might be included because it fits into a broader, purely formal, pattern that needs no motivation beyond its aesthetic appeal for an audience. There is at least some evidence (see Hammel 1972) that children's stories and folktales experience a sort of evolutionary selection for iterative formal symmetries even in a literate tradition, and it would be reasonable to assume a similar principle operates in myth.[15] Were this so, a "mytheme" might be motivated by showing it possesses the appropriate formal properties, while its "meaning," which is to say its contribution to some message the myth is thought to convey, would remain largely incidental.[16]

At quite another level, Lévi-Strauss believes some of the disjointedness of American myths can be explained by supposing that, rather as in a kaleidoscope, they are continually being reassembled in varying patterns from the broken shards of aboriginal canon.[17] Without access to these, an orphaned and rearranged piece seems to make no sense

15. Hammel offers a quite remarkable analysis of the increasing structural symmetry gained by the story of Goldilocks over the course of its publishing history. Though he is interested in deriving meaning from this as well, one can dispense with this in appreciating the evolving pattern.

16. It sometimes seems that for Lévi-Strauss myth is never to be understood in purely formal or aesthetic terms. "Unlike mathematics," he writes (1981:650), "myth subordinates structure to a meaning, of which it becomes the immediate expression." Elsewhere (1963b:640), however, he suggests that "the retrieval of meaning seems to me, from the point of view of method, to be secondary and derived."

17. This belief, announced at the outset of *The Raw and the Cooked,* resurrects imagery from *Tristes Tropiques,* where Lévi-Strauss suggested (1974:178) that the particular

because the context in which it first made some has been lost. We must presume time wears on any oral tradition since it is constantly subject to the vagaries of memory, transmission, reception, and innovation. In such circumstances, the only way to motivate the orphaned mytheme would be to recover the appropriate part of the canon, and this is one of the aims of *Mythologiques*.

Finally, returning to the theme of "The Structural Study of Myth," meaning might be found for particular mythemes by showing they are part of a message coded beneath the apparently disjointed narrative. The more heroic the effort needed to decipher the message, however, the more baffled we will be as to the fashion in which it is being "communicated." Similarly, the more recondite the analysis, the more we will hope for external evidence to support it. The sociological mode of justification utilized in "The Structural Study of Myth" is continued in *Mythologiques*, and the question we will pose is whether in this more substantial context it is any more effective. The texts involved are certainly obscure, and the strategy thus has the initial advantage of providing a meaning where otherwise there might be none.

These three techniques—formal, canonic, and sociological—can be illustrated by looking at the way Lévi-Strauss interprets a Tukuna myth (from the Solimões region of the upper Amazonian basin) that inaugurates *The Origin of Table Manners* (1978). "Monmanéki the Hunter and His Wives" (M_{354} in the numbering of *Mythologiques*) tells the story of a young man who marries five times in monogamous sequence, his first four partners being animals and his last a human. All five leave him; not, however, for any fault of his own but because of criticism or abuse by his mother. To give some of the flavor of the myth and illustrate the peculiar details that require motivation, we quote the account of the first marriage as originally recorded by Curt Nimuendajú (1952:151):

Monmanéki's parents belonged to those first people fished for by Dyai and Epi [two culture heroes]. His only occupation was hunting. On the way, coming and going, he passed a frog who would dart into its hole at his approach, and each time Monmanéki would urinate into the hole. One day he saw a good-looking girl standing before the hole. Monmanéki looked at her and saw that she was pregnant. "I have become pregnant because of you," she said. "How can that be?" asked Monmanéki. "You always pointed your penis in my direction, and so I became pregnant," she replied. Then he asked her to come to his house and live with him. His mother also thought the girl pretty.

---

customs, games, or dreams of a community are merely selections "from an ideal repertoire that it should be possible to define."

They lived together and she accompanied him on the hunt. He used to catch for her a kind of black beetle that formed her only diet. When his mother saw these beetles in the house, she said, "Why does my son soil his mouth with such filth?" He, however, ate only meat; his wife ate the beetles. The mother threw them out, putting peppers in their place. When Monmanéki called his wife to the meal, she placed the little pot on the fire and began to eat from it, but the peppers burned her mouth. Then she ran away and hopped into the water in the form of a frog. Her little son, who had remained behind her, wept. She learned of this from a rat, but said in reply that she would have another child. However, at night she returned to the house and stole the infant from the grandmother's arms.

Monmanéki repeats this process with three more animal-women: an arapacu bird he meets by requesting a drink; an earthworm upon whom he is inadvertently about to defecate; and a macaw of whom he requests beer. After the encounters each turns into a woman, is taken home, and quits him after being criticized (and in the second case mutilated) by his mother. The fourth wife he unsuccessfully pursues on a rather long journey down the Solimões, which Lévi-Strauss relates to the origins of fish, their seasonal migrations, and the astronomical signs used to predict them. Then Monmanéki marries "a girl of his own people" who has an unusual and quite successful method of catching fish: she separates the bottom half of her body from the top, leaves the former on the riverbank, and crawls out into the water, where her torso attracts fish by its "odor of flesh." These she collects in her arms, swimming back to connect with her nether half on the shore. No one knows of this technique until her mother-in-law, searching for her upon the assumption she is shirking domestic duties, discovers her bottom half on the river bank and removes part of its spinal column, without which the girl is unable to make herself whole again. When Monmanéki eventually comes looking for her, she (i.e. her torso) leaps upon him from a tree and clings to his back. She proceeds to snatch his food from him, consume it, and defecate, leaving him both famished and soiled. Eventually, desperate from hunger, he manages to separate himself from her by means of a ruse, upon which she climbs a tree, turns slowly (babbling the while) into a parrot, and flies away. With this, the myth concludes.

If we want to picture these events, the images will likely come in part from Bosch, and in part from Dali, Magritte, or Ernst. The surreal aura is characteristic of the genre, as is the indelicacy that combines sadistic and Rabelaisian themes, offered deadpan and without the slightest effort to moralize. Perhaps what is most striking is the general absence—there are several exceptions—of what we would consider appropriate emotional responses to the events as they unfold. Provoked by their mother-in-law, the wives seem justified in abandoning Monmanéki, but the curiosity is that he never addresses his mother's behavior nor shows any concern with it. If the myth might perhaps be about the difficulty of pleasing in-laws, it certainly does not direct us to this interpretation, seeming rather to shrug its shoulders. A dreamlike quality and flatness of affect characterize most of the text: only the frog-wife's child registers a spontaneously appropriate response, and his mother's reaction is at first perplexingly casual, as if it were an afterthought.

In trying to puzzle out what is going on here, we notice first that the suppression of affect and absence of psychological motivation are counterbalanced by the attention to certain themes and variations in the marriages: the first and third wives are chthonic, the second and fourth aerial, the fifth terrestrial; Monmanéki meets the first and third in the process of relieving himself upon them, the second and fourth in the act of requesting food, while the fifth both takes food from and defecates upon him; the first and third stand out as producing children, the fourth as the only one to whom Monmanéki appears emotionally attached, while the fifth becomes physically attached to him; and so on. Lévi-Strauss explores these patterns in great detail: clearly, the arrangement does not seem incidental—a point to which we will return.

The first wife raises a number of questions: why a frog? Why impregnated by such an odd means? Why a beetle eater burned by peppers? Why return for the child, having indicated disinterest? and so on. To explain these features Lévi-Strauss goes very far afield, assembling myths from North America in which frog-women behave in quite intriguing ways. In certain myths, for instance, they are married over great physical or social distance (wedded, for example, to a godlike Moon); women so married are sometimes (in still other myths) impregnated by elongated penises or ingenious prostheses; frog-women in some myths lose "silent chewing contests" by noisy, sloppy eating, unfortunately having chosen to consume *charcoal;* failing in these contests, they are driven from their husbands' homes; otherwise, rejected for instance by a Moon-husband, they leap onto his face, attach themselves to him, and become his spots; and, finally, these frog-women are notorious for returning to kidnap their children.

All this is highly suggestive. There seems to be something of a frog-woman motif in North American myths, one allusion to which we may have stumbled upon in Monmanéki's first wife: a "distant" (hyperexogamous because animal) woman, she is impregnated at a remove, brought home to encounter buccal difficulties (charcoal here being split into *black* beetles and *hot* peppers), and absconds with her child after feeling rejected. Further, the theme of the clinging woman, sometimes associated with the frog, returns in the Tukuna myth, though now deferred until the final human wife. What are we to make of such astonishing correspondences? Lévi-Strauss is not entirely clear about the mechanism that might account for these similarities between the myths of peoples separated by great distances, but were there ever a canonical mythic text for the aboriginal migrants to North America, it is not inconceivable that shards of it might be carried by inertia over the long migration to the Amazonian basin. One general thesis of *Mythologiques*, to which we have alluded, is that South American myths are "eroded" forms of canonical texts still surviving relatively intact among the Klamath-Medoc and Salish tribes of the Northwest so that, for instance, some sense can be recovered for the Bororo "Bird-nester" myths with which the journey of *The Raw and the Cooked* began by reference to just these texts. The inherent difficulties of such a thesis have to be played off against the interpretive aid it offers: without the North American frog-wife motif we are certainly not going to be able to make much of the specifics of Monmanéki's first wife.

On the other hand we might see some of these as loosely constrained by the themes and variations played out across the sequence of wives. The attribute "frog" is given by chthonic requirement; the method of impregnation by the "eliminative" requirement; the return for the child by the need to distinguish the first from the third wife; and so on. We cannot get very far with this, but on the other hand it is hard to avoid concluding that the wives are being differentiated from one another and yet joined together in an elaborate architectural form, independent of whether this might "mean" anything. Lévi-Strauss tries to gloss the pattern several times without much conviction: perhaps there is a sequential order to the wives that symbolizes a development from hunting, through gathering and cultivation, to fishing. But in the end he concludes (1978:37) that "although structural analysis brings out the hidden pattern of the hunter Monmanéki's story, this pattern is still only perceptible to us on a formal level. The narrative content remains arbitrary." To get beyond this and find a message in the pattern, he first notes (1978:44) that the story "has a surprising affinity with themes which occur in northern regions of North America and even in Siberia. . . . The Koryak, the Eskimo, the Tsimshian and the Kathlamet all have versions of the story about a man who marries a succession of animal creatures and loses them one after the other, often through a misunderstanding caused by their different, non-human diet." He then combines this point with further North American examples where spurned women punish their male tormentors by clinging to their backs to arrive at a first gloss for the succession of Monmanéki's wives and its denouement: "Monmanéki the hunter at first appears to have a dilettantish approach to marriage. He is a kind of hyperbolic Don Juan who, not being content, as we say in French (but already using sub-specific differences) *d'aller de la brune à la blonde* (to flit from brunette to blond), extends his amorous curiosity to a great variety of animal species, such as batrachians, birds, and invertebrates" (1978:73). From this it would follow that "The Tukuna hero's clinging-woman [the human wife] forces herself upon him to punish him for having been a woman-chaser: he is an *insufficiently shy husband*, taking the place of the *excessively shy bachelor* [who spurns women] in the North American versions I have listed" (1978:74).[18] Thus within the mythic system of the Americas, the Tukuna version maintains certain thematic constants while transforming two terms of the canonic texts—bachelor into husband and sexual timidity into Don Juanism.

This is intriguing, but we might easily question whether the characterization it offers of our protagonist is apt. Monmanéki indeed marries a variety of animal women, but whether out of "amorous curiosity" is debatable. Actually he seems an erotic zombie, simply stumbling across his eventual wives in the course of his daily routine. Two of these, in fact, are arguably the sexual aggressors. And unlike a Don Juan he quits none of them voluntarily, the onus for their departure being shifted to his mother (who seems monotonously able to find fault). On the surface of the text, then, Monmanéki seems the opposite of a woman chaser: characterologically passive, he lets women *occur* to him and *chases* only when the fourth wife, of whom he was apparently fond, departs. Because of this it seems hardly likely the Tukuna would interpret (by our conventions, anyway) Monmanéki's predicament with his fifth wife as a punishment for waywardness. The more obvious gloss—although we are quite thoroughly at sea—is that he gets what is coming to him for brooking motherly meddling. In its absence he would presumably have remained married to the pretty frog.

Here Lévi-Strauss's recourse to North American motifs, whatever its value with regard to motivating the frog-woman, suggests an interpretation quite unsupported by anything in the text, or at least sanctioned only by the brute fact of successive wives. To carry the meaning he suggests, Monmanéki must be cloaked with attributes derived from very distant myths, which must somehow have subliminal purchase upon the

18. We should note that while most "clinging woman" stories include a spurned woman, she is not always spurned by an "overly-shy bachelor"; nor is it the spurned woman who always does the clinging. For an illustration, see the story of "Clotkin" in Bloomfield (1930). This tale is M_{367} in Lévi-Strauss's numbering, but is not much discussed by him.

Tukuna. Yet before we have time to question this, Monmanéki's story is assimilated to a still-broader category in relation to which the issue of his character is incidental. Lévi-Strauss notes that the physical attractiveness of the animal wives is commented on by the myth, whereas that of the human wife is not. This suggests a quite different moral unrelated to the Don Juan theme:

What do the myths proclaim? That it is wicked and dangerous to confuse physical differences between women with specific differences separating animals from humans, or animals from each other. This anticipatory form of racialism would be a threat to social life, which demands, on the contrary, that as *human beings,* women, whether beautiful or ugly, all deserve to obtain husbands. When contrasted in the mass with animal wives, human wives are all equally valid; but if the armature of the myth is reversed, it cannot but reveal a mysterious fact that society tries to ignore: all human females are not equal, for nothing can prevent them from being different in their animal essence [meaning attractiveness?], which means that they are not all equally desirable to prospective husbands. (1978:76)

Here the sequence of Monmanéki's animal wives, each from a different species and each (of the first three, at least) having her beauty commented upon in the myth, is opposed to the human wife whose looks are ignored so as to derive a moral more abstract than the one that womanizers will find their retribution. The result is ingenious and surprising, though expected in the sense that through it the myth finally achieves the traditional Lévi-Straussian format in which a socio-ideological conundrum—the differential aesthetic value of women as set against the social and ethical necessity of their equality—is figured through the opposition of animal wives to human ones. Again what Jameson styles the "political unconscious" seems at work.

The reading achieves its effect by offering an intelligible linkage between phenomena the myth appears to "stress" without any rationale—marriage being marked by repetition, physical attractiveness by several comments, and so on. At most the text itself presents certain formal, but essentially meaningless, contrasts between the terms, distinguishing, for instance, the animal series from the final human wife, but without making it clear what bearing this has. Yet though Lévi-Strauss implies (e.g., "the myths proclaim"—a curious choice of words, since the myths "proclaim" nothing at all) that the message coordinating these distinctions into an intelligible structure is somehow present in the text, albeit elaborately encrypted, this misrepresents: here, as with the reading of Oedipus, the final interpretation, though roughly in tune with the canonical and formal data he has unearthed, is by no means entailed by them. The impression that the moral is being read off the encrypted surface of the text by someone who has cracked its code is mistaken: what we have is simply one gloss among many possibilities.

Is it the "correct" one? In puzzling over this we should note that though assumptions about the trans-American character of the mythic system (with all the difficulties these raise) are involved in producing the gloss, its warrant resides in the sociological domain. The myth presumably serves a social function in that it encourages the Tukuna to believe that for matrimonial purposes women must be treated as a class rather than as individuals of variable worth. There is a problem here, however. The Tukuna are exogamous by moiety, and thus face another "threat to social life" in the erotic domain, one arising from the demand that attractions to individual women (or men) of a prohibited category be suppressed. Half of all women are for Tukuna men sexually (and a fortiori connubially) unavailable, and it seems reasonable to assume this social incest taboo occasionally conflicts with preferences activated by "beauty." In other words, attractive women (and men) from the prohibited category may excite interest that must be dampened if the taboo against fictive incest is to be maintained. Women are not "all equally valid" for purposes of marriage, though the beauty of some might cause Tukuna to regret this.

If, having started down this speculative path, we return to the myth, we may wonder whether the Tukuna are perhaps being alerted that, though alluring, men and women of the forbidden moiety are inappropriate marital partners. Though this message is quite different from the one Lévi-Strauss adduces, it is "structurally" as sound as his and would seem of greater immediate sociological relevance.[19] On the basis of the text, however, there is little to choose between them—and in fact no way to do so, since neither actually "decodes" anything. Consequently, the meaning of this myth remains mercurial.

Lévi-Strauss's interpretations clearly "make sense" of mythic features it is otherwise difficult to account for, but in doing so leave us confronted with most peculiar intentional agents. It is not just that the messages of myths are individually so ingeniously encrypted as to undercut

19. Despite the sentimental appeal of Lévi-strauss's gloss, we may wonder whether, in practical terms, the variable attractiveness of individuals any more interferes with marriage in tribal societies than it does in ours. Assortative mating seems to handle most of the misfortunes we face in this regard, while in tribal societies the frequent conjunction of preferential female infanticide, polygamy, and the status gain to be had upon marriage seem to overcome the reservations of most prospective husbands, so there isn't much reason to see the issue as having salience in the life of primitive communities.

their communicative function (see n. 21 below), but that the whole set of them is assumed to form a system operative across the Americas.[20] For instance, the set of North and South American myths of which Monmanéki's story is a part, though "heterogeneous in content and geographical origin, can all be reduced to a single message, of which they effect transformations along two axes, one stylistic and the other lexicological" (1978:84). Yet just how we are to conceive of the agent effecting these transformations is unclear. It is because Lévi-Strauss consistently indicates myths are acting on their own—thinking themselves in men—that some have inferred them to be the product of a transpersonal entity such as a "universal mind."[21] Less vaporously, it can be suggested that myth is the product of an individual competence that is collectively shared, just as speech is the product of shared linguistic competence. Under this analogy, once an individual acquires the potential for mythmaking, his or her behavior will be governed systematically, allowing myths to be transformed in regular ways so as to respond to historical or ecological change, but never so as to permit idiosyncratic departures from the original system. An advantage to the analogy is that it might explain how people can be quite unaware of what myth "is doing" through them: just as a person can produce well-formed sentences although quite unaware of the rules of grammar, so mythmakers can

20. Perhaps the best discussion for geographically proximate tribes is in "Relations of Symmetry Between Rituals and Myths of Neighboring Peoples" (1976:238–255). For a discussion of the distribution of the core myths taken up in *Mythologiques,* see *The Naked Man* (1981:590–598)—which, however, neglects both history and mechanics. The issue of historical linkages is hard to assess. On the one hand it seems hard to imagine that peoples whose languages have diverged so radically (or were so different to begin with) would show much continuity in their mythic motifs. Further, evidence from present-day contexts of story telling (see Goody 1977:29) suggests that relatively rapid innovation occurs. On the other hand, mappings of North American myth indicate the broad geographical dispersal of many motifs and of some entire myths, while folktales in European societies often show quite striking constancies. Thus it is not beyond possibility that certain characteristics of, say, our frog-woman are traditional, and that their presence in a Tukuna myth might adequately be accounted for simply by inertia. On this issue, the reader might want to consult Thompson ([1929] 1966) where the distribution of entire myths and their individual motifs is discussed. Certain myths, such as that of "Star-Husband," can be found almost anywhere on the continent. The actual mechanics of this are not understood, as far as we are aware, but the breadth of distribution lends some support to Lévi-Strauss's suppositions. On folktales, see Thompson ([1946] 1977).

21. "Mythological analysis," he argues in an oft-cited statement (1969:12), "has not, and cannot have, as its aim to show how men think . . . it is doubtful, to say the least, whether the natives of Central Brazil, over and above the fact that they are fascinated by mythological stories, have any understanding of the systems of interactions to which we reduce them. . . . I therefore claim to show, not how men think in myths, but how myths operate in men's minds without their being aware of the fact."

automatically produce well-formed myths without being able to articulate how it is done. The system would thus run quite well "on its own" without conscious intervention. This notion is enchanting in its own right, since it envisions all of us potentially, and mythmakers specifically, giving voice to an obscure metalanguage whose powers we begin to glimpse through Lévi-Strauss's work.[22] Yet he has not been able, or has never chosen, to draw aside the veil that would expose this metalanguage to the light of day. Consistently alluded to, it remains an occult entity, dubiously warranted (see Seung 1982).

Are we left, then, with nothing more than strange intenders, and thus with no further insight into myth? Here we should note that, quite apart from his difficult hypotheses about unconscious messages, cryptic mythic codes, trans-American systems, and so on, Lévi-Strauss may have discovered something fundamental and important about myth: its formalism. With regard to this, Dan Sperber (1985:84) has suggested that "the facts brought out by Lévi-Strauss—all those odd correspondences and regularities—could possibly be accounted for as optimal properties for 'untamed' thinking (more specifically, for storage and retrieval, in the absence of memory stores made available by writing). The study of myth could then throw light on little-known aspects of the human mind." Orally transmitted tales may be selected for episodic structure because of the aid this provides to memory. In such a context, systematic variation across episodes might serve memory as well, while providing a (possibly subliminal) coherence to the whole, an abstract thread by which episodes are bound together. Thus each of Monmanéki's wives shows systematic differences from the others—differences that may be both mnemonically helpful and aesthetically satisfying. None of this, however, need signify anything and thus be in need of interpretation.

We are now somewhat nearer a speculative answer to the question with which Lévi-Strauss began: why it is in myth that anything can happen? Perhaps this is because what happens in them is selected less for psychological goodness of fit or narrative entailment than for formal propriety. We are misled by our conventions of reading just as we would be if we expected a psychological motivation for the juxtaposition of motifs in Islamic art. Yet this argument is simply negative: myths are allowed to show narrative anarchy because they are patterned according to quite different criteria. Yet what of the possibility that narrative anar-

22. The competence metaphor, of course, does not explain how myths address themselves to the local sociocosmological difficulties Lévi-Strauss calls upon to decipher them and to warrant his results.

chy has its own positive appeal? We should note before proceeding that similar anarchy can be found in contemporary art at both the highbrow and the popular level. Some Fellini films, David Lynch's *Eraserhead,* or Marcel Carné's *Zéro pour conduite* show properties that seem quite "mythic." And this is even more evident in the early Mickey Mouse cartoons or the "Silly Symphonies," where transmogrification and narrative disjunction are commonplace.[23] In such genres, we ourselves seem to appreciate just the possibility that "anything can happen." Could myth be capitalizing upon this?

G. S. Kirk (1975) has argued that fantasy and dislocation are the distinguishing features of myth, meaning by "fantasy" simply the incorporation of the fantastic and by "dislocation" the sense we get that myth develops as a narrative through quite wrenching changes of setting or physical form. That is, radical metamorphosis is its primary constant, from which comes the impression that anything can happen, just as Lévi-Strauss argues. In speculating about the cause of this, Kirk (1975:283) first attends to the context of oral composition:

> It is possible, for instance, that these qualities occasionally arose as an incident of the tradition of story-telling itself, whereby themes were displaced or carelessly amalgamated in ways that seemed somehow effective, and so were preserved, or that stimulated the teller to unplanned flights of the imagination. It is possible, too, that certain tales made use of materials derived from dreams, and reproduced their imaginative and chaotic qualities. . . . The reason for such similarities might also be the dependence of each manifestation (dreams, myths), on the subconscious mind, so that fantasy and dislocation would enter directly from that source.

Dreaming certainly suggests itself as the paradigmatic experience after which myth might be patterned, though attributing both myth and dream to unconscious sources, while perhaps etiologically correct, does little to clarify why the format should dominate myth the way it does.

Rodney Needham (1978) has also pointed to dreams as the likely paradigm for the structure of myth. The latter is for him characterized by metamorphosis, taken both as the translation between forms (frog into woman, and so on) and between settings (the same phenomenon Kirk captures in "dislocation"). In both dreams and myths we face an absence of constraint by narrative psychologic or physical possibility.

---

23. Robert Sklar (1975:200) writes that "the early Mickey Mouse and Silly Symphony cartoons are magical. Freed from the burdens of time and responsibility, events are open-ended, reversible, episodic, without obvious point. Outlandish events occur without fear of consequence. There is no fixed order of things: the world is plastic to imagination and will. Yet its pliant nature also renders it immune to fundamental change."

Needham views the result more or less as a "primordial" consequence of imaginative activity unfettered by any procedural rules, and seems to suggest that the metamorphic inconstancy of myth derives from imaginative anarchy—the "natural" condition of the political economy of the mind.

However this may be, the impression of anarchy or structural weakness derives from the same nonlogic for which it seems reasonable to take dreams as the model. But why dreams? One line of speculation might be that since dreams offer themselves as a common experience of the extraordinary—to waking habits of thought, at any rate—if one were looking for some way to highlight the special status of stories of origin, of the legendary time and space in which they take place, dreams would certainly provide what was required.[24] But further, and here borrowing from Goody's (1977) provocative analysis of the consequences of writing, preliterate societies largely lack means apart from such imaginative anarchy to plumb the rich possibilities of semantic structures. In other words, the semantic density we relish in poetry and the elaborate developmental patterning we relish in the novel have inscription as their precondition. Writing broadens the vision of the compositional moment, extending it across the whole of the text and allowing one to edit in the direction of increasing profundity and richness. Without writing, on the other hand, certain forms of structural richness are impossible: as Goody remarks, while stories and orchestral performances are possible in any society, novels and symphonies are not. Nor is *Un coup de des.* In the mnemonic economy of oral composition, the normal way to "spin out" a story is to repeat incidents with minor variations, throwing a series of tests before the hero, for instance, all of which have a similar form. Both Perseus and the Three Little Pigs undergo consecutive trials, just as Monmanéki runs through consecutive wives. The endurance of oral invention, it seems, is poor, and thus the long oral story is almost always, as we have already noted, episodic.

If these ruminations are on the right track, it seems reasonable to conclude that the major avenue to richness and fascination in mythic composition is just the developmental weakness that allows anything to happen. To transform myths into well-groomed stories with beginnings and ends, or with clear, sequentially unfolding morals, or to have them

24. Unsystematic inquiries on our part suggest that some people—what percentage we cannot tell—have almost exclusively "banal" dreams with few "mythic" characteristics. Differences in the character of dreaming in different individuals invite speculation about possible differences in susceptibility to "myth" as well as in the tendency to produce it. It is certainly hard to imagine a Silly Symphony—or Monmanéki's story—being produced by someone whose dreams are banal.

indulge in commonsensical psychology, would be to destroy precisely the attribute that makes them intriguing to their audience, if perplexing to us. Their strangeness is allowed by and relies upon their *formal* integrity, and they use such peculiar patterns as we find among Monmanéki's wives not to make a point or code a message, but simply to charm the audience with niceties of counterpoint, embellishment, and variation. In this regard, Lévi-Strauss's analogy between myth and music, stated at the outset of *The Raw and the Cooked,* seems particularly apt, though he does not draw what would seem the appropriate conclusion: myths may mean much less than he imagines. Rather, they exploit the few techniques available to them to excite wonder and enjoyment. In short, their narrative weakness is not something to be overcome through interpretation: it simply *is.* But if so—and we are merely speculating here—we are left without anything to explain.

Of course all the above criticisms and speculation may be ill-conceived, since Lévi-Strauss, quite as we would expect, works in an ambiguous epistemic register that leaves unclear the criteria by which he should be judged. On the one hand, he chides analysts of literature for engaging in a "play of mirrors" without access to external verification (see 1976:274–276), thus seeming to place himself in our naturalistic camp, but on the other suggests his efforts be judged by the criterion of coherence—the traditional hermeneutic standard. In the latter regard he says that "The value of the epistemological model offered by structuralism to the human sciences cannot be compared to the [naturalistic] models available so far. Structuralism uncovers a unity and coherence within things which could not be revealed by a simple description of the facts somehow scattered and disorganized before the eyes of knowledge" (1976:ix). The same point is made at the conclusion of *Mythologiques* (1981:562–563), where warrant is seen as an issue internal to structural analysis rather than something to be won naturalistically. By these lights his analysis is clearly a success since, despite the involved paths his interpretations take, they do generate an impression of unity for American myths—symbolized by his concluding argument (1981:561–624) that all of them in the end turn out to be saying the same thing. In any event, having opted for coherence as a criterion, Lévi-Strauss can easily dismiss the queries we have been raising and win epistemic space for his findings, albeit at the cost of somewhat weakening their purchase upon us.

Lévi-Strauss's choice here was not forced upon him by lack of more traditional naturalistic possibilities: as Swanson (1976) has shown, there are comparative strategies that can warrant relatively deep interpretations of myths. Rather, he seems to be expressing a virtuoso disinclination to probe systematically into—and thus perhaps disenchant—the mechanisms he implies are at work. And this stance seems perfectly intelligible in terms of his broader ambitions for structuralism, which might best be described as "Orphic."[25] We began this chapter with an epigraph from Henry Reynolds, an early and minor seventeenth-century poet and critic who in his *Mythomystes* confuted scholars who had placed literature and science in opposition to one another. Reynolds sided with those who, like Pico della Mirandola, were convinced that both the Christian Scriptures and the myths of antiquity had encoded within them the secrets of natural philosophy. All that stood between us and their Orphic wisdom was the key that would unlock the meaning hidden beneath their surface. Myth held a promise, as yet unfulfilled, that he framed in the following way: "Suppose a man . . . should be at pains of running through all the Fables of the Ancients, and out of them shew the reader, and lead him by the Finger as it were (who can yet discover nothing . . . in them) to the speculation of the entire Secret of our Great God of Nature in his miraculous fabric of the world" (quoted by Sewell 1960:79). This is what *Mythologiques* has attempted, though in a secularized version. The analytical paradigm it employs, furthermore, can be traced back to the same Renaissance Neoplatonism that inspired Reynolds—an argument we have developed at length elsewhere (Schneider 1979) and need only summarize briefly here. According to Neoplatonism, the apparent diversity of the world belied its underlying unity. Having originated through systematic transformations of a primordial mix of matter and mind, all the supposedly dissimilar elements of the world were potentially transmutable into one another, a notion that laid the spiritual foundation for alchemy. Understanding this allowed one to perceive a system at work in what had seemed nothing but endless and chaotic empirical difference. Furthermore, the harmonious functioning of this system was seen as a model for the ordering of human affairs. In Orphic science, then, nature spoke to man is a way that erased the boundaries between nature and culture, a theme Lévi-Strauss expresses in *The Savage Mind* (1966:247) when he argues that the goal of the human sciences must be "not to constitute, but to dissolve man," a process that involves "the reintegration of culture in nature and finally of life within the whole of its physico-chemical conditions." The systematic order Lévi-Strauss finds in myth is thus only the working out at the level of culture of principles and processes that are laid down by nature. All myths are systematic

25. George Steiner (1967) was perhaps the first to note Orphic tendencies in Lévi-Strauss's work.

transformations of a primordial message spoken by the world itself. In contrast to the Sartrean dictum that "hell is other people," myths assert that "sound humanism does not begin with oneself, but puts the world before life, life before man, and respect for others above self-interest: and that no species, not even our own, can take the fact of having been on this earth . . . as an excuse for appropriating the world as if it were a thing and behaving on it with neither decency nor discretion" (1978:507–508). This Orphic moral and the analytical strategy that "decodes" it have surfaced occasionally in Western culture. Goethe's scientific efforts (to which Lévi-Strauss links his own) served, along with German *Naturphilosophie,* to rekindle Neoplatonic themes in the Romantic period, for instance. Indeed, Blake's conviction that the entire world was in some sense contained in each of its elements, even down to a grain of sand, had similar origins.

The Orphic backdrop of Lévi-Strauss's work helps us understand his urge to discern miraculous messages "writ obscurely" in the fabric of myth, and through them the entire moral Secret of Nature. Yet the effort combined such virtuosity (in the standard sense), intellectual scope, and assurance that it could not easily be emulated. Lacking the therapeutic applications available to Freud, it was essentially stifled by its own brilliance. Though Roland Barthes continued the search for semiotic *systems,* the idea of system itself came to be challenged by deconstruction, and had its Orphic moral undermined by Foucault's dark (and similarly occult) investigation of regimes of "power." If structuralism's reign was brief, however, it served better than any inquiry since Freud's to open prospects of a world beyond our present understanding. And though Lévi-Strauss's premier position among French intellectuals was not entirely a function of the enchantment that ensued, it is difficult to understand the surge of interest in culture since the sixties in its absence.

To summarize our argument here and in the last chapter, Geertz and Lévi-Strauss find meaning conveyed by components of culture not normally thought capable of doing so. Like the kabbalist Abulafia, they "decode" messages concealed in specific aspects of artifacts or practices—line in Yoruba sculpture, the formalisms of myth—breathing semantic life into them. Each in his own way calls for radically reorienting our thinking about culture and communication, opening vistas where strange and quite unanticipated powers are at work. Rather than stopping to query these with the most highly esteemed naturalistic tools, however, they move on to further examples, making their case more by accretion than by penetration (by *Darstellung* rather than *Erklärung*), a habit we have associated with earlier virtuoso devotees of enchantment. At the same time, by adopting epistemic registers that at once seem to require and yet to ignore naturalistic warrant, they ambiguate their findings, leaving us unsure whether these are meant as some form of "science" or as edification. They flirt with an imaginative genre which, like literature on occasion, draws strategically upon empirical evidence in search of realism, while at the same time establishing themselves in epistemic territory normally closed to this.

The focus in which we have tried to hold them will by now either have stabilized for the reader or not: thus we will either have defamiliarized them or shown ourselves narrow-minded and epistemically antediluvian. Whichever the reader decides, the sociologically intriguing point is that our analysis is open to these varied evaluations. Over the next three chapters we offer a rough explanation of why this should be, developing a sociology of enchantment while considering further the status of culture as referential ecology.

The Social Bases of Enchantment

There are indeed some operations of the mind, which may be best performed by the single strength of men's own particular thoughts. . . . But there are other works also, which require as much aid, and as many hands, as can be found.

Thomas Sprat, *History of the Royal Society* (1667)

As we noted at the outset, the enchanted character of cultural inquiry is now theoretically to be anticipated. Weber himself recognized (1946:142, 155) that the grip of science was tenuous and circumscribed, but like many of us he may still have overestimated its sway. Even academic culture, as we have seen, often traffics in very odd goods, causing us to wonder whether the gulf that seems to separate us from figures like Aubrey actually exists. His habits of thought perhaps live on in less evidently exotic clothing, camouflaged as it were within our present forms of inquiry.

Yet this is less unusual than it might at first appear. Taking a broader view than we have, Richard Shweder (1977) suggests that some of the apparent cultural distance between ourselves and people like the Azande studied by Evans-Pritchard is produced by the questionable assumption that they think "magically" whereas we do not. From Shweder's point of view, however, "magical thinking is an expression of a universal disinclination of normal adults to draw correlational lessons from their experience, coupled with a universal inclination to seek symbolic and meaningful connections (likenesses) among objects and events. Magical thinking is no less characteristic of our own mundane intellectual activities than it is of Zande curing practices" (1977:637). Some evidence for this comes from cognitive science, which uses various experiments to demonstrate that the decision-making processes of untutored individuals differ systematically from those that are optimal according to "rational" criteria, sometimes taking on "magical" overtones (see Tversky and Kahneman 1983; Gilovich et al. 1985). And some comes from research into the empirical basis for the attribution of personality characteristics, which seems grossly underdetermined by evidence. For instance, Shweder's research shows that people often attribute traits to others less on the basis of their observations than on their preconceptions about "what should go with what." People seem to believe, for instance, that individuals who "give loud or spontaneous expressions of delight or disapproval" should also "talk more than their share of the time at table" and vice versa. Indeed, these preconceptions dominate their actual experience, which is retrospectively distorted to accommodate them.[1] Shweder takes this to indicate that "resemblance and likeness are intuitive concepts while correlation and contingency are not. It is easy to confuse the conceptual connections among one's descriptive categories with observed connections among the objects or events described" (1977:641). When Azande reflect this confusion in using bird droppings to treat ringworm on the basis of visual similarities, we call the result "magical thinking," yet when we experience it with regard to character traits, the result seems normal and easily accommodated within our supposedly "rationalized" existence. The latter has come about, however, not by a general transformation of our everyday ways of thought, but by the domination of particular areas of experience—perception of disease etiology in this instance—by institutions capable of sustaining less intuitive means of gaining knowledge. Because of these institutions, "we" appear to think scientifically and Azande magically, though outside quite narrow limits this is not the case. Believing in the superiority of our everyday cognitive habits, we mistake, argues Shweder, "a difference in the content of thought for a difference in mode of thought" (1977:638).

Likewise with enchantment: the striking differences of content that separate now obviously enchanted works from those we have looked at effectively mask similarities in habits of thought. They all exhibit, for instance, a somewhat promiscuous interest in finding, to use Shweder's words, "symbolic and meaningful connections . . . among objects and events." Indeed, so do most of us most of the time, and it makes sense to see our proclivities as "natural," at least in the sense that they are quite generally shared in the absence of formal tuition and persist in the face of counterevidence. Thus far our argument simply parallels Shweder's; but we stress in addition the positive attraction of enchantment, as well as variations in its quality. Things become enchanted not faute de mieux, but in part because of the enjoyment of finding the mundane cloaked in the trappings of the unusual, the ineffably rich, or the mysterious. This occurs both on a popular level where, for instance,

1. In reanalyzing a field study where observers were asked to monitor a group of people and record such behavior, Shweder found that the actual correlation between spontaneous expressions of delight/disapproval and monopolizing table talk was minimal. However, when the observers were asked to evaluate specific individuals in retrospect, they correlated these behaviors strongly. In other words, their preconceptions about what went with what dominated and displaced their actual experience. (Other research suggests these preconceptions themselves have no empirical basis, but are instead based upon semantic intuitions of similarity: see Shweder and D'Andrade 1980.)

reports of prodigies enliven daily existence, opening it to possibility—
e.g. "Doctors find three-pound frog in boy's stomach"—and on a more
sophisticated one where we encounter peculiar vehicles of meaning or
strange intenders. Neither phenomenon arises from a simple disinclination toward less intuitive modes of thought; instead, they are often
sought out, and for the same reasons one might prefer well-seasoned
food to bland. Sophisticated forms of enchantment, furthermore, generally call for virtuosic performances (in the standard sense): quite striking intelligence and enormous stores of knowledge have gone into *Mythologiques*, for instance, whereas tabloid stories about prodigies can be
generated in quantity by bureaucratically organized means. Consequently, even when doubts arise about the substantive contributions virtuosic efforts make, they often display a degree of intellectual prowess
that excites wonder on its own.

The seductiveness of enchantment, combined with the brilliance of
its sophisticated forms, goes some way in explaining the appeal of figures like Geertz and Lévi-Strauss. In fact we might argue that enchantment is so ubiquitous and attractive that our problem becomes less to
explain its presence than its absence. Of course in suggesting this we do
not imply that enchantment somehow predominates in everyday life,
since by definition what we think of as "mundane existence" must be
free of it. Its proper habitats are those nonordinary realms where puzzling, novel, or otherwise "questionable" phenomena impose themselves upon us. In dealing with these realms, enchanted responses have
long been customary, whereas we might view naturalistic inquiry precisely as the attempt, by now quite successful within narrow limits, to
disenchant portions of them. This is accomplished by providing explanations (in the rather strict sense we developed in chapter 2) for what
might otherwise be treated according to virtuoso canons.

However, the success of naturalistic investigation in providing explanations depends upon its capacity to establish relatively firm boundaries
between itself and enchanted forms of inquiry, so that the latter's influence can be restricted. The "mature" sciences have been quite effective
in this regard, having developed firm boundaries that are well policed:
intrusions by alien forms of discourse are in these circumstances quickly
identified and aggressively challenged.[2] Where boundaries are not
erected, in contrast, no relevant distinction is made between enchanted
and disenchanted inquiry: they are seen as interchangeable, as giving

2. For a relatively recent instance of boundary defense, see the response of physicists
to the inclusion of parapsychologists on a panel at the 1979 meeting of the American
Academy for the Advancement of Science (*New York Times*, 9 January 1979, 3:3).

equally plausible accounts of the world. Further, in cultural sciences such as anthropology, where boundaries are weak when they exist at all, efforts to strengthen them will often be seen as misguided, closed-minded, or simply beside the point. To understand why, we must begin by investigating the conditions that permit boundaries to be constructed.

We will follow recent custom (see Gieryn 1983a) by referring to efforts at constructing boundaries as "boundary-work." In hoping to monopolize epistemic prestige and access to resources for knowledge production, "science" must continually differentiate itself from competing forms of inquiry. If we turn to the relatively recent past, for instance, modern science, having begun as "natural philosophy," only managed to escape from the organizational umbrella of the philosophical faculties of European universities over the course of the nineteenth century. During that time it contended with religious institutions to distinguish its approach to and competence in explaining worldly events. The individual sciences had to differentiate themselves from both philosophy and religion as modes of knowledge production capable of explaining the natural order. In fact the number of fronts upon which demarcation of this sort proved necessary was quite large: magic and other forms of "pseudo-science" had to be isolated, claims from common sense or amateur investigation impugned, distinctions between pure and applied research developed, and so on (see Gieryn 1983b).

Perhaps the first thing to remark about such boundary-work is that, although an everyday occurrence, its philosophical basis is problematic, having lately fallen into disrepute. As Larry Laudan (1983:9) notes:

From Plato to Popper, philosophers have sought to identify those epistemic features which demarcate or mark off science from other sorts of belief and activity.

Nonetheless, it seems pretty clear to many of us, particularly the philosophers among us, that philosophy has largely failed to deliver the relevant goods. Whatever the specific strengths and deficiencies of certain well-known efforts at demarcation . . . it can be said fairly uncontroversially that there is no demarcation line between science and non-science, or between science and pseudo-science, which would win assent from a majority of philosophers.

Various qualities once supposed uniquely characteristic of the sciences—such as the provision of certain knowledge, demonstrability, methodological rigor, cumulativeness, verifiability, falsifiability, and so on—all have the awkward consequence, when made into necessary and sufficient definitional criteria, either of designating "unscientific" some forms of investigation that accord with our common intuitions about science or of accepting into science ones that don't. To revert to an earlier example, research in parapsychology is sometimes conducted with a degree of methodological rigor that would shame most efforts in the social sciences, and yet none of this weakens the conviction that it is beyond the pale. Similarly, strictures against ad hoc hypotheses, often invoked to cast aspersions on psychoanalysis or astrology, are routinely flouted in accepted sciences without much comment. Whether or not these criteria come into play, in other words, seems to depend on whether one wants to denigrate a particular notion or discipline. Accumulated cases of this sort can imply that "science" is an arbitrary collection of disciplines unified only by their success in monopolizing epistemic prestige. "Knowledge," in short, is defined by power.[3] Yet this conclusion offends some persistent intuitions, such as that there are relatively obvious differences between astronomical and astrological practices, or that there are paradigmatic cases (such as physics) that can be used to hierarchically order even the legitimate sciences (but cf. Cole 1983). Fortunately, by drawing insights from the strong program in the sociology of science and combining them with arguments from chapter 2, we can sketch an intermediate position that allows us to recognize both the integrity of the sciences and the frequently shoddy, if not dishonest, way their boundaries have been justified.

Among strong programers, H. M. Collins (1985) has perhaps most effectively demonstrated that the knowledge used to conduct experiments in vanguard scientific inquiry is significantly "tacit" (see Polanyi 1958). In particular, when new experimental equipment is introduced the know-how involved in running it is often difficult to acquire, so that we may be unable to determine whether our results reflect something "out there," bugs in the apparatus, or merely our clumsiness in using it. Furthermore, even when we get an apparatus to "perform," how this has been done often proves impossible to articulate—and so much so that the transfer of experimental competence between laboratories sometimes requires the transfer of competent personnel.

The knowledge involved in drawing boundaries around the sciences, we suggest, is similarly tacit. Rather than being philosophically articulable as a parsimonious set of principles, it consists of numerous intuitions, developed in the course of induction into a research community, that act in complex ways when an individual tries to decide whether a specific practice is "science" or not. Intuitions of this sort connect with and might be seen as a generalization from the same knowledge that allows us to judge between more and less propitious research agendas within any field. Such knowledge is presumably based upon extensive acquaintance with successful and unsuccessful paradigms of research, from which one distills a practical "wisdom" that can be applied to novel cases. Thus a good mentor should be able to steer an aspiring student toward or away from particular agendas because of a "feel" for the likelihood of their success, even though explicating the basis for this might prove taxing or, indeed, impossible. A similar process occurs, we suspect, when people make distinctions between what is science and what is not. In a sense, what is "not science" is whatever would prove radically imprudent as a research agenda *within* science. Would a psychology student be well advised to invest heavily in researching astral determinants of character? Clearly, the student's prospect is one of extremely high risk undertaken in pursuit of high potential gain. If such determinants can be shown, the student will be seen as an innovator of the first order, a revolutionary figure; if not, the student will appear to have been misguided from the outset. Exactly *how* we conclude (blind prejudice aside) that such research is very risky, however, is hard to determine. Like a craftsman telling an apprentice that a proposed solution to a problem isn't going to work, we may find it troublesome to explain just *why*. Judgment in such instances is based upon "feelings" for fields and research strategies which develop in part beneath awareness. Furthermore, they cannot easily be justified to neophytes, who by definition lack the experience upon which they rely.[4]

Granted that the frameworks in which such judgments are made are intuitive, vary across disciplines, are localized, and change with time, we can still get some loose impression of the factors involved. In a mature science, prejudice against a line of research will presumably increase, for instance, when it does not articulate with established theory, but instead infers yet-to-be-observed agents; finds the "signal" in its data difficult to discriminate from the noise; pursues mercurial effects present in some instances and not in others; relies upon disfavored forms of evidence, such as anecdote; operationalizes its theoretical constructs arbitrarily; or has not taken adequate precautions against experimenter effects.[5] (Some of these principles, not unexpectedly, resemble those by which we de-

---

4. This sounds rather like Charles Taylor's "hermeneutic insight" as discussed in chapter 1. Yet the difference is that, as with most forms of craft knowledge, practitioners usually find themselves in spontaneous agreement as to the "sound" strategy to choose. Were interpreting intersubjective meanings a craft (as opposed to an art), spontaneous agreement about them might also be had.

5. Compare Harriet Zuckerman's (1977:112) discussion of I. Langmuir's criteria for "disreputable error" by scientists, as well as Larry Laudan's (1987:23) list of "typical methodological rules."

fined rich and occulted domains to begin with.) To these epistemic criteria have been added procedural ones requiring, for instance, peer review (which permits application of epistemic norms prior to publication), availability of raw data upon request, and so on. Of course such prescriptions are too vague to be of much practical use, so that craft knowledge is required for their effective application in any specific case. Their crude or formulaic use would often fail to discriminate, for instance, between vanguard and retrograde investigations of problematic phenomena—between, say, the pursuit of "dark matter" on the one hand and of "telekinesis" on the other.[6]

Even greater care is needed to identify "deviant science" when it is produced in an otherwise orthodox milieu. To cite only one case, Nobel laureate C. G. Barkla, famous for his work on the K and L series of secondary X-ray emissions, went on to identify a third ("J") series that proved mercurial. Rather than drop the research, Barkla took it further, developing a new theory to account for his difficulties. These continued to prove substantial. In a summary account he noted (1925:1049 n. 24, cited by Wynne 1976:322) that

Attempts to discover the difference between the conditions of experiments which showed, and those which did not show the J phenomenon have so far been unsuccessful. The J phenomenon occurs sometimes, and at others it does not. . . . Sometimes the J discontinuity occurred day after day; at other times it could not be observed for a comparable period. More remarkably still, at certain times the J effect appeared and disappeared before our eyes, while we were unable to detect any change in the conditions.

For this and other reasons "the prevailing view in physics," as Brian Wynne (1979:72) has written, "was that Barkla was pursuing an obscure and fantastic interpretation of . . . results . . . which could be explained away in the newly orthodox terms of Compton's quantum theory of X-ray scattering." In consequence, he was increasingly seen as a deviant prosecuting an idiosyncratic program, though because of his prestige and the security of his position, efforts to neutralize him proved less than effective.[7] Our interest, however, is in illustrating how a low

6. As noted before, in the mature sciences occult entities like dark matter are "theory driven"—that is, they flow from mismatches between theory and observation, filling up "gaps" that would otherwise seem to impugn theory. Phenomena like telekinesis, by way of contrast, are "observation driven," usually flowing from anecdotal reports, and are often left untheorized.

7. Barkla, who became head of the Department of Natural Philosophy at Edinburgh in 1913, received the Nobel Prize in 1917 for work conducted between 1905 and 1912 on X-ray scattering. Despite heavy criticism of his J series work in 1921–1922, however, he continued to publish findings and produce Ph.D.s. Though most of the latter either

signal-to-noise ratio for a frustratingly mercurial phenomenon contributed to Barkla's dismissal from the community of reputable thinkers.[8] Researchers who, like Barkla, persist in pursuing what the community gradually deems artifactual face reputational collapse and eventual ostracism.

Some of the same criteria that help scientists decide whether a colleague has become deviant are employed to designate certain investigations "nonscience," "pseudo-science," "quackery," and so forth, making them disreputable. Finding themselves unable to adequately explicate the basis for such judgments, however, scientists may sometimes reach for the simpler criteria offered by philosophers of science. Though we now realize these do not live up to their promise, they have acted as a convenient means by which mainstream scientists express their dismay at colleagues or competitors who cling obdurately to apparently ineffectual research agendas or, worse, investigate psychic faculties too weak or undependable to help us beat the odds in Vegas. Whether the boundary that separates the two is seen as one between better science and worse, between orthodox and deviant, or between science and some antithetical pseudo-science is largely a matter of degree and context. In competition for epistemic prestige, it is in the interest of "science" to magnify the distance between itself and competitors, but in the interest of the latter generally to minimize it. In this circumstance, philosophically unconscionable name-calling is unfortunately common (and entirely irrational behavior not unknown).[9] Yet were this eliminated and less prob-

---

abandoned physics altogether or the J phenomenon in particular directly upon receipt of their degrees, that they were approved by external examiners reflects, Wynne suggests (1979:75), a desire on the part of the community of physicists "to avoid . . . *official* manifestation[s] of conflict with Barkla, arising from the general need for science to avoid overt conflict where it can." In tacit exchange, Barkla muted his prosecution of the J phenomenon case and reduced his profile in the scientific community. Rather than change his ideas, he continued to seek empirical support for them until his death in 1944. Thus his deviance was delicately managed on both sides.

8. As recent experience in replicating the Pons-Fleischmann "discovery" of cold nuclear fusion indicates, novel phenomena will often have a weak signal and appear mercurial unless and until the techniques by which they are revealed can be fine-tuned and made to produce consistent results. Until this happens it will be unclear whether scientists are encountering a "real" phenomenon or some will-o'-the-wisp eventually to be dismissed as an artifact. For a consideration of the specific case, see Crease and Samios 1989; for general discussion see Ackermann 1985; and for a sociological treatment see H. M. Collins 1985.

9. For instance, sociologists who study deviant science sometimes experience a sort of "contact stigma" and fall prey to the ridicule usually reserved for deviant science itself. See Westrum (1982).

lematic distinctions employed (Laudan [1983] suggests one between well-confirmed and poorly confirmed notions) the same boundaries would in practice be maintained.

These rather lengthy reflections are necessary if we are to understand the basis for a boundary between enchanted and disenchanted discourse. Obviously, this is not something that is formulated with an easy stroke or two. Rather, it originates in complex intuitions derived from craft experience and can only be forwarded (honestly, at least) through subtle, context-sensitive argument. Further, the criteria involved are not given once and for all, but evolve over time as new research paradigms enter the canon and others are discarded as ineffectual. All this places boundary workers in a particularly delicate situation. They would *like* to argue that the differences they point to are *discriminable in principle* even when their audience fails to recognize them in practice.[10] In boundary-work, however, this will only be true for those who share the matrix of craft experience which made the result "evident" to begin with. Thus though it may appear "obvious" to us in retrospect that Newton's physics and his alchemy made odd bedfellows, Newton himself would have been quite unable to appreciate this. In order to do so, he would need to be effectively "modernized" by acquaintance with our matrix of assumptions. Similarly, readers not convinced by the examples of enchantment we have offered are not failing to recognize something before their noses, but instead lack the craft experience (or reject the argumentation) through which it is put there. Granted, however, that the perception of boundaries is relative to particular background assumptions, our argument does not imply that the latter are purely arbitrary and the differences without pragmatic basis, any more than one's inability to perceive ultraviolet radiation or continental drift implies these are illusory.[11] Instead, we argue that enchantment and disenchantment are indeed discriminable in principle—but not by everybody: the distinction between them, though based on such differences

10. To use an analogy, marginally different shades of color are normally discriminable even though a given community fails to linguistically mark, and thus commonly to perceive, the distinction between them. One assumes, however, that were the attention of the community aroused, the difference would be spontaneously noted and agreed upon. Similarly, one might like to imagine that careful inspection of epistemic examples would reveal self-evident differences among them, easily generating consensus as to which were enchanted, say, and which not.

11. If not arbitrary, however, neither are such judgments inerrant: Barkla's incorrigibly mercurial J phenomenon was no more improbable, in the end, than stones falling, irregularly and always anecdotally, from the sky. The "rehabilitation" of meteors at the turn of the nineteenth century shows that once-enchanted phenomena occasionally reappear, in disenchanted form, to be welcomed into the bosom of science.

as the mercuriality of their subject matter, has a socially conventional as well as a conceptual side, indicating that when and whether it will be utilized must be understood in part by sociological means.

Intuitive criteria (nevertheless based pragmatically in craft experience) cannot be used to erect a boundary unless most members of the relevant community agree with the discriminations that result. In the mature sciences agreement is easily had, whereas in other (e.g. the cultural) sciences it is not. This is due in part to differences in referential ecology, but it has a social-structural component as well. Boundaries are, after all, means of social control, and the capacity to exercise this is dependent upon community structure. We noted before, for instance, that the prevalence of prodigies in peasant communities could be accounted for in part by their insularity, which is to say the absence of travel and of social ties outside one's place of residence. By narrowing the scope of experience and largely eliminating the capacity to gather foreign intelligence, insularity leaves communities incapable of corroborating, and thus exercising control over, imported information. Thus what we think of as structural features of community life can act as a barrier to disenchantment. Before we explore these further, however, it may help to review the major points of our argument thus far.

To begin with, we take enchantment to be a "natural" condition of thought, not just because of a preference for seeking "symbolic and meaningful connections . . . between objects and events" rather than explanations of them—Shweder's point—but because of the seductiveness of the result. Consequently, it is not enchantment we seek to explain, but its opposite. For disenchantment to occur, a cognitive boundary must be formed that isolates certain ways of interpreting the world and sets them in opposition to others. This demarcation does not rely upon the simple criteria sometimes advanced by philosophers of science, however, but instead upon complex and partly intuitive ones assimilated in the course of induction into the disenchanting disciplines (and perhaps originally developed as much through trial and error as anything else). Enchanted ways of construing the world have characteristic properties—occultness of operative principles, mercuriality of effects, and so on—that cause them to be seen as imprudent paths to knowledge, but only by those who have adopted the assumptions of these disciplines. Those who haven't are apt to see only narrowmindedness and authoritarianism in such an estimate, and thus argue it is merely a ploy in the politics of epistemic prestige. The question thus becomes whether we can understand the conditions that favor one or the other side in this dispute. Where does disenchantment prosper and where does it not? To approach this topic, we will call first on a tradition of theorizing that explains boundary formation in terms of social structure. Our preliminary investigation will be very general, dealing with the development of boundaries in various milieus and articulating with quite broad theories of social control. We will then focus on the boundary between enchanted and disenchanted discourse and review an instance where it proved impossible to draw.

Sociological interest in boundaries began, of course, with Durkheim ([1895]1964), and has flourished recently in the works of Douglas (1966), Erikson (1966), Bergeson (1984), DiMaggio (1987), Fisher (1990), and Gieryn (1983a, 1983b) among others. From our perspective, the relevant feature of this tradition is that it views the manner in which cultural domains are crosscut by boundaries as an effect of certain features of group life, such as the density and intensity of social relationships. Let us first consider, however, what it means to have a cultural domain intersected by boundaries. Following an argument by Paul DiMaggio (1987), we can look on "art," for instance, as a cultural domain that is differently articulated in different societies and different eras. One can imagine art being little differentiated, in which case few distinctions between styles, genres and strata would be recognized. (One might even imagine a hypothetical circumstance in which no division is admitted between art forms, so that painting, music, dance, and so on would all be lumped together as a single activity.) Most commonly, however, numerous distinctions *are* made and specialization occurs within the various arts. But further distinctions can be drawn: between the fine arts and the crafts; between original works of art and reproductions; between highbrow and popular arts; and between various genres and styles within any of these. In each case a boundary must be drawn on the basis of principles (once again quite likely intuitive) that produce the relevant discriminations. Among other qualities, such boundaries vary in number, in location, in scope, and in strength (or impermeability). The strength of a boundary reflects the degree to which it has been "cathected," which is to say that its maintenance has become an emotional issue, with violations seen as a species of pollution. To cite only one example, the segregation between the repertoires of the Boston Symphony and the Boston Pops is today firm enough that mixture of the two would be experienced by many as a minor abomination, an unnatural congress between species. Yet the segregation of elite and popular orchestral repertoires in America is largely a product of the late nineteenth and early twentieth centuries, occurred in different places at different times, and seems to vary in rigidity according to the relative fragmentation or consolidation of elites (see DiMaggio 1987:446; and for a different example, Beisel 1990). What many today take to be a "natural" division had to be socially constructed by boundary workers over the course of many years.

These boundary workers resemble the "moral entrepreneurs" who in Howard Becker's (1963) analysis are responsible for generating public support for specific definitions of deviance. The same sort (if not the same degree) of effort that goes into promoting a distinction between normal and abnormal sex, between licit and illicit drugs, or between "victimless" and victimizing crimes, for instance, goes into creating a distinction between classical and popular orchestral music. Yet more is needed in such circumstances than entrepreneurial effort and skill: only a fertile social context is apt to bear fruit in a new and firm boundary.

What factors determine the fertility of a given context? The Durkheimian perspective suggests that cultural boundaries both express and help constitute distinctions among groups within the relevant sector of society. Their stength, furthermore, should be roughly proportional to the density and intensity of group life, which itself can be influenced by intergroup relations—as when hostilities produce cultural "walls" between combatants or sociable relations erode them. The overarching system of boundaries would thus be affected by the pattern and quality of intra- and intergroup relations. DiMaggio, drawing inspiration from Blau's (1977) structuralism, has explored some of the patterns of interaction. If boundary systems vary, for instance, in their relative differentiation (number of partitions), degree of hierarchy, and strength, this is likely due to such features of social structure as relative social heterogeneity (the number of groups), complexity (role differentiation by occupation, gender, etc.), inequality, status diversity, structural consolidation (the degree to which different parameters of status are correlated), and insularity (the ratio of intra- to intergroup sociability), among others. DiMaggio argues, for instance, that social heterogeneity and status diversity increase the differentiation of boundary systems while structural consolidation decreases it. Similarly, inequality, structural consolidation, and insularity all add to the hierarchy (invidiousness) of a boundary system. Its strength, in turn, is positively related to structural consolidation, but negatively to status diversity (controlling for inequality) and complexity. Finally, these various dimensions of boundary systems are related to one another: the more hierarchical, the stronger are boundaries; while the more differentiated, the weaker and less hierarchical. To illustrate only one of these propositions, DiMaggio (1987:449) writes that "boundary strength of genre classifications is primarily a function of structural consolidation. Where persons occupy similar positions on all dimensions of status, genres are highly classified. Thus, urban elites institutionalized the high/popular classification during a period in which family standing, wealth, occupational status, educational attainment, ethnicity, and political influence were uniquely congruent." Lesser consolidation (and/or insularity and status heterogeneity) would have made for a less fertile context in which to promote this particular boundary.

If the dimensions we have just considered seem abstract and bloodless, they are nonetheless one way of getting at quite concrete aspects of social life. Some degree of structural consolidation, for instance, is a precondition for the meaningfulness and vivacity of rituals within invidiously distinguished groups. Without it, neither country-clubbers nor ghetto dwellers would find much point in banding together to develop a rich expressive life; without it, neither cotillions nor street corner ceremonies, debuts nor dapping, would be in fashion: the identities established through these events and statuses would simply cease to be meaningful. Like the structural components that support a building's facade, permitting it to have a particular character, abstract features of social organization determine or constrain the character of lives. Cognitive boundaries like the one that divides the orchestral repertoire come in practice to be used as social discriminators as well, dividing the public into various groups on the basis of taste. As DiMaggio notes, it is by exchanging information about tastes that strangers generally form impressions about whether they have enough in common to "get along" with one another. Cognitive boundaries thus get turned into real social boundaries as well, forming the basis for group life. In situations where boundaries are few (or very many), nonhierarchical, and weak, group life does not generally have much intensity—which is another way of saying it has little hold on us. Where it does have a hold on us, in contrast, both social and cognitive boundaries tend to be strong. Nor is this surprising since, as we noted before, boundaries are preconditions for social control, and it is through social control that groups actively exercise their hold on us.

It seems, then, that structural variables influence the cognitive and social construction of boundaries as well as their maintenance through social control. This is only to be expected, of course, since a boundary can be strong—one of the dimensions of concern to us—only when the means exist to enforce it. We would expect a society of undifferentiated but cosmopolitan equals to create few boundaries and weak ones at that, because in such a circumstance individuals would be maximally independent of one another, and thus little subject to social control. Alternatively, societies that are differentiated, stratified, and insular tend to have many and strong boundaries, the latter in part because the dependence of individuals upon others exposes them to control.[12] In the same vein, it would be reasonable to conjecture that where boundaries are frequently and freely ignored—that is, where control in practice has broken down—there will be little incentive to support them simply as cognitive niceties. Their salience will decline and their very meaning eventually evaporate.[13]

Before we train this analytical framework on the boundary separating enchanted and disenchanted realms, it may help to briefly review certain of its features. Boundary construction begins with *cognitive* discriminations: someone first has to *conceive of* ways of differentiating the music conducted by John Williams from that by Seiji Ozawa, for instance. Once this has been done, the matter can be promoted before a broader public—a campaign that may fail, of course, in which case the boundary will possess no social significance, or succeed, in which case it will be used to keep separate things that are now seen as distinct from one another. The stronger this boundary, the more stepping over it will excite public concern, with violations of the strongest boundaries being seen as profoundly polluting and thus as occasions for outrage. Sociological and anthropological study of this phenomenon, though still in its early stages, suggests that the impulse to draw boundaries conceptually as well as the entrepreneur's success in promoting them correlate with various features of group life. Furthermore, at least one dimension of boundaries, their strength, can be looked at from the reverse angle of social control: wherever the capacity to exercise this is weak, as it is when individuals are autonomous, so will be the boundaries. Indeed this is unsurprising, since social control and boundary formation are linked together in the same analytical framework and respond to similar structural variables.

With this in mind, let us turn to a historical case. We saw in chapter 1 that John Aubrey, whose credulity and appetite for marvels now seem so striking, was a member of the Royal Society—an organization we think of as the progenitor of a new and more skeptical frame of mind. The ease with which this could occur, with which people moved between milieus now thought antagonistic, indicates that in the seventeenth century the boundary between enchanted and disenchanted

12. "Mutual dependence" among investigators will turn out to be a defining characteristic of "mature" sciences when we discuss them in chapter 7.

13. DiMaggio's argument implies that noninvidious and weak cognitive boundaries would be maintained in differentiated, egalitarian societies if only because they facilitate recognition and communication. Granting this, a very high rate of boundary violation (or creation) will, however, weaken their capacity in this regard.

realms either could not be conceptualized or, where conceived of, had little force. In the present instance, the latter seems to have been the case: efforts were made at drawing the distinction, but they failed. To see why this was, we need more information about Aubrey, the social setting of his inquiries, and the nature of the Royal Society. Then we can assess how these relate to the expectations our broad argument about boundaries has created.

As we have noted, Aubrey belonged to a category of natural philosopher known as "virtuosi," the term we appropriated to designate researchers who pursue enchantment.[14] We now want to examine its original application. First developed as a role in Italy among noblemen and courtiers during the sixteenth century, the virtuoso engaged in an intellectual form of conspicuous consumption which was attuned specifically to his "caste" circumstances.[15] Supernumerary nobles, finding little demand for their talents in military or governmental posts, could achieve a modicum of distinction by acquainting themselves with antiquities, with the arts and their history, and with the oddities and rarities of nature. The scope of their interests was determined largely by the requirement that they not be utilitarian, thus avoiding the pollution that would attend unseemly labor.[16] By knowledge of antiquities and the arts, men could express their connection to a glorious past whose inheritors they were, while by accumulating curiosities and marvels—the "uncommon" among nature's offerings—they could demonstrate prepotent acquaintance with the world. Thus the acquisition and display of certain edifying objects and knowledge came to be institutionalized in a role.

Its development was encouraged by European exploration and trade,

14. Throughout what follows we will consistently use the term "virtuoso" anachronistically so as to avoid repetitive qualification in the text. As the scholarship cited hereafter indicates, however, contemporaries often used this designation indiscriminately to refer to anyone who investigated nature, and both virtuosi and their detractors among the "new scientists"—whom for convenience we will often style, again anachronistically, simply "scientists"—were lumped together when natural philosophers were discussed. This latitude in the extension of "virtuoso" is one manifestation of the phenomenon we want to explain.

15. See Houghton (1942). Our subsequent analysis relies extensively on this source and four works by Michael Hunter (1975, 1981, 1982, 1989). Brief discussions of individual virtuosi, their cabinets, and specific national traditions will be found in Impey and MacGregor (1985) and Kenseth, ed. (1991)—both of which have the advantage of extensive illustration.

16. Aubrey was unusual among virtuosi in having utilitarian ambitions. In this regard see Hunter (1975:104–112). Olmi (1985) brings forward interesting information about cabinets assembled by members of the third estate in Italy.

which increased access to novelties, by the artistic flowering of Mannerism with its promotion of the bizarre, and by widespread elite and popular interest in monstrosities (Kenseth 1991a, 1991b; Park and Daston 1981). At the same time, in Italy and elsewhere, wealthy professionals, merchants, and scholars vied with the aristocracy in assembling "cabinets" for display, so that *Wunderkammern* began to proliferate. On being popularized in England (as through *Peacham's Compleat Gentleman* of 1634) the social base of the role expanded similarly, being taken up by the educated among urban and rural gentlemen of means. Yet it still retained its cachet in courtly circles, with Charles II himself, for instance, being an amateur virtuoso who found diversion in the proceedings of the Royal Society.

If we restrict ourselves to the natural philosophical component of the role, its ambitions were broad if perhaps shallow, combining a somewhat mindless empiricism with a taste for the peculiar or miraculous. This was expressed in "natural histories" compiled for various localities in which folkloric, geological, antiquarian, meteorological, and other miscellaneous data were presented alongside prodigies, monstrosities, calamities, and other sensationalist information in a sort of omnium-gatherum intended as a contribution to knowledge. (Aubrey's posthumous *Natural History and Antiquities of . . . Surrey* [1719] and *The Natural History of Wiltshire* [1847] were of this stripe.) It was expressed as well when natural philosophy was taken up as reputable entertainment, with virtuosi performing curious and instructive experiments or collecting cabinets of odd and rare items that were guaranteed to amaze and divert. At least by midcentury, furthermore, this latter aspect of the role had become something of an occupation, as educated individuals of lower station developed particularly striking collections, the display of which earned them a living (see Altick 1978; MacGregor 1985). John Evelyn, for instance, himself one of the foremost amateur virtuosi, was captivated by the cabinet of a certain Signor Rugini:

which abounded, above all, "in things petrified, walnuts, eggs in which the yolk rattled, a pear, a piece of beef with the bones in it, a whole hedgehog . . . [as well as] divers pieces of amber, wherein were several insects, in particular one cut like a heart that contained in it a salamander without the least defect." Almost as fascinating were actual monstrosities—pearls and stones of unnatural size, "a cock with four legs," "a hen which has two large Spurs growing out of her sides." And complementing such miracles of nature were the artificial miracles of man, the surprising inventions like hydraulic organs, [or] singing birds moving and chirping by the force of water. (Houghton 1942:193, quoting Evelyn, *Diary and Correspondence* 1:221,97–98,23)

Less ambitious collections were assembled by many virtuosi, while the outstanding cabinet of the Tradescant family, later to become the core of the Ashmolean Museum at Oxford, contained "a natural Dragon" and "two feathers of the Phoenix tayle" (Houghton 1942:195, quoting *Musaeum Tradescantianum* 6,2). Elsewhere, one might find a mermaid's body and other expressions of the mirabilary's zeal for collecting.

Though all this strikes us today as quaint, the Baconian mission that animated so much of seventeenth-century British natural philosophy had authorized the collection of wonders as a means of establishing the extremes or limits enquiry must take into account (see Park and Daston 1981). Yet it did so with the aim, which virtuosi often ignored, of advancing a theoretically informed and generalizing explanation of them. The disenchanting effect of the latter was resisted by virtuosi, and to Houghton (1942:195) this made them "anti-Baconians, reluctant to serve the cause of science at the expense of romantic wonder. . . [and willing to stop] at the very point where the genuine scientist begins." While this opinion is perhaps too harsh, and in any event is meant to apply only to an "ideal type" of virtuoso, it does accurately convey the distaste many of them felt for drawing aside the veil of mystery that added so conspicuously to the appeal of their knowledge, experiments, and collections.

It seems, then, that virtuosi acted as socially recognized repositories of enchantment. It was through them that the strange, mercurial, and inexplicable phenomena of nature (as well as the more ingenious of human contrivances) were brought before a wider public, and a premium in this context quite naturally attached to the more sensational and occult objects or experiences. That these could serve as well to help map the terrain of Bacon's "new science" only legitimated virtuoso interests the more. These easily encompassed apparitions, meteors, phoenix feathers, and so on, and marked them out for virtuoso investigation.

Not just because they were so numerous among those interested in nature, but because they were socially prominent as well, it was to be expected that virtuosi would be included in the Royal Society when it took shape in 1660. Eight of those who either founded the Society or were voted members before 1663 were active virtuosi, and their outlook was congenial to significant numbers among the more casual members.[17] Thus, as Hunter (1975:136) suggests:

17. As to social standing, among the active virtuosi Sir Kenelm Digby, Elias Ashmole, John Evelyn, and Charles Howard—a courtier, two government officials, and a nobleman, respectively—were particularly well situated (see Hunter 1982:159–82).

Among minor supporters of the Society, an ability to believe in [astrology and alchemy] and a wish to study them, like Aubrey's, seems to have been the norm. The Society's papers, like Aubrey's letters, reveal them taking an interest in a miscellaneous range of subjects, from natural phenomena like earth tremors and prodigies to magic and prognostic dreams. . . . [A]mong scientific enthusiasts of the Restoration there were more whose interests were of this heterogeneous and uncritical kind than there were rigorous mechanists like Oldenburg and Ray.

Furthermore, the Society's long-unfulfilled expectation of patronage from Charles II guaranteed virtuosi a place quite independent of their investigative and organizational contributions, which in any event proved considerable. Thus in almost all respects one could argue that the position of the virtuosi within the institutional and reputational structure of seventeenth-century British natural philosophy was un-problematic: in a very practical sense they were indistinguishable from those who surrounded them, so that enchanted inquiry subsisted along-side disenchanted.[18]

The only reservation we need enter here is that the public ideology of the Society, as produced by (or under the supervision of) certain key members, was hostile to and dismissive of virtuoso values, if not of the virtuosi themselves. Though Thomas Sprat's *History of the Royal Society* (1667) and Joseph Glanvill's *Plus Ultra* (1668), which were the first and most influential efforts of the Society at propaganda, were aimed explicitly at scholasticism and the dominance of traditional authority in natural philosophy, they also indirectly impugned the sensationalist, antiutilitarian, and untheoretical orientation of the virtuosi. More di-rectly, Nehemiah Grew, in his catalog of the Society's Repository (origi-nally a virtuoso cabinet), was

sarcastically dismissive of phenomena that had preoccupied virtuosi such as the strange power of the *Echineus remora* . . . [and] made short work of items like the sticks formed in such shapes as that of a St. Andrew's Cross, straightfor-wardly rationalising them with the words: "'Tis probable, That these were bound together (as may be any other) when they were young, and with the Barque pared off, where contiguous; and so, by a kind of ingrafting, became

---

18. The strongest demonstration of this will be found in Hoppen, who concludes (1976:266–267) that "at most levels of ability, and among most types of social and profes-sional background represented in the society—physicians, aristocrats, clergymen, aca-demics, lawyers, courtiers, landed gentlemen—there was a significant element who saw the society's work in an extremely eclectic and catholic light. . . . The minutes, correspon-dence, and publications of the society show it quite unselfconsciously juxtaposing many seemingly distinct intellectual traditions."

coalescent." (Hunter, 1989:145, quoting Grew, *Musaeum Regalis Societatis* [1681], preface)

Occasional remarks of this sort were accompanied, as Shapin and Schaffer (1985) have shown, by vigorous efforts on the part of Boyle to advance the experimental method as a generator of "facts." Appeal to facts, he hoped, would obviate vaporous theoretical disputes (such as that between vacuists and plenists) and combat the "dogmatism" of figures like Hobbes. Though his experimentalist propaganda did not have the virtuosi directly in mind, its effect was to promote a preference for demonstrability in the search for knowledge that was inimical to their concern with mercurial phenomena. It seems clear, then, that the scientific and propagandistic core of the early Society had conceptualized, and publicly demonstrated its commitment to, a boundary between the values of the new science and those of the virtuosi.

Having tried to propagate this boundary, however, they found it did not prosper. Unchastened virtuosi continued to play an active part in the Society and contributed to the *Philosophical Transactions,* its journal. New virtuosi continued to be accepted as members throughout the century, and with the ascendancy of Newton (president 1703–1727) and Sir Hans Sloane (secretary 1693–1712 and president 1727–1741) found leadership less directly antagonistic. Just as important, furthermore, contemporary usage failed to distinguish the "new scientist" from the "virtuoso," with both hoist on the same petard in contemporary satires.[19] Thus though enthusiasm for the role seems to have declined gradually after 1680, this was not because an invidious distinction had arisen between virtuosi and scientists. Instead, Houghton (1942:211–219) cites a complex of factors, including a weakening antipathy to utilitarian concerns and an increasing disregard for learning among the nobility, that slowly shrank the audience for conspicuous intellectual consumption of the virtuoso sort, which came increasingly to be seen as "pedantry." (Kenseth [1991a:54] adds that the very proliferation of *Wunderkammern* seems to have markedly deflated their prestige value: the marvelous was becoming commonplace.)

The failure of boundary-work by the scientists was further guaranteed by the circumstances of the Royal Society. As a voluntary associa-

---

19. Best known of these, of course, was *Gulliver's Travels,* though it was not published until 1726. More contemporary were Samuel Butler, who made glancing remarks in *Hudibras* (1678) and more pointed ones in poems like "The Elephant in the Moon" (which, however, was published only posthumously), and Thomas Shadwell, whose play *The Virtuoso* (1676) was the most damaging (see Nicolson 1965:114–175 for a thorough treatment of the latter two figures as well as other critics).

tion dependent upon members' dues, it could not be particularly discriminating in its recruitment. Thus high-status individuals whose interest in natural philosophy was somewhat casual were welcome as long as they made their annual contribution to the treasury, while even those who did not were kept on the lists until an endowment allowed some culling in 1682.[20] As Hunter (1989:206) argues, the difficulty of keeping the Society afloat financially

> meant that the virtuoso membership on which it depended for income from subscriptions could have a deleterious effect . . . so that instead of research the Society's priority became the amusement of Fellows. In the reform of 1673–75, for instance, part of the Council's object in providing "experimental entertainments" was to make the meetings "more considerable" and thereby attract more subscriptions. Moreover, the kind of spectacular and novel experiments that appealed to most of the virtuosi were not necessarily the most scientifically significant.

To these very practical considerations ideological ones could be added. Part of the original appeal of Baconism lay in its tolerance of diversity and its expectation that differences between investigators could be settled by discussion and experiment. Aggressive boundary work on the part of the scientists against the virtuosi—even were it not financially suicidal for the Society—would have violated this ideal, signaling a lapse into the very sectarianism the new science aimed to transcend. Further, we can note that with regard to one issue that divided these camps— whether natural philosophy should have technological or economic utility—the ambitious expectations of the scientists proved unwarranted. Though they promised immediate and quite spectacular payoffs from investigations undertaken by the Society, the latter proved singularly devoid of technological or commercial return (see Hunter 1981:87–112). Thus the "proof of the pudding" that might have significantly buttressed their case simply did not materialize.

These specific features of the historical setting go far in explaining the inability of the scientists to distance themselves from the virtuosi, but our sociological reflections can contribute as well.[21] We suggested, for instance, that a group of undifferentiated but cosmopolitan equals

20. Four fellows who were in arrears had been removed from the lists in 1662 and several more in 1675, but the majority of expulsions occurred in 1682 and 1685. See Hunter (1982:98–99).

21. With regard to the difficulties of the scientists in forging still other boundaries, see Wright (1981) and van den Daele (1977). A useful perspective (and review of the literature) on the institutionalization of science in the seventeenth century will be found in Wuthnow (1980).

would create few boundaries and weak ones at that, adding that the independence of such individuals would stymie whatever attempts at social control might occur. Looking at seventeenth-century natural philosophers in this light, we find that their relative lack of differentiation, especially in comparison to today's scientists, is striking. The scope of any given investigator was normally extremely broad, with the most productive of them making contributions in a variety of (what would later be seen as) fields. Granted the low cognitive costs of entry into most branches of inquiry outside mathematics—the only significantly theoretical field in the period until Newton's development of mechanics—this is just what we would expect. Lack of role differentiation was reflected as well in the omnibus character of the few available scientific journals: thus the Royal Society's *Transactions* presented material that would today be scattered among hundreds of specialized organs. Individual breadth of purview combined with this dearth of vehicles to produce frequent juxtapositions of subject matter that today seem striking: plant physiologist Nehemiah Grew appended a "Comparative Anatomy of Stomachs and Guts" to his catalog of the Royal Society's Repository (1681), while John Ray surveyed metallurgy in an appendix to his *Collection of English Words* (1674).

Similarly, though we have hitherto spoken as if virtuosi and scientists were easily differentiated—so that in this respect distinct roles would be evident—this was not necessarily the case. Houghton's portrait of the virtuoso limns an ideal type rather than a modal one, and many of the individuals active in the Royal Society appear to have had an ambiguous allegiance to the values he outlines. Or perhaps we should say that their allegiance might shift from one context to another: Aubrey, for instance, though "credulous," could summon both skepticism and empirical diligence in his effort to plumb the origins of the Avebury megaliths. And what appears here (in retrospect) a sort of split personality would later be evidenced even more dramatically by Newton. Indeed, an ability to switch back and forth between investigative "moods" that today seem inimical is one of the interesting features of the period and, as Hoppen (1976) has shown, characterized even those figures we view as most firmly in the camp of the "scientists."

Given the lack of role differentiation, it is not surprising that the social networks of the natural philosophers were cosmopolitan. Recall that in the restricted sense we are giving cosmopolitanism, it refers to the ratio of in-group to out-group social relations. Were investigators restricted in their spheres of communication, so that, for instance, virtuosi dealt only with virtuosi and scientists with scientists, the ratio would be high. As the institutional contribution of the virtuosi alone would suggest, however, neither they nor the scientists formed insular groups. John Evelyn's term as secretary of the Royal Society and frequent participation on its Council, where he was joined intermittently by Charles Howard, Dudley Palmer, Edmund Wylde, and Kenelm Digby—all virtuosi—is symptomatic of the organizational integration of the two camps. And organizational patterns were matched by friendship ties: Aubrey, for instance, counted Hooke, William Petty, John Pell, Seth Ward, and Christopher Wren among his closest friends, and joined Hooke in his experiments during the years the two lived at Gresham College (see Hunter 1975:46). Thus despite the fact that the scientists monopolized the very few paid staff positions in the Society (Hooke as curator of experiments, for instance), their activity brought them into regular contact with virtuosi. As with any organization, the Society had its cliques and cabals, but these appear to have been fluid and motivated by issues tangential to the ideology of inquiry. What insularity did exist bears only partially on our concerns. The difficulty of travel made participation in the Society by anyone not resident in London problematic, and provincial correspondents frequently lamented their isolation. But among the virtuosi, rustication seems to have correlated with eccentricity: "Country virtuosi were more prone than London ones to become old-fashioned and eccentric in their views, humbly admitting that their ignorance of the latest scientific theories was greater than those closer to the centres of learning realized, while Hooke wrote off one such figure as 'a simple asse'" (Hunter 1981:80–81).[22] Isolation, of course, is not quite what we mean by insularity, but one might approach this from the opposite side by suggesting that the cosmopolitan connections of the London virtuosi served to moderate the tendencies to eccentricity that were built into their interests and methods.

If low levels of differentiation and insularity clearly discouraged boundary formation, the question of inequality is rather more complex. Here multiple and potentially independent dimensions—among them caste (or estate), wealth, education, and scientific reputation—are involved. Further, it is unclear whether additional features of the relations among natural philosophers should be considered. Is it important, for instance, that the Royal Society was in principle a democratic institution, or should we note that participation in its discussions correlated with social prestige? Rather than become bogged down sorting these

---

22. Hahn (1971:52) finds a similar relation between provincialism and eccentricity in France. In contrast to their Parisian brethren, "provincial societies remained for a long time the carriers of a charming but old-fashioned ideal of general culture better suited to amuse the mind and the senses than to harness the specialized wisdom of man."

matters out, it seems best merely to register some relevant observations. On the one hand, differences in reputation within natural philosophy (though it is difficult to assess these without Whiggish contaminations) seem to have favored the development of a boundary, since figures like Boyle and Hooke (and thus the side of the "scientists") were dominant. Similarly favorable to boundary creation would be the superior social standing of the virtuosi, though this factor would work against the invidious distinction sought by the scientific camp. Since these particular dimensions seem to cancel one another out, perhaps the best way to characterize the situation is to suggest that within the community of natural philosophers structural consolidation was minimal—a circumstance not favorable to boundary formation.

In all these regards the conditions under which natural philosophy was produced in the seventeenth century were even less conducive to disenchantment than those under which culture is studied now. As today, the educational requirements for entry into the field were high, but the capitalization of inquiry was low, with major outlays required only of those who needed private libraries, laboratories, or cabinets.[23] Work could be (and frequently was) undertaken in isolation and the results communicated in social gatherings or by mail. Until groups like the Royal Society were formed, the production of scientific knowledge was by and large very little organized and thus quite autonomous. In such circumstances we would expect considerable cognitive differentiation, with individuals disagreeing as much over the aims of inquiry as over results, so that natural philosophy as a whole would resemble a patchwork quilt made out of diverse and potentially antagonistic pieces. Robert Hooke, one of the scientists, hoped the Society would bring more order to this picture by acquiring monopoly control over the production and distribution of knowledge. He

felt it necessary that the Society's benefits should be exclusively limited to its Fellows, so that active membership would be obligatory for any with serious scientific interests: "there must bee somewhat to be had by those that meete & are regular members which others must want." To achieve this he would even have overturned the Society's Baconian commitment to the free dissemination of knowledge, arguing that "Nothing considerable in that kind can be obtained without secrecy because els others not qualified as abovesaid will share the benefit." (Hunter 1989:57)

23. Shapin and Shaffer (1985) point out that the air-pump, an instrument of great significance in Boyle's campaign to establish a realm of "facts," was so expensive to produce (and difficult to operate successfully) that few scientists could afford one. This seems to have been the exception, however: microscopes, telescopes, prisms, and other apparatus were within general reach.

Yet because the conditions in which natural philosophy was produced were so autonomous, it is hard to imagine just what could fill Hooke's demand for "somewhat to be had . . . which others must want." That he would propose an artificial restriction on the dissemination of information only underscores the Society's inability to generate knowledge that was spontaneously in demand. Further, the Society's weakness as an organization, coupled with its financial dependence on a numerous and heterogeneous community of inquirers, made his aspirations doubly implausible. Thus no orthodoxy with regard to a research program, though sometimes wished for by the scientists at the core of the Society, could be achieved. In fact this would have to wait for the nineteenth century, when the Society was reformed so as to focus on "professional" science (see below). Unable to exclude enchantment from their discipline, the scientists were reduced to some private grumbling at, and occasional public mockery of, virtuoso values—neither with much effect.[24]

As our discussion has made clear, structural factors like role differentiation, equality, cosmopolitan contacts, and autonomy in knowledge production are only part of the complex of circumstances that made boundary-work ineffective in the early Royal Society. Had Charles II shown different intellectual tastes and sided with the scientists, for instance, their case might have been both more aggressively prosecuted and more effective. Similarly, had their Baconian mandate been less inimical to (and their experience less recent with) sectarianism, a more vigorous effort to stigmatize virtuosi might have been launched.[25] Finally, had virtuosi not served as potential allies in the "battle of the books," which was the main front on which the scientists were engaged, the latter might not have been so patient.[26] Taking all these factors together, it seems clear that the matter was "overdetermined" and that the relative contribution of structural factors cannot be isolated and

24. Because it is tempting to think this a sad state of affairs, we would do well to wonder just what an effective boundary would have accomplished at that time. As Charles Webster (1982:12) has noted, "the worldview of the Scientific Revolution should be viewed as a diverse phenomenon, the result of a dynamic interplay of forces which emanated from many different directions. All of these forces contributed to the process of creativity and change, and none of them deserves to be written off *a priori* as a useless intellectual encumbrance from a discredited magical past." We return to this issue in chapter 7.

25. This does not mean it would have succeeded. Brian Vickers (1984) has discussed the relatively vigorous campaign during the sixteenth and seventeenth centuries to impugn the analogical habits of reasoning integral to Hermetic or Neoplatonic science, which nevertheless remained strong (see Hoppen 1976) throughout our period.

26. Thanks to Michael Kennedy for suggesting this point.

weighed. Nevertheless, the evidence is in the direction anticipated and fully congruent with our expectations.

Exactly how circumstances changed with time to permit the formation of a boundary is as yet little understood. As we have noted, it seems likely that the specific interests of seventeenth-century British virtuosi were abandoned in the eighteenth century (at least by active scientists) in the absence of aggressive boundary-work against them. Houghton sees the virtuoso role as having died out by around 1720, though we find the designation itself used for some time. Collin Russell (1983:80–85) remarks that E. M. da Costa, a secretary of the Royal Society, made notes on "virtuoso" collections between 1747 and 1788, but by this time their contents had become prosaic: the sensational items of the past were replaced by seashells, rocks, and fossils. Yet this seems to have occurred less because sensationalism had been successfully disparaged by scientists than because elite interest in it waned for reasons Houghton and Kenseth allude to above. It may also be that more marvelous items in virtuoso cabinets were replaced in function by new instruments of science such as the microscope and the telescope. The enthusiasm of Samuel Pepys (an amateur installed as president of the Royal Society is 1684, but better know for his *Diary*) suggests how powerful the influence of these "gadgets" themselves may have been (see Nicolson 1965:22–27). The ability of amateurs to personally view the "minute bodies" Hooke described in his *Micrographia* (1665) must have dramatized scientific "progress" quite effectively, and done so in a way that would have brought enthusiasts to devalue the older cabinets. In 1675 Emanuele Tesauro was already mourning the loss of celestial mysteries caused by the introduction of the telescope.[27]

The apparently spontaneous retreat of virtuoso concerns (difficult to gauge, as we shall see, both as to depth and width) in the absence of aggressive boundary-work illustrates the historical and sociological complexity (or muddledness) of the processes by which boundaries arose. In trying to explain the correlative issue of the "decline of magic" in the seventeenth century, Keith Thomas (1971:641–663) first remarks the rise of the early natural and social sciences and cites interesting examples of boundary-work on their behalf, but then points to cases of apparent "backsliding" to indicate that the effect was not uniformly progressive. He eventually concludes that the waning of "magical"

---

27. See Kenseth (1991a:54). On the other hand, the Society continued to act (perhaps somewhat ritually) as a clearinghouse for reports of prodigies. Hall (1984:224) writes that "the last 'monstrous lamb' (described by A. Carlisle, FRS 1804, a distinguished surgeon) was published in 1801."

worldviews, though perhaps encouraged by contemporary achievements in mechanical philosophy and by certain social and technological innovations that made life more predictable, is better attributed to the promise of the new science than to its accomplishments. Yet exactly how this promise captured the fancy of cultural elites so as to make virtuoso ambitions appear passé remains somewhat obscure (but see Stewart 1992).

Furthermore, it would be wrong to give the impression that virtuoso concerns died out with the onset of the Enlightenment. As late as the 1780s, as Robert Darnton (1968:33–34) has shown, they were strong on the Continent, where the picture of a bizarre and impossible monster supposedly discovered in Chile could amaze readers of the *Courier de l'Europe*, and where "serious scientists had long been publishing accounts in the *Journal des Scavans* and the *Journal de Physique* of marvels like talking dogs and basilisks whose looks killed quicker than bullets." Parisian enthusiasm for popular science made it "the mecca of the marvelous in the eighteenth century" (1968:48) and thus an attractive venue for figures like Cagliostro and Mesmer. Nevertheless, despite offering a ready market for anecdotal marvels, the later eighteenth century gravitated more than the seventeenth to theoretical speculation about universal principles acting in the form of subtle fluids. Inspired in part by Newton's systematics and in part by experiments with electricity, investigators competed with one another to announce the discovery of invisible agents capable of explaining human and macrocosmic behavior. Thus at the end of the century, when *Naturphilosophie* brought a sense of the narrowness of scientific vision into the academy, the matters in dispute bore little resemblance to their seventeenth-century forebears (see Esposito 1977). Prodigies and other peculiar phenomena had given way to cosmic schemes demonstrating the systematic integration of forces at work in the world—forces that, however mysterious, were themselves regular in their consequences.[28]

Perhaps a second difference in the later eighteenth century was the aggressiveness with which academic science sought to promote its (tenuous) boundaries. Mesmer's enormous success in Paris, for instance, caused the appointment of a royal commission (drawn from the academies and numbering Lavoisier and Franklin among its members) which concluded on the basis of various experiments that "the effects of mes-

---

28. A striking example is Lorenz Oken's *Elements of Physiophilosophy* (1847); he begins by generating the world out of mathematical oscillations around a primordial Nought, and then systematizes the results so thoroughly that, 637 pages later, he is able to speculate about the psychology of snails.

merizing could be attributed to the overheated imaginations of the mesmerists" (Darnton 1968:64). Yet this degree of skepticism seems to have been selectively applied in that the academies could voice approval for theories, such as that of Nicolas le Dru, that in retrospect seem difficult to distinguish from Mesmer's. Further, as was to be expected, proponents of subtle fluids responded by circulating anecdotal and clinical evidence of their successes and sought to establish pedigrees by finding analogies to their theories in the works of Locke, Bacon, Bayle, Leibniz, Hume, Newton, Descartes, and La Mettrie. The consequence was that even those who rejected Mesmerism, like Condorcet, found themselves unable to persuasively articulate their reasons for doing so (Darnton 1968:30,39,61).

If boundaries between enchanted and disenchanted inquiry remained somewhat fluid in the eighteenth century, however, the problem seems to have gradually developed into, and then become domesticated as, a conflict between amateur and professional. For instance, Hahn (1971:44) notes that the Berlin academician J.-H.-S. Formey

made it a special point to single out [the] problem of *demi-savoir* as one of the academies' major concerns. According to Formey, academicians were, by the very nature of their enterprise and their position, the only legitimate possessors of the key to knowledge. By that very token, they were responsible for stamping out the pretensions of "this legion of half-wits, not even worthy of being called dung-piles . . . who dishonor the Republic of Letters."

While ambitions to be epistemic legislators had perhaps always been stronger among Continental than among British academicians, professional scientists in the Royal Society also felt their luster dimmed by association with amateurs. This problem was only "solved" with the reforms of 1830–1848, in result of which the Society took on its modern role of recognizing exclusively professional eminence (see Hall 1984). Perhaps these reforms could be linked with the aggressive prosecution of *Naturphilosophie* by Continental laboratory scientists like Dubois-Reymond during the 1830s to signal the cementing of prejudices that are in force today.[29] In any event, it was only in this period that the production of scientific knowledge became well enough organized to successfully police its boundaries.

We need to add here, however, that the strength of this boundary can be affected by broader cultural and political developments. Even within the "mature" sciences, as Anne Harrington (1991) has argued,

29. Even in this period, however, a later-to-be-ridiculed enterprise like phrenology achieved significant popular and elite support. See Cooter (1984).

explicit programs of enchantment have arisen when scientists found traditional scientific norms spiritually limiting. A dramatic example was the
growth of "holistic" research agendas in German biomedicine and psychology in the period between the wars. Figures like von Uexkull, von
Manikow, and Goldstein championed forms of vitalism as a way of expressing characteristically German modes of thought so as to combat
the prevailing spiritual deadness of science. Mandarin ambitions to develop (or recapture) a value-laden and thus spiritually satisfying method
of inquiry in the image of Goethe's—ambitions Weber (1946:143)
scathingly characterized as those of "big children in university chairs"—
turned research programs in distinctly irrationalist directions so as to
uncover vital universal principles similar in many respects to Mesmer's
animal magnetism.[30]

Thus the boundary between enchanted and disenchanted inquiry in
the study of nature is complex both in its history and in the forces that
have caused it to strengthen and weaken. If it now takes some effort to
summon up the circumstances in which Newton divided his research
between (what we see as) physics on the one hand and alchemy on the
other, some of his contemporaries would have shared our difficulty in
this regard while others would not have. Yet though we must admit that
the exact course of events by which our prejudices have been shaped is
as yet unclear, their sociological underpinning is not. The transformation of the natural philosopher (an undifferentiated role performed by
cosmopolitan but independent intellectuals largely in solitude) into the
natural scientist (a differentiated role performed by insular and highly
interdependent intellectuals collectively) has permitted relatively firm
boundaries to be drawn where none could be in the past. This was not
quite what Thomas Sprat had in mind when he contrasted "operations
of the mind" best performed individually with those requiring "many
hands," but it was the crucial distinction. The result, at least among
educational elites, has been the disenchantment of the natural order.
On the other hand, where "mature" sciences have not developed—
where, that is, the structural conditions of knowledge production remain much as in the seventeenth century—enchantment, it seems, is
still the norm.

As we will see in chapter 7, there is more to be said about the social
bases of enchantment, at least in the study of culture, but before addressing this we need to take up a question left in abeyance too long—

---

30. For the social, cultural, and political context of these developments, see Ringer
(1969).

Culture as Referential Ecology

*If we had a keen vision and feeling of all ordinary human life, it
would be like hearing the grass grow and the squirrel's heart beat,
and we should die of that roar which lies on the other side of
silence.*

George Eliot, Middlemarch

The relative enchantment of an area of inquiry, we argued much earlier,
is a function both of its organization and of its referential ecology. We
have just considered organization, but have all along deferred important
questions about ecology. One might reasonably argue that the frequency with which strange phenomena are discovered at work in culture
points to something more than the investigative autonomy of their discoverers. Perhaps culture as referential ecology is itself quite strange, the
sort of terrain that hinders or perhaps precludes more organized efforts.

An argument to this effect has been made, albeit in an edifying register, by literary theorists of deconstructive persuasion. And whether one
accepts their rationale or not, one may still conclude that culture consists of essentially slippery terrain that prevents all but the loosest organization of interpretive communities (or ensures that individual autonomy could be decreased only by authoritarian means). For instance, the
social constructivism of Stanley Fish (1980, 1989a) sees meaning as
constrained not by features of culture itself, but simply by the conventions of a local community. So well socialized are most of us that we
come to see our own conventions as natural, and (quite unaware of alternatives) believe ourselves able, through them, to see the "objective"
shape of an artifact. In this circumstance interpretations wildly at vari-
ance with ours will be deemed "strange" or the product of a peculiar
intender—but this is just how our own would be characterized from
the opposing perspective. Once we realize that interpretive standards
are relative to local communities and vary considerably across space and
time, we will be driven to conclude that culture *has* no contours, no
variation which would make inquiry into it more or less difficult. Instead, it is found more or less difficult only as given communities *make*
it so. Obviously, then, it is wrong to consider it in terms of referential
ecology.

Against this relativism, as we noted earlier, realists like E. D. Hirsch
(1967, 1976) have found in "authorial intention" a possible basis for
consensual inquiry into meaning. On this argument, we can obviate the

problem posed by strange intenders by sticking to commonsensical ones (like ourselves) and looking for evidence of what they had in mind. If an artifact conveys *a* meaning, it can only be the one *intended* by the person who produced it. (Allowing strange alternatives will in practice lead to such variable results that any hope of consensus is lost.) Intention has the character of a historical "fact," and it can be warranted by the same techniques historians use to establish other facts. As we suggested in chapter 2, furthermore, intentions (or reasons) may vary in perspicuousness, with some being compellingly simple and others less scrutable. In this light, intention allows us to think of culture both as *having* contours (contra the relativists), and as showing variation in them that may either facilitate or impede inquiry (contra relativists and deconstructors). The idea of a referential ecology thus makes sense when it refers to the substrate of intentions underlying and expressed through culture.[1]

These positions are the current form taken by the paradoxical intuitions of chapter 1—that meaning is at once both bounded and indeterminate—and it will pay us to look at them in some detail. Doing so will allow us to establish a basis for culture as referential ecology, and in the process show that what is normally viewed as a conflict between theoretical positions is instead a struggle between different practices that, joined as they have been under the same disciplinary umbrella, have perhaps not fully realized the antithetical nature of their aims. Ambiguous epistemic registers, and thus enchanted discourse, thrive in part because of this confusion—which is endemic to cultural studies but most easily delineated in literature.

Perhaps we might begin by looking at some of the arguments that make the relativist position so compelling. One of these is comparative and historical in nature: when we cast a glance broadly over the history of interpretive practices, it is argued, we are struck by their variety and mutual incompatibility. Clearly the aims that interpreters bring to texts show more than marginal differentiation; instead we meet wholesale differences, many of which seem quite strange to us. Thus, as we noted, interpretive practices like *gematria* may be employed so that further lev-

---

1. On the other hand, overtly politicized forms of deconstruction, which make more-than-edifying claims about how the world works, are symptomatic of the very enchantment we are studying. Adopting an ambiguous register like that of Geertz and Lévi-Strauss, they hope through understanding the workings of phenomena like "difference" to achieve desired political change. Such a position, in which a relativism so reflexive as to consistently pull the rug out from under its own feet is taken as a point d'appui from which to understand and change the world, Fish (1989a:322–324; 1989b:307) dismisses as "antifoundationalist theory hope." We note it as an interesting florescence of virtuosity.

els of textual meaning can be plumbed. Our tendency to look upon this as eccentric and parochial, as something we have perhaps finally "gotten over," is belied by similarly eccentric but academically respectable interpretive practices like structuralism and deconstruction.

The radical nature of exotic methods of reading and the apparent "violence" they work on texts both stimulate and undercut appeals to "common sense" so as to avoid a relativist conclusion. Some critics challenge relativism by pointing out that "if we don't know exactly what such and such a text means, at least we know it does not mean . . . (outlandish example)." The offense to common sense the example constitutes, however, diminishes as we multiply the number of unusual interpretive practices with which we are acquainted, since these suggest that if the text does not mean something outlandish now, we need only wait long enough to find that—somewhere, for some interpretive community—it *will*. Thus an argument such as Wayne Booth's (1974:242 cited by Fish 1989a:184) to the effect that texts have "a structure of meanings, an order which rules out some readings as entirely fallacious, shows other readings to be partially so, and confirms others as more or less adequate," is convincing only within the limits of a particular community. The more varied the practices we become familiar with, the less convinced we will be that texts *have* this sort of structure, and rather than assume it to be somehow in them prior to and independent of interpretation, we will see it as the artifact of necessarily local conventions. Our particular interpretive practices are all that stand between us and whatever outlandish constructions common sense finds a text unable to bear.

The point to such arguments, as we shall see, is not to encourage whimsy in interpretation, but rather to disturb parochial assumptions that are more or less forced upon us by our having conventions in the first place. But with the parochial bathwater, relativism seems to toss out our baby—referential ecology. If culture is, as relativists seem to imply, a "white noise" (or featureless terrain) that only acquires character through interpretations,[2] and if interpretations vary dramatically, then there is nothing *before* interpretation to see in ecological terms. We get "whited out." Moreover, we needn't look outward or backward, surveying exotic interpretive communities, to arrive at this conclusion,

2. To avoid misrepresentation, we must add that for Fish culture can never actually be confronted as white noise because there is simply no preinterpretive way of getting at it. Because it is impossible to stand outside *all* interpretive conventions and still find culture to be meaningful, it always has some character or another. Yet none of this is, so to speak, its own. He says of a legal document, for instance, that it is "neither ambiguous nor unambiguous in and of itself. The document isn't *anything* in and of itself" (1989a:301).

since it is fostered as well by experience with disagreements among people who inhabit roughly the same community and thus subscribe to more or less similar conventions. Fish has examined some of these controversies, with characteristic acumen, in prosecuting his relativist case. For instance, he cites (1980:339–342) the variety of opinions as to William Blake's "Tyger" poem: for some the tiger is a holy figure, for others the symbol of "rapacious selfhood", and for still others both good and evil or beyond good and evil. Yet each of the participants in this controversy forwards evidence assumed to conclusively demonstrate his or her case, and the discussion abounds in phrases like "It is obvious that . . ." or "Surely the point is that . . ." which Fish takes to be interpretive whistling in the dark. The degree of dissensus in this and other cases suggests to him that the interpreter's desire to ground a reading in evidence that is prior to and independent of it, so that an appeal can be made "to the facts of the matter," is mistaken. What will be seen as evidence in the first place is dependent on interpretive aims, and there is nothing prior to these aims to which a reading might be anchored— the same conclusion we arrived at by the route of comparing interpretive communities. Thus we are confronted with white noise whether we look on the matter comparatively or locally.

The case Fish presents (with a resourcefulness we have been unable to illustrate in so short a space) seems unarguable—and in fact is frequently allowed by realist opponents. The dispute is fueled less by opposition to the theoretical arguments for relativism than by objections to specific interpretive practices that find sanction in them. For though Fish insists that his position has no implications for literary practice, others take relativism to underwrite just the forms of interpretation that exercise realists. The significant argument, then, is not between theoretical forms of relativism and realism—the day is more or less conceded to the former—but between a "practical" realism and specific interpretive practices grouped under the relativist umbrella.[3] (Nevertheless, this is sometimes forgotten and relativism itself attacked more or less by way of proxy.) If we can get beneath the resulting smoke, however, we can detect features of the dispute that bear on our concern with referential

3. The tenets of "practical" realism will gradually be developed over the course of this chapter, but it might help here to indicate that they include (1) that expressive culture has an intentional (causal) structure investigable by naturalistic means and invariant across interpretations of what it means; and (2) that when this structure is relatively poor and perspicuous, mundane interpretive strategies prove successful enough for communication to occur. Practical realism would meet opposition from latter-day structuralists, New Historicists, deconstructors, and Geertzian "thick descriptionists."

ecology. Perhaps we can begin by addressing some of the worries relativism commonly raises. (Of necessity, we will treat arguments and examples that will be familiar to some readers, who may prefer to skim until conclusions are drawn.)

One worry, already alluded to, is that the specific practices relativism is sometimes thought to sanction yield willful or whimsical interpretations and thus lead to anarchy, to a loss of authority, in interpretive communities (see Hirsch 1967:2). As Fish (1980:346–350) rightly points out, however, truly whimsical interpretations—of the sort that would warrant concern—could only occur where there were no interpretive *communities* to begin with. Each of these has developed its conventions through painstaking arguments that proved convincing to serious and sophisticated inquirers. To think of their products as whimsical demands that we discredit entirely the habits of thought involved, a judgment that would render the interpreters "mad" rather than merely willful. Relativism thus never encourages interpretive idiosyncracy or anarchy, but at most a pluralism of strategies each of which would require, indeed could only exist on the basis of, constraints on the will of individual inquirers.[4]

A second worry, with regard to which we cited M. H. Abrams in chapter 1, is that relativism makes impossible "anything we would count as literary or cultural history." This is a more interesting possibility, for while it could be argued that relativist pluralism actually ensures a space for just such historical inquiry, it also raises a question as to why one would think to engage in it. If culture is really "white noise" to which color is (unavoidably) added by interpretation, why would anyone approach it from a realist position rather than from some potentially more edifying perspective? Why not the most interesting or politically correct interpretation rather than the one best warranted by historical research? It is in grappling with this question that practical realism both advances our understanding and falls into serious problems as an interpretive program. If we are right, it draws rhetorical sustenance from an alliance with the explanatory naturalism practiced by the "scientific" cultural disciplines, while being unwilling to curtail its interpretive ambitions in

4. We should point out, however, that Fish is insufficiently sociological in his approach to interpretive communities, for he seems to suggest (see 1989a:126–132) that they all exercise the same degree of constraint over interpretation, whereas in fact the constraint varies with their ability to control individual members. He is also insufficiently anthropological in that he fails to recognize the importance of cross-cultural regularities in folk (or "commonsense") interpretive strategies both at the perceptual level (see below) and at the conceptual level (see Atran 1990).

the way strict allegiance to naturalism would require. Once we see our way into and through this problem, we should understand how culture can be seen as referential ecology.

"The theoretical aim of a genuine discipline, whether scientific or humanistic," says Hirsch (1967:viii–ix), "is the attainment of truth, and its practical aim is agreement that truth has probably been achieved." If literary interpretation is to rank as a "genuine" discipline, then, it may have to adopt many of the warranting standards by which its scientific brethren render their constructions of the world probable. The role that terms like "validity," "knowledge," and "consensus" play in Hirsch's argument, as well as the damage he sees them done by "willful arbitrariness and extravagance in academic criticism" (1967:2), suggest the degree to which his ambitions are congruent with those of other naturalistic endeavors. If he does not go on to explicitly argue that literary interpretation is cumulative and progressive like the sciences, he certainly covets the epistemic and social circumstances in which they seem to settle disputes by discovering data strongly favoring one or the other side. Similar discoveries in literary studies would not mean arrival at Truth in any absolute sense, Hirsch makes clear, but simply the surmounting of past errors, and though our view of these could always be changed by radical innovations in understanding, these latter would themselves proceed not so as to shift our ground entirely but so as to preserve elements of the past even as we advance. Regardless of how far the analogy between interpretation and science as "genuine" disciplines goes, however, Hirsch is clearly anxious to borrow from the prestige of the sciences to advance his case: indeed, were this entirely inappropriate it would make the laborious and often intrinsically unrewarding efforts of literary historians hard to fathom. Why else brave the archival dusts if not to contribute to our "knowledge"? Would this be worthwhile if the results were not as "sound" as those of the sciences—if one were not, in other words, pursuing a "genuine" discipline?

One decides for or against such a vision for literary interpretation in moral terms, Hirsch argues (1967:26). We will be drawn to it only if we see it as a worthwhile vocation, as a way of intellectual life more appealing than the alternatives—such as those that from Hirsch's point of view sanction "arbitrariness and extravagance." Let us allow this appeal, which is simply that of science itself. The question then becomes more practical: how do we go about acquiring "knowledge"? Hirsch argues that if interpretation is unable to arrive at "determinate meanings" for cultural phenomena, the project will necessarily falter, being unable to achieve consensus. At the time *Validity in Interpretation* was written, the doctrine of "semantic autonomy," which allowed a text to mean all the things it could be interpreted as saying according to current grammatical and semantic conventions, stood in Hirsch's way. The problem with it, he points out, is that "the task of finding out what a text says has no determinate object, since the text can say different things to different readers" (1967:11). While public conventions place some limits on possible sayings, within these literary phenomena are left too mercurial (more specifically, not equipresent enough) to be plausible objects of a consensual discipline. If cultural phenomena are to have determinate character, as we have already found Hirsch arguing, this can only be grounded in authorial intentions, a possibility we might opt for on "the sensible belief that a text means what its author meant" (1967:1).[5]

Hirsch's argument occasionally winds up in minor difficulty (particularly when the topic of unconscious intentions arises), but as long as we accept his aims its main thrust turns out to be as hard to argue with as Fish's relativism. If texts (or cultural phenomena more generally) are thought to *express* something, it seems clear that they make manifest an internal state of the people who produce them—a state we can conveniently summarize in terms of intentions. To put this somewhat differently, but in terms Hirsch also uses, if we want to know why a text took the particular form it did—why it turned out to be one thing rather than a host of alternatives—we will look to the reasons behind and embodied through it. The act of its production is always a phenomenon of determinate shape that could in principle be known just as thoroughly as any other historical phenomenon. But it will occur to us, referring back to chapter 2, that knowledge of this sort would allow us to *explain* the product, deriving it *causally* from the intentions of its author. More specifically, the knowledge that allows us to judge a particular interpretation "valid" is at the same time the knowledge that will account for it according to naturalistic canons. In other words, valid interpretation can be had only through explanation, and from this point of view Hirsch's thesis that "genuine" scientific and humanistic disciplines share

5. Significant portions of *Validity in Interpretation* are given over to making clear what this does *not* mean. It does not require, for instance, that the ambiguities authors frequently intend somehow be resolved, but only that their nature be specifiable and thus determinate. Nor does it require that texts successfully convey what their authors "have in mind" (or hope to achieve), since it is possible to bungle attempts at communication. Finally, it does not require that authors have always in mind everything their texts can be seen to imply, though it does demand that they assent to whatever implications we draw from them. We should note that though Knapp and Michaels (1982) point out that all interpretations of what a text is saying must assume authorial intentions, their argument is somewhat disingenuous with regard to Hirsch's broader project, which hopes to exclude factitious characterizations of the author—or what we have previously styled "strange intenders."

the same goal acquires more force: they are all equally interested in the causes of things.[6]

A brief example here might help. Hirsch discusses (1976:23–25) the interesting case of an originally anonymous pamphlet of 1702 titled *The Shortest Way with the Dissenters?* It counselled brutal suppression of religious heterodoxy and was read as such by some contemporaries. Yet its tone was so extreme as to allow the possibility that it might have been meant ironically, so as to impugn the repressive desires of the orthodox. When Daniel Defoe, a dissenter, was discovered to be its author, the ambiguity—straightforward vs. ironic—was cleared up in favor of the latter, and Defoe pilloried (literally) for his temerity. Here we have a case of a text that, according to public conventions of interpretation, can be (and was) read in conflicting ways. Just as we may wonder whether a person is being sarcastic with us or not, and thus find ourselves annoyingly unable to attach determinate meaning to his or her words, so we cannot on the basis of textual evidence find a determinate meaning for *The Shortest Way with the Dissenters?* Determinacy can only be provided by research into the intentions a text embodies. Once we know these were Defoe's, however, we can be reasonably sure (barring *quite* odd possibilities) that the text *was* ironic. A different provenance, on the other hand, might lead to the opposite conclusion. The text thus could have gotten to be the way it was by two quite different routes (or causal paths). Historical information clears the matter up, allowing us to decide *validly* that the route was ironic, and precisely because Defoe's intentions explain how it took the shape it did. Explanation thus provides determinacy.

In principle, then, "genuine" literary interpretation is a discipline whose hypotheses about textual meaning aspire to empirical warrant, and in the process show a causal link between intention and expression. This link is the only way of giving determinacy to meaning and thus of decreasing its intractability as a subject for research. Valid interpretation makes meaning equipresent, and its appeal would be not unlike that of an instrument able to give precise measures of some phenomenon that had previously proven elusive. Of course this is not everyone's ambition for interpretation, since the very idea of naturalistic warrant for determinate meaning proves offensive to many. But the more relevant question here is whether realism "works," or rather, whether it works well enough to attract our (moral) commitment. If the scope of realism—meaning by this the amount of culture we can comprehend and motivate on its

---

6. Again, we are following Toulmin (1970) here, but the matter is controversial: compare Collin (1985:57–103).

basis—turns out for reasons of practice or principle to be limited, then one might judge it too restrictive for comfort.

But how are we to determine its scope? A serious effort in this direction would require another book, but we can point to some cases that are suggestive, and begin through them to roughly delimit the referential ecology of culture. The first of these has been discussed interestingly by Hirsch. He points out that relativists themselves see certain domains of meaning as quite unproblematic. Both the visual recognition of printed language and the aural recognition of speech involve interpretive practices (albeit preconscious ones) whereby highly variable phenomena are reduced to "types" and thus made capable of determinate signification. As he writes:

Any two speakers of a language make different sounds, often recognizably different ones, and yet they can perceive the different sounds as being linguistically identical, as being the self-same phoneme. Since we are all aware of regional accents, we are not surprised to hear very different noises being made when, say, the pledge of allegiance is recited. Yet we do not doubt that these different noises are representing the same, self-identical words. (1976:28)

Thus at the level of graphemic or phonemic perception, where various typefaces or sounds are judged the same for purposes of interpretation, culture appears—even to relativists—to be quite stable and equipresent. (Of course one might demonstrate some limits to this experimentally, showing that "degraded" sounds or letters eventually become subject first to controversy about meaning and then to incomprehension—a state often experienced by those grading handwritten exams—but these cases are of such theoretical insignificance as to be uninteresting.) Moreover, there would be little disagreement as to why meaning at this level is so unproblematic: the alternative is evolutionarily and anthropologically impossible. Speech itself would never have become a vehicle of communication were phonemic interpretation characterized by dissensus to the same degree as the scholarly interpretation of texts. What constrains the former, with great effectiveness, is the threat of permanent communicative breakdown (and consequently of human extinction); and what liberates the latter, just as effectively, is its absence. From an anthropological or sociological perspective, then, determinate meaning thrives when much is in the balance; indeterminacy when nothing is at stake.[7]

---

7. Needless to say, it is possible to imagine circumstances where so little weighs in the balance that an interpretive community might fall deeply into controversy over phonemes or graphemes. Like the bank officials in Woody Allen's *Take the Money and Run* who disagree over whether a robber's note says "I have a gun" or "I have a gub," we can drive dissension to any interpretive level we wish and note that there is nothing in the phenom-

Hirsch hopes to work outward from this beachhead of determinacy where relativists for the most part must agree with him. To do so he needs to show that the lessons of the phonemic case are applicable to interpretation in general, and that the latter always has something important—i.e. "knowledge"—at stake. Rather than trace his arguments out, however, let us provisionally concede them and see what happens. We may still conclude that the results to be expected from realism will not prove fully adequate for literary interpretation, since both practical and theoretical difficulties stand in Hirsch's way. The practical difficulty is that, for various reasons, we often lack the knowledge of authorial intentions that would warrant claims about determinate meaning. It may be denied us by living authors for reasons of principle (poems should not mean but *be,* etc.), or by departed ones by happenstance (as when available documents offer no clue to intentions). The latter problem has been nicely illustrated by Fish. Whereas Hirsch, for instance, argues for the determinate irony of *The Shortest Way with the Dissenters?* basing his case on Defoe's authorship and quite reasonable assumptions about possible intentions, Fish looks at Swift's "Verses on the Death of Dr. Swift." Interpretations of this poem by contemporaries such as William King found some of its lines "a little vain," which causes Fish (1989a:188) to note that "the poem's textual history begins with the conviction that in lines 307–484, Swift is engaged in an indecorous act of self-praise. That conviction was not repudiated . . . but took a new and diagnostic form in the speculation of John Middleton Murry that at the time the poem was written, Swift's mind was already failing." Critical opinion, having previously been uniform in viewing these lines as defective either in moral or intellectual terms, has only recently changed. In 1963, Barry Slepian showed that the lines could be read ironically: in purposely praising himself, so it is suggested, Swift shows himself subject to the universal vanity he has proclaimed in earlier sections of the poem. Clearly, this gives us quite a different sense of what his intentions may have been.

While other interpretations have since been offered, Slepian's is now broadly accepted. This is not, Fish suggests, because it rests upon newly unearthed empirical evidence about Swift's frame of mind, but rather because it gives integrity to a work previously thought to lack it: the lines once thought defective can now be seen as part of an interesting

ena themselves that prevents this. In philosophical terms, then, relativists could as easily establish their bailiwick here as at higher levels of interpretive practice. In practical terms, however, it is hard to imagine anyone putting up with such "nonsense," at least apart from comedic designs—which deconstructors sometimes exploit to great effect.

argument, thus providing us with a more estimable poem—a salutary outcome for those who appreciate Swift, and one that accords with our desire for tonal unity. From the "empirical" or historical point of view, nevertheless, there is still nothing to choose between King's "vanity," Murry's "failing mind," or Slepian's "irony." Though we will be tempted to deduce Swift's intention from the ironic interpretation, this would be calamitous in an empirical discipline: intentions may be evidence for an interpretation, but *not* the other way around. As Fish (1989a:296) notes in another context:"One cannot read back from the [text] to the intention (for that would be possible only if [texts] were meaningful apart from intention, or, to put it more precisely, had as part of their meaning a specification of the intention behind them)." But they don't. Of course one might use the ironical reading to stimulate new historical research into Swift's frame of mind, but the limits of "knowledge" here—and thus in Hirsch's terms the practical limits of a "genuine discipline"—are set by the potentially available data, which in this instance prove insufficient.[8]

We have looked here only at one case—obviously the argument between Hirsch and Fish relies on more than Defoe v. Swift—but it suggests that requiring empirical evidence of authorial intentions so as to arrive at determinate meanings would significantly constrict the scope of literary interpretation, though to what degree is a matter for speculation. In part it would depend on just how hard-nosed one wanted to get and on whether hypothetical interpretations would be countenanced as a stimulus to research, but even in a soft-nosed version the likely effect on humanistic disciplines would be bracing indeed. The limits of valid interpretation would be set both by the amount of information about intentions and by their relative richness. The latter poses a particularly troublesome issue, because it is the richest texts that most stimulate the interest of interpreters. The probability, then, is that realist interpreters would have to retreat to considering poor texts of well-documented provenance. A second, more theoretical or speculative set of considerations has to do with the degree to which knowledge of an author's intentions allows us to understand a text's meaning. We introduced this question in chapter 2 when we pointed out that the processes by which

8. There may of course be occasions in which competing "coherentist" justifications of interpretations can be adjudicated among on the basis of historical evidence. For instance, a perfectly coherent interpretation of a text could be shown wildly anachronistic. But when such judgments rely upon vague and general impressions of what a specific time and place were "about," one coherentist interpretation will be used to "validate" the other, thus precluding appeal beyond the hermeneutic circle. Clearly the latter circumstance is one Hirsch needs to avoid.

expressive phenomena are produced are sometimes not very perspicuous even to their authors. When the decisions involved in producing
expressive phenomena depart from canons of rationality, knowledge of
how they were arrived at may not help us understand what the phenomena mean. Perhaps more interestingly, however, even when authorial intentions *are* perspicuous they may prove insufficient to the task.
Though we have the option here of deciding that at some extreme the
phenomena simply become meaningless, to go this route will place beyond interpretation items that many people clearly believe meaningful—a possibility we welcomed anent symbolism but find less satisfactory in the present case.

The issues here are quite difficult and do not allow for definitive treatment. Perhaps they may best be approached through a thought experiment we borrow from Richard Rorty (1979). Though the experiment
is fanciful and indulges in science fiction, it manages to bare issues that
could otherwise be addressed only in a cumbersome fashion. Imagine,
then, some future time in which we have developed a technology to
investigate intentions. Rather than seek verbal reports on them, or perhaps probe them psychiatrically, or ferret them out by means of "truth
serums," our technology gets to the heart of the matter by monitoring
the brain processes that constitute cognition. Since everything that we
think (along with the unconscious activity that contributes to thinking)
is embodied in neurophysiological processes, a "cerebroscope" (Rorty's
term) that could observe our brains in detail without causing damage—
imagine a vastly souped up nuclear magnetic resonance imaging machine—would be able to view our intentions as physical happenings inside us. In fact, when we suggested earlier in this chapter that expressive
culture makes "manifest an internal state of the people who produce"
it, we actually had in mind for "internal state" just this sort of neurophysiological description. Of course a cerebroscope would be of little
practical use unless it was coupled with a sophisticated explanatory neu-
rophysiology, but the two together would generate quite awesome possibilities. Scientists viewing us with the device and understanding quite
thoroughly how our brains worked would, in fact, be able to predict
and explain anything and everything we might do. For instance, to the
extent that our brains process what we are going to say somewhat before
we actually say it, these scientists would be able to beat us to the punch,
predicting our words an instant before we could blurt them out. And
the same would be true for our interior monologues: an instant before
we recognized that we were thirsty and could use a beer, investigators
would be able to predict the precise interior language through which
this condition and the attendant desire would dawn upon us. The sup-

position here is simply that every "sentence in the language which any-body bothered to form could easily be correlated with a readily identi-fiable neural state" (1979:71) and, on the basis of this knowledge, predicted by means of the cerebroscope.

Though literary realists might well loathe the idea of this instrument and its attendant neurophysiology, the knowledge it could afford them should nonetheless prove seductive in principle. Though Hirsch never considers intentions in terms of brain processes, he should admit that the latter provide the bedrock of "hard" data that seem to guarantee literary interpretation, albeit prospectively, a place alongside the sciences in their quest for knowledge. To return to our previous case, were Swift before us now and composing the verses on his death, we could tell by means of a cerebroscope whether they were vainglorious, a symptom of mental decay, or ironic—even if Swift were to prove, like T. S. Eliot, unforthcoming under interrogation. In a cerebroscope we have the ulti-mate tool for snooping into intentions, and thus for deciding on the determinate meaning of texts, if we are to follow Hirsch's earlier argu-ment. Though it gives him an investigative power he might choose to shun—images of secret police should already have occurred to the reader—it also makes his case in the strongest possible light. In fact it suggests that everything about culture is in principle explicable, since all of it is borne by natural processes investigable beneath the semantic level.

But a problem still remains, for it is not yet clear that being able to explain culture in this way would allow us to understand it. Better phrased, there may still be limits beyond which cerebroscopes and neu-rophysiology prove of little benefit. Suppose we allow that they promise to decide Defoe v. Swift in Hirsch's favor and pass on to a harder case. Recall here our discussion of Mallarmé in chapter 2. We speculated there that it would not help much to seek out the intentions behind "Un coup de des" if it had in fact been composed significantly on the basis of aesthetic intuitions about the "fittingness" of specific words. Here a cerebroscope would indeed be able to explain each "choice" Mallarmé made; and yet this neurophysiological knowledge would be of no aid in evaluating what the poem *meant*. This remains after we explain it just as ineffable as before we set about doing so. Even less occulted locutions, when sublime, present us with the same problem. Consider, for instance, the epigraph for this chapter from George Eliot.[9] Would a cerebroscope help us understand what it means? We could cer-tainly tap into, and fully explain, Eliot's interior monologue at the time

9. Quoted from *Middlemarch* without citation by Donoghue (1981:14).

she produced it, and we might find in the process that she chose grass and a squirrel's heart for her similes because the first grew slowly and the second beat fast, thus offering a nice contrast. We might even deem the choice perspicuous because it is at least faintly rational. We would then be able to account both in neurophysiological and in "human" terms for the presence of "grass" and "squirrel's heart" in the passage. Yet we do not get any closer through this knowledge to understanding precisely what the sentence as a whole *means*. It seems to acquire no greater determinacy, however thoroughly we understand its intentions.

Hirsch might well respond that it does, or does well enough to suit his aims for interpretation. He might achieve from the cerebroscope enough evidence to "disprove" certain willful and extravagant paraphrases of Mallarmé or Eliot, for instance, though this claim might be disputed for reasons we will address momentarily. Yet knowing the intentional basis of sublime or ineffable cultural products certainly does nothing to reduce their sublimity or ineffability, qualities that invite varied and divergent paraphrase. Such invitations, extended to us by the richness of the phenomena before us, are responsible in part for the intrigue of literary interpretation as a vocation, and thus enter into our moral deliberations as to its proper aims alongside goals like the acquisition of knowledge. In any event, what is at stake here is whether texts have the capacity to "mean" more than they intend, an issue that has been puzzled over both in literary theoretical and in anthropological contexts.

For our purposes, the most interesting literary-theoretical discussion of the problem is by Paulson (1988). Drawing upon information theory and discussions of complex systems in the natural sciences, he argues that while for *instrumental* communication "noise" degrades messages and thus is incapacitating, for *aesthetic* expression it serves to enrich the "message," allowing it to be characterized in a variety of ways. Though in instrumental contexts noise normally intrudes into communication from without, while in aesthetic contexts it is often intentionally built into the product or develops as an inevitable outcome of language used "literarily," with it comes an excess of potential meaning that will be appreciated in the latter if not in the former situation. As Paulson (1988:130) writes:

It is precisely [the] autonomous complexity of language . . . that makes it possible (and necessary) to speak of noise in verbal texts, and a fortiori in literary texts. The uncertainties of literary language arise out of the properties of language itself as a system. Language's unreliability as a communicative instrument is due to ambiguities, overlappings, and uncertainties that occur because it has its own, internal, self-referential laws, its own features, which are not those of the message one seeks to send through it . . . [and which] are exploited in the literary text.

This means, as he goes on to note, that literary texts are not very good vehicles of instrumental communication, though it is precisely because of this that they are effective vehicles of aesthetic expression. Noise allows different textual meanings to organize themselves more or less spontaneously in the effort of interpretation, giving us the impression that a text is "rich" while precluding agreement as to its meaning. (Here the "chaos" of myths and dreams—the sense that anything can happen—may be viewed in terms of a low signal-to-noise ratio.) Thus though what we gain through interpretation is "a form of knowledge," it is not "identical with knowledge *of* the text" (1988:139) as this might be conceived of naturalistically. While we might hope to describe an instrumental message adequately by paraphrasing it, this ambition seems ill-suited to literary texts.

Paul Ricoeur perhaps had a similar thought in mind as he strove to open a field for hermeneutics above and beyond science. He argued that "This is the strength and weakness of hermeneutics; its weakness because, taking language at the moment when it escapes from its enclosure, it takes it at the moment when it also escapes a scientific treatment. . . . But this weakness is also its strength, because the place where language escapes from itself and escapes us is also the place where language comes to itself, the place where language is *saying*" (1974:66–67). The allusive and somewhat obscure way Ricoeur puts this dramatizes his point. It is unclear just when and where he believes language "escapes from its enclosure": perhaps it fails to do so in instrumental circumstances where its structural poverty normally makes it perspicuous (at least by pragmatic canons of interpretation), but succeeds in literary ones where structural and semantic entailment are weakened, as Paulson's argument would suggest.

The anthropological route to the same end follows from Sperber's analysis of symbolism discussed in chapter 3. Even in impoverished circumstances, whether a message has a determinate meaning depends on whether one reads it symbolically. Here it would be worth quoting Sperber (1975:109) at length:

Some utterances are clearly and absolutely symbolic: liturgical formulae, invocations, myths, figurative idioms, etc., either because they have no other interpretation than their symbolic one, or else because all other interpretations are absurd. We might therefore be tempted to define symbolism by what these

utterances have in common either in their form or their content and by what
opposes them to non-symbolic utterances. But there is no non-symbolic utterance which is not capable, in some conditions, of becoming symbolic. It takes
only, for example, recognition in the utterances:

No entry,
Keep left,
What is the pun about the fiddler?

respectively of a sexual allusion, a political allusion, and a Spoonerism, to give
them a symbolic value that they do not normally have.

This last point might be argued with, since the sample utterances
constitute rather poor symbols with few interesting paraphrases (according, once again, to mundane canons), but the general stance
Sperber takes certainly helps us make sense of our difficulties with
George Eliot's notion about the rapturous threat posed by the sounds
of life. In evoking the sublime, her language slips into symbolism—as
does Ricoeur's when he writes about the liberation of language. Phras-
ing the latter's argument now somewhat differently, we could suggest
that when language, in becoming symbolic (or from Paulson's point of
view, in becoming "noisier"), ceases to mean, it begins to "say," and
that what it says cannot be reduced to what it intends. This remains
the case even though we can in principle explain it fully (that is, show
"scientifically" how it took exactly such and such a form) in terms of its
intentions, driving the issue back (if forced) to its basis in neurophysiological data.

From our perspective this is a happy state of affairs because it allows
a full and potentially complete scope to naturalistic explanation while
blocking any worries we might develop about "scientism"—taken here
as a concern that effective explanation might strip us of the ineffable as
an enjoyable component of the human condition. As Rorty (1979:123)
writes: "The secret in the poet's heart remains unknown to [scientists],
despite their ability to predict his every thought, utterance, and movement by monitoring the cerebroscope. . . . We can know which
thoughts pass through a man's mind without understanding them. Our
inviolable uniqueness lies in our poetic ability to say unique and obscure
things, not in our ability to say obvious things to ourselves alone."[10]
Perhaps this might be revised to say that the "secret" lies not in the
poet's heart but in her language, yet it amounts to the same thing.

Unless we are mistaken, the capacity of culture to remain obscure as

10. Paulson (1988:141) arrives at the same conclusion, but then adds, "If we could
"explain" fully a single text . . . that text would in effect lose all its potential cultural
interest." Yet this would be a possibility only if a literary text could be objectively explained
at the level of its meaning—something our argument suggests is unlikely.

to its meaning even when it has been satisfactorily explained in naturalistic terms serves as the ground out of which all the problems we have discussed grow. The examples we have looked at suggest that though the intentional foundation of symbolic or literary expression stands as an appropriate object of "knowledge" in Hirsch's sense, what it *means* does not, and it is in the apparent tension between these conclusions that difficulties arise which invite enchanted inquiry. Certainly if Sacks, Taylor, Geertz, Lévi-Strauss, or other contemporary virtuosi were seeking some phenomenon that seemed to *demand* the ambiguous epistemic registers they adopt, symbolic or literary expression would be it. In this light, their investigations appear one way of responding to the widespread and entirely legitimate intuition that culture cannot be adequately understood by science alone. Yet what naturalistic methods cannot in principle grasp is a matter not for some new (if always different) blend of science and edification, but for edification pure and simple, for interpretation quite unconstrained by naturalistic canons. What *cannot* be explained does not remain still to be explained by some new method, though its meaning remains open to edifying construal. This continued openness does not show naturalism as failing, as somehow coming up short with regard to culture; on the contrary, it might meet with complete success, but in the process reveals an aspect of culture it simply makes no sense to pursue in naturalistic terms.

This conclusion bears just as strongly upon the ambitions of realism in literary interpretation. When its naturalistic premises are fully recognized, realism is seen to face the same difficulty in probing "the secret in the poet's heart" as do scientists with cerebroscopes. Once intentions have been plumbed to the depths empirical investigation allows, something remains that cannot be reduced to them—at least when we are dealing with "unique and obscure" phenomena. In these circumstances we cannot expect to achieve interpretive consensus as to meaning on the basis of historical evidence: our subject matter is too mercurial and occulted to allow for this. Yet if we forego our desire for "knowledge" and content ourselves with edification, much remains to be discovered beyond concerns with "validity."

To put this differently, in cultural disciplines "meaning" appears caught between the determinate empirical pole of intention on the one hand and the indeterminate hermeneutic pole of "saying" on the other. Traditionally, inquirers inclined to realism have sought to draw meaning as close to intention as possible, while their most aggressive opponents, such as the deconstructors, have driven it toward "pure saying," toward the liberation of which Ricoeur speaks. The realist case appears strong first because instrumental communication would be impossible on any other basis, and then because it works so well in the vast majority of everyday circumstances where nothing "unique and obscure" is involved. The relativist case, on the other hand, appears irrefutable whenever we compare exotic interpretive practices or have to deal with rich phenomena such as symbolism. Rather than look on these positions as conflicting, however, we should view them as the outcome of ultimately incommensurable but nevertheless quite compatible practices, one naturalistic and explanatory and the other edifying and interpretive (see Rorty 1979:379–389; Margolis 1990). Just as science cannot tell us everything we need to know about the world in order to live in it, neither can edifying discourse. Each has an independent role to play, with realists in this case seeking to explain expressive culture and relativists interpreting the myriad possibilities of what it says to us. Yet because these quite different aims wind up being pursued in the same academic discipline (and occasionally by the same person), they are assumed commensurable—whereupon they quite naturally appear to conflict, and thus set us to squabbling over the direction in which meaning is to be drawn.

A Solomonic judgment might be appropriate here, however: cut meaning in half and give it to both. Or rather, simply get rid of "meaning" as the site where intention and saying are falsely supposed in conflict, thus allowing them to go their separate ways. At present the reasons the two are forced together in dubious union are institutional rather than epistemic. Were a separation effected, the disagreements over culture as referential ecology that have been our focus would disappear. If we looked at culture in terms of its intentions rather than its meaning, none of the points made by relativists (which are devastating when addressed to meaning) would have any purchase. The intentional structure of culture is as much a natural phenomenon as anything studied by the sciences; and sometimes, as with rational activity, this structure is extremely simple and perspicuous—a fact upon which the success of much everyday communication relies. At other times, however, it can become very rich; and yet this need not entail that it also be mercurial or fail of equipresence. In fact the mercuriality of meaning resides in what is "said" rather than in what is intended. When we don't separate the two, experience with rich cultural phenomena (or with poorer ones as worked up by exotic interpretive practices) can easily give rise to the impression that culture is ontologically enchanted. Restricted to its intentions, however, it is no more (but of course no less) enchanted than any other domain of nature.

From this perspective, at least, the relativist argument is not damaging to realism. Though cultural phenomena may be interpreted in the most various and conflicting ways according to the standards of different communities, this has no effect on the intentions that originally gave rise to them, which remain invariant across construals. When we are able to discover these, we can successfully explain the phenomena. At the same time, however, this "knowledge" offers no way to determine what the phenomena are saying, first because it will often, even in its own terms, prove insufficient to underwrite a satisfyingly comprehensive interpretation, and then because the conventions upon which it depends simply are not part of the hermeneutic "game." Thus the ambition of realism to regulate meaning on the basis of intention falls by the wayside just as does the relativist attack. The role Hirsch gives intention in sorting valid from invalid construals is one it cannot sustain—at least in the rich circumstances that cause him to call upon it in the first place. The assumption that has driven the dispute between realism and relativism— that we say what we intend, or intend what we say—need only be abandoned for the argument to appear without much point.

Of course in ordinary circumstances and according to ordinary usage, intending what we say and saying what we intend seem both possible and desirable. Were things otherwise, as we have noted, communication itself would be unlikely. But like so many assumptions that serve us well in everyday life but get us into trouble when subtlety is called for, this one causes mischief when we import it into cultural studies—where rich phenomena are frequently at issue. Intentions cause and can be viewed as mapped onto these phenomena, but have no necessary bearing on what they say. Similarly, viewed from the opposite direction, the readings given phenomena in the course of edifying investigation need have no relation to their intention. The two are seen as inseparable only because they are traditionally conflated in the notoriously vague concept of meaning. Yet our point is not to develop a philosophical distinction that could keep intention and saying separate, but merely to suggest that the practices by which the two are investigated and the canons by which results are evaluated are different—and that ignoring this fact leads to fruitless controversy. Unfashionable though it may be in an era when the blurring of disciplinary boundaries is trumpeted, there is good reason to keep the subject matter of "knowledge" separate from that of edification.

Having developed a distinction between "intention" and "saying" to get this far, we want to drop the latter term immediately because of its infelicity. Henceforward we will simply use "meaning" to designate the component of cultural objects appropriately dealt with in hermeneutic or edifying terms, leaving "intention" to naturalistic investigation. Expanding now upon our previous discussion, we can say that what a cultural phenomenon *intends* is the entire range of causal events by which it came into being and which in ideal circumstances could be shown "mapped onto" it by naturalistic means. What it *means,* on the other hand, is the set of paraphrases and higher-level interpretations it has been (or might be) given. By defining intention in this way, we link together the complex of articulable reasons ("authorial intention" *sensu strictu*) through which an object came into being with the accidents of composition (perhaps explicable only at the neurophysiological level) and the unconscious determinants that molded its character. Understanding these would give us an "idiographic," or historically particular, explanation of the object's genesis. But we want intention to encompass additionally whatever "nomothetic" factors contributed to its development, factors that could be revealed only by generalizing disciplines like psychology, sociology, and anthropology. In other words, we are including in the concept of intention everything that went into making a cultural object what it is. Our extention for the term is thus far broader than Hirsch's, and deliberately so: we want to connect inquiry into authorial intention as a *cause* of culture—the underlying, if unstated, premise of Hirsch's realism—with all the other forms of "genetic" investigation, since only through contributions of both sorts could we develop satisfactory explanations of cultural phenomena.

Similarly, we want meaning to be viewed in the most capacious light. Though Hirsch dismisses the doctrine of semantic autonomy, which allows a text to mean anything within the range of possibilities opened by the meanings of its component words (relative, of course, to an imaginable context), we want meaning to encompass not just the semantic possibilities, but all the paraphrases generated by "exotic" interpretive strategies that rely on strange intenders. The latter may indeed express themselves through vehicles that in an instrumental mood we might deem nonsemantic, like the Balinese cockfight. In our new dispensation for the term, it would be perfectly reasonable to speak of the "meaning" of cockfights, read in an edifying mood as symbolic expressions of Balinese sensibility. The result will be essentially contestable; or at least we can say that the stability of meaning relative to a particular observer will be a function of sociological variables—the number of interpretive communities to which the observer is exposed, their power to exercise social control, and so on. Meaning will perhaps appear unitary and "obvious" where one community possessing uniform and highly specific standards is firmly in control, but more mercurial the more plural the circumstances. Where pluralism flourishes and interpretation is a competitive enterprise, meaning will fail dramatically of equipresence.

Taking the opposite perspective, when we confine ourselves to poor phenomena and exclude exotic vehicles and strange intenders, meaning and intention will appear largely to coincide. Or, to put this somewhat more accurately, one paraphrase of a phenomenon will almost always best represent its proximate intentions. Such correspondence presumably encourages realist programs for interpretation in general. For richer phenomena, however, a singular paraphrase can be designated only by fiat, and can be sustained in an interpretive community only by specific patterns of control, patterns that are likely to be authoritarian. Collectivities of interpreters who, to refer back to our discussion in chapter 5, are independent equals will "naturally" show significant variation in their results—a phenomenon we might think of as the Protestant Reformation syndrome in interpretation.

If we need a summary analogy for the point of view put forward here, we might draw on the study of chaos. Just as a fluid in motion may go through a phase transition from a state where its behavior is predictable to one where it isn't, so cultural objects, as they grow richer in their intentions, go through a phase transition whereby their meaning becomes indeterminate. Whereas transitions in fluids occur at a fixed point, however, transitions in cultural objects are relative to the interpretive strategies by which meaning is discovered. Everyday strategies may yield indeterminacy only for phenomena of significantly rich structure, while exotic ones may yield it for even the poorest (or, indeed, preclude it even for the richest). Though it seems odd to think of the intentional structure of an object as somehow "splitting off" from its meaning as it grows richer, this simply indicates that at some point we will have to pursue explanation beneath the semantic level (perhaps, in some science fiction future, by means of cerebroscopes), since there will be *too much* meaning "in the poet's heart" to be circumscribed. Once again, however, this is not an indication that explanatory inquiry has somehow failed—it might succeed completely—but rather marks the point where meaning becomes solely a matter of edification.

By laboriously untangling the argument between realism and relativism in literary studies, we have gradually managed to develop a basis for culture as referential ecology. We need now to consolidate it and explore some of its implications. To begin by restating our conclusions, there is no reasonable relativist objection to viewing culture as referential ecology as long as we conceive of it in terms of intentions rather than meanings. In doing so we make no foundational claims for realism, but instead simply establish the subject matter for one particular investigative practice—naturalistic explanation—among many equally valuable ones. When Hirsch describes the moral value of valid literary interpretation, it is from the ethical profile of this practice that he draws his themes. Yet (not surprisingly) he seems unwilling to accept certain of its constraints, even though they are integral to its moral worth, because they interfere with certain disciplinary tasks of literary interpretation—such as construing rich texts even when empirical warrant for the results cannot be had. No doubt hewing closely to a hard-nosed version of interpretive validity would quite radically—and adversely—alter the character of literary disciplines; but on the other hand straying far from this ideal lessens the moral weight of Hirsch's challenge to relativism. One can't easily have it both ways. Our solution is to preserve the ambition to validly describe and explain cultural objects in terms of their intentions, but to foreswear using the results to regulate what they *mean*. From our point of view, practical realism entails foregoing the desire to regulate—at least outside one's own house. At the same time, by yielding sway over meaning, practical realism establishes a plausible framework within which to explain culture. One might reject this as a retrograde ambition, but not as an epistemically dubious one. Hirsch has shown that the arguments by which this is done wind up in a crushing inconsistency, unable to give an account of how they could be communicated in the first place.[11]

Having established a restricted domain for practical realism, we can use it to view culture as referential ecology. Reserving for the moment the issue of exotic interpretive strategies, we find considerable areas of culture where referential consensus as to the proximate intentions of expressive objects (or components of them) is achieved quite easily. For instance, Hirsch's morphemes and graphemes in spoken and written expression, Darwin's facial expressions, common expletives, stick figures, rude gestures made in stereotypical circumstances, and so on, all seem easy to interpret. Their relatively unproblematic character we correlate with their structural simplicity—which is to say the poverty of their intentions. To say that referential consensus is easily achieved in these circumstances is to indicate that the phenomena in question are highly "codable." Not only do individuals find designating and characterizing—giving meaning to—them unproblematic, but the results tend to agree spontaneously across coders. In these circumstances, the impression that expressive phenomena mean no more than they intend will be very powerful. Codability declines, however, as the intentional structure of phenomena grows richer, with the most sublime phenomena powerfully impressing us with their capacity to mean more than they intend.

11. For general support for this position see Livingston (1988), who explores the philosophical literature extensively.

If we reflect upon this, it will be apparent that when different coders spontaneously agree about the intention of a cultural object, they must share criteria for assigning it that, however intuitive, they are might in principle prove specifiable. For instance, that we all agree about the intentions of phonemes across speakers in simple, everyday speech suggests we share heuristics (or coding protocols) for assigning the variable phonetic performance to uniform phonemic categories. So reliably and repeatedly are these heuristics used that they can be preconscious, though in principle we should be able to ferret them out and specify them—perhaps well enough for computers eventually to achieve voice interface with us. Similarly, we all use roughly the same heuristics to interpret more complex instances of language, at least in instrumental contexts where something is in the balance—and thus assign meaning in predictable ways. We might be able (though significant difficulties arise here) to specify the heuristics we use well enough for a sophisticated machine to mimic us, producing the same paraphrases of the language we come up with by more intuitive routes. Yet for richer phenomena—particularly the "unique and obscure" of which Rorty speaks—the problem of successfully specifying the heuristics is not just exceedingly difficult but in all likelihood impossible.

More or less by definition, our difficulty here corresponds with the contours of our referential ecology. As the material we must code grows richer, we find that alternative heuristics seem plausible, or that the ones we devise prove less reliable across coders.[12] Increasingly, then, meaning will seem mercurial and fail of equipresence. Yet the phenomena we are trying to code, though they have certainly become more complex, don't share this fate: they go on being just as brutely there as their structurally impoverished brethren, but in an "extrasemantic" condition—as objects from which meaning has been "liberated." No doubt speculation about what they mean may give us clues as to their intentions, but it may just as easily lead us astray. By the same token, even a thorough understanding of their intentional structure—what made them what they are—would not satisfy us as to what they meant.[13]

12. This problem bedevils attempts, such as that by Jones in *The Romantic Syndrome* (1961), to specify at a relatively high level of abstraction the characteristics of genres or expressive "periods" like Romanticism. The higher the level of abstraction, the more coders will find the phenomenon in question "bleeding" outside the circumference of its usual application. For an example, see Schneider (1991).

13. Of course this argument makes certain assumptions about the interpretive community involved. Clearly, it must exercise enough social control to put certain coding practices beyond question, since otherwise its members would be unable to communicate with one another. But it can't exercise so much control as to eliminate dispute among

Professional interpretive communities seem to spring up spontaneously only on significantly rich referential terrain. Or at least we can
say that without such an assumption it becomes hard to explain certain
regularities in their behavior. For instance, granted how easy it is, in
principle anyway, to see rich meaning in intentionally poor phenomena,
why is it that the stick figures of child artists are not more frequently
exhibited by galleries and museums? Or, to elevate the question somewhat, why is it that today's New Historicists, in seeking out instances of
"resistance" in Renaissance literature, find it regularly in the works of
Marlowe or Shakespeare rather than in those of lesser lights? Or, finally,
granted that a urinal signed by Duchamp is a work of art, why is it
that the signing receives more critical comment than the resulting work?
Clearly, nothing in principle impels these emphases, and exceptions to
them could easily be cited; yet they occur with such consistency as to
demand explanation. Perhaps we can account for them in purely political terms, ascribing the exclusionary behavior of museums, New Historicists, and art critics to their elitism, but this only defers our difficulty.
Educational elites discriminate on the basis of aesthetics that incorporate something like intentional richness in the first place. Why? Presumably because rich objects—the "noisier" ones, in Paulson's terms—bear
up under the weight of repeated interpretive scrutiny better than do
poor ones, barring externalities.[14] Thus though the world *may* be symbolically contained in a grain of sand, as Blake suggested, the attention
of professional interpretive communities is commonly diverted from
sand piles to structurally more complex phenomena.

Since they are members of such a community, the same goes for anthropologists. Sperber (1975:3) has suggested that he and his kind by
and large ignore the rational and gravitate to the symbolic: "My assis-
tant says he is tired in the middle of the afternoon and goes to lie down.

---

them, since then it would no longer appear to practice interpretation, having made it all
"preconscious," something that could be done by a machine. Between these extremes,
however, there is a great deal of latitude for variation in the quality and quantity of control
exercised—factors dependent upon the structure of the community, as previously discussed.

14. For some empirical evidence in this regard from the psychology of aesthetic appreciation, see Nicki (1983). In general it seems that, as measured by such gross standards
as preference for or time spent viewing an object, appreciation is a nonlinear (inverse U)
function of complexity: we most gravitate to objects in between simplicity on the one
hand and chaotic complexity on the other. Exactly how an object's complexity relates to
its differential appreciation by "taste publics" has apparently not been much researched,
but see Gans (1974) and Bourdieu (1984) for interesting discussions of the stratification
of taste.

What a waste of time! He awakes, feels bad, and suspects the evil eye. Not such a waste after all." No wonder, then, that Geertz is intrigued by the cockfight, so inexplicable in utilitarian terms. Its intentional structure is certainly complex, though quite likely in ways neither he nor we yet understand. Yet its complexity makes it a viable symbolic vessel for the meaning he finds in it. In contrast, as we argued in chapter 2, the structure of rational action is often too simple and perspicuous to bear such concern.

By the same token, the terrain upon which cultural *sciences* would be apt to flourish will be poor. If the natural sciences got their start in the hospitable circumstances provided by repetitive phenomena of extremely strong structure, there is no reason to believe cultural sciences might begin differently. To some this will be a disheartening thought, since it implies that precisely the phenomena of greatest spontaneous interest to us—those of "rare and obscure" meaning—will prove inauspicious grounds for the sort of consensual knowledge Hirsch holds up as a disciplinary ideal. Yet for very practical reasons, consensual knowledge is apt to be had first of cultural items that are produced and consumed in quantity: in literature, for instance, of genre works like romance novels (see e.g. Radway 1984), or of isolated features of items that occur repetitively and show variation from one place or time to another (see e.g. Griswold 1981).

But this leads to the topic of the next chapter. In establishing a basis for culture as referential ecology, we at the same time developed (not inadvertently but without comment) a perspective through which it *might* become disenchanted. The study of intentions allows us to explain cultural artifacts according to naturalistic canons, thus disenchanting them, while edifying inquiry into their meaning would occur in a register that does not provoke enchantment in the first place. If the ambiguous middle ground—where strange phenomena are presently discovered by virtuoso practitioners of the interpretive "sciences"— were to be abandoned, the study of culture would become disenchanted. What is possible, however, is not necessarily either likely or desirable. For culture to be disenchanted, the study of it would have to change dramatically in organization, and it is the prospect of this we must address by way of conclusion.

The Future of Enchantment

In our midst there is a host of enchanters, forever changing, disguising and transforming our affairs. . . . So, what you call a barber's basin is to me Mambrino's helmet, and to another person it will appear to be something else.

Cervantes, *Don Quixote*

Don Quixote recognized the relativity of interpretive communities and chalked it up to enchanters—under whose spell he remained until he found himself, on his deathbed, once again Alonso Quixano. In preceding chapters we have explored the circumstances in which enchantment flourishes, suggesting parallels between Mambrino's helmet and cultural phenomena like myth or the cockfight-as-text. Might we also wake one day disenchanted? As was just argued, this is possible in principle: a division of cultural studies into exclusively naturalistic and edifying endeavors that complement but do not compete with one another would eliminate the ambiguous register in which enchantment currently resides. Yet this outcome seems unlikely in practice: for culture to be disenchanted, for instance, naturalistic inquiry would need to differentiate itself from the enchanted variety, a development that would require it to become significantly more mature—and there is at present little indication it will.

One reason for this, developed in the preceding chapter, is that the referential ecology of expressive culture—its intentional foundation—is often forbiddingly difficult, especially for the phenomena that most solicit our interest. Though there may in fact be determinate structure to culture that supports its mercurial meanings, this often proves difficult to uncover. Further, the task itself generates little communal devotion, a fact explicable in terms of the way inquiry is organized—our second concern. We began to analyze this in chapter 5 and now return to it, focusing on the attributes of disciplinary maturity.[1]

---

1. In addressing the relative maturity of fields of inquiry we should caution that though physics and chemistry will sometimes be mentioned, these are obviously not models for naturalistic inquiry into culture. If there are such, they would be "historical" fields like geology and paleontology—which are considerably less mature. Increasingly, for instance, paleontology has had to confront the dramatic impact of historical accident on its subject matter (see Gould 1989), which is to say (in the terms of chapter 2) the extent to which its referential ecology is weakly structured, so exposed to extrasystemic influences as to make it "systematic" only in an extended sense—at least in comparison to physics

"Maturity" as a descriptive characteristic of disciplines has both epistemic and organizational dimensions that influence one another. Its epistemic indices are complex and have been variously described. In terms of the analysis provided in chapter 2, for instance, mature naturalistic disciplines can be thought of as good at providing explanations of things, often having a significant store of these on hand. In contrast, immature ones simply haven't developed many explanations and don't seem very deft at doing so. (Disciplines uninterested in explanation are normally similar in epistemic and organizational terms to immature explanatory ones.) It has been customary to think of this difference as symptomatic of the presence or absence of a "paradigm," though this notion is perhaps too vague to be of much use. We could substitute for it the matrix of craft knowledge discussed in chapter 5, whereby groups of inquirers develop similar intuitions about what constitutes fruitful or barren research agendas and, in the process, demarcate the boundaries of their field—but this does not go far to eliminate vagueness itself. Alternatively, we could take a more analytic tack, already alluded to, and suggest that maturation is a process by which disciplines acquire theoreticity on the one hand and sedimented research procedures on the other. Recall that by theoreticity we mean the way in which "scientific knowledge differs from, and surpasses, everyday knowledge. . . . It is the dimension measuring the integrative, organizing power of knowledge systems, their power to compress information into an easily surveyable form" (Collin 1985:60). This property allows us to rank disciplines very roughly in terms of scope and integrative ability: immature ones have little of this, resembling, as we have said, a quilt patched together from a congeries of independent insights, while the most mature have a good deal, allowing much of their knowledge to be linked together through a parsimonious set of underlying principles. Sedimented research procedures, on the other hand, refer to the accumulation and embedding of standardized vocabularies, techniques, and instruments by a discipline (litmus paper, for instance, being a well-sedimented means for determining the pH of a liquid). Sedimented practices become unproblematic and thus are automatically employed: to question them would be to question principles at a fairly deep level in a discipline's theoretical structure (see Latour 1987). Unsedimented procedures, in contrast,

---

or chemistry. Thus referential ecology can set limits on the aspiration of a field to maturity, and it would be wrong to think the latter a normative concept measuring disciplinary success. Instead, it is a descriptive concept that registers certain dimensions of disciplinary variation. As our analysis develops, it will become clear that maturity is both impossible for and entirely unwanted in edifying inquiry.

can easily be questioned without threat to the conceptual edifice, should much of one exist. Maturity can thus be judged, again roughly, by the ratio of sedimented to unsedimented practices—a measure that will correlate to some degree with theoreticity. Epistemically, then, mature disciplines show high theoreticity, a high ratio of sedimented to unsedimented procedures, and significant explanatory scope.

However we characterize the cognitive aspects of maturity, the phenomenon itself allows for an interactive development of theory, method, and evaluative norms that is generally evolutionary in character (Laudan 1984; Richards 1987:574–593). In this process effective research agendas gradually win out over competitors that are less advantaged, and thus pass on their heritage to successor agendas. Such a pattern of development contrasts sharply with that of the least mature disciplines, which at the extreme is better described as sectarian or fashionable than as evolutionary. Sectarian fields multiply and isolate critical standards, preventing commensuration across the whole, while fashionable ones allow research agendas to compete for attention largely on the basis of innovativeness and of stylistic distinctiveness. In the latter case, little is passed on to successor agendas, especially since they must differ from predecessors both in substance and form, while in the former attention is directed away from the *development* of theory, methods, and norms and toward incessant quarrels over first principles or historical inquiry into their development.

Mature research agendas function differently. Latour and Woolgar (1979), drawing on ethnographic research in a biochemical laboratory, argue that they operate by transforming equally probable constructions of the world into unequally probable ones. In other words, when alternative and similarly attractive ways of viewing things are available, investigators work to alter their relative warrant. To accomplish this, write Latour and Woolgar (1979:241), "the technique most frequently used by our scientists was that of *increasing the cost* for others to raise equally probable alternatives." Thus an investigator who, for instance, is willing to devote heroic amounts of labor to substantiating a particular fact or theory may well be able to drive from the field competitors who are unwilling to sacrifice as much. Similarly, use of a costly but effective new instrument may force others to back away from opinions that are cheapened thereby. After the costs of maintaining opinions have been raised, poorly endowed alternatives generally fade in the presence of their now more heavily capitalized brethren. This framework cannot account for all that goes on in inquiry, since occasionally "cheap" opinions do succeed, but as a general rule it seems serviceable. Over the course of time the expense of simple entry into some fields—experimental particle physics, for instance—becomes so high that it is no longer in reach of individuals or institutions but only of countries (or consortia thereof). And the same principle applies, if less drastically, to well-worked humanistic or social scientific terrain such as Shakespeare or the French Revolution.

From this point of view, the immaturity of seventeenth-century natural philosophy was guaranteed by its cheapness. It was no more costly, for instance, to explain the "remarkable" Saint Andrew's crosses in the Royal Society's repository by naturalistic means than by enchanted ones, thus making these notions equivalently plausible. In such circumstances, Grew's sarcasm about virtuoso credulity could have little practical effect. Similarly, Newton's mechanics and his alchemy could easily coexist because they were equally undercapitalized. (Boyle's air-pump, by way of contrast, raised a barrier against entry into the arena where pneumatic "facts" could be made: see Shapin and Schaffer 1985.) Of course it would be easy to get carried away with the impression of quantifiability here when we often have little way of measuring costs, but the instances discussed by Latour and Woolgar suggest that on many occasions a relatively rigorous treatment is possible. In any event, we find in their analysis a possible mechanism of selection by which mature disciplines evolve, as well as a hint as to why enchantment falters in competition: in practical terms it is not a particularly attractive investment, given maturation as a goal.

Whether maturation is a gradual or a discontinuous process remains unclear, as do the factors that initiate it.[2] Further, precisely where the process begins, or even whether it is appropriately seen as having a beginning, is hard to determine. It is tempting to see in Hooke's "somewhat to be had . . . which others must want" a first impetus to development, and add that once some "takeoff point" has been reached (as a theory of economic development used to argue) the accumulated capital of a discipline is somehow sufficient to initiate sustained growth.[3] As

2. In some fields, relatively abrupt increases in theoreticity occur that are sometimes interpreted in terms of paradigm formation. Most recently, as we noted, geological knowledge was both expanded and integrated by the development of a plate tectonic model, though whether this constituted paradigm formation depends on how one wants to use the term. Significant amounts of knowledge had certainly already been accumulated by geologists and remained relatively unaffected by the new theory, as did many well-sedimented research techniques. It would seem inappropriate, then, to view this particular development as marking geology's transition from immature to mature status. Instead, it appears that here (as elsewhere) occasional leaps forward are made in a process that is without clear stages or well-defined junctures.

3. For a discussion of various models of scientific change used by historians of science, see Richards (1987:559–593).

suggested in chapter 1, however, such an internalist reading of maturation ignores the possibility that the organizational capacity to establish
cognitive standards may sometimes have to *precede* epistemic accumulation. For maturation to accelerate significantly, one might argue, the
attention of researchers must be focused on appropriate referential
niches. In this light, the problem Hooke and his fellow scientists faced
was that they could not dissuade virtuoso colleagues from investigating
mercurial and occult phenomena, however inauspicious these might
have been as the matter of a mature discipline. Clearly, the study of precognition—a favorite virtuoso concern—is no more likely to precede
cognitive science to maturity than was meteorology to precede classical
mechanics. But though this principle seems evident to us (and quite
likely was to Hooke and his kind), it will prove impossible to impress
upon autonomous knowledge producers understandably drawn to the
more seductive, if less tractable, niches. Until organizational mechanisms are in place that can direct the community's attention to profitable
research topics and *organize* skepticism with regard to results, the evident attractions of exotic niches will always stand as a barrier to maturation.

In the final analysis, instances of pristine maturation, being perhaps
weakly structured themselves, may be better suited to detailed historical
treatment than to sociological generalization—as chapter 5 suggested.
About the correlates of maturity itself, however, we now know a good
deal. The research on this topic has been reviewed at length and theoretically integrated by Richard Whitley (1984), whose work in turn has
been summarized and extended by Stephan Fuchs and Jonathan Turner
(1986).[4] The latter have developed a summary model, which we borrow
with several modifications, whose final variable is perceived maturity.[5]
Eight factors, some epistemic and some structural, interact to affect this:

4. Randall Collins (1975:470–523), we should note, seems to have arrived independently at conclusions similar to Whitley's.

5. We have introduced two modifications, one cosmetic and the other more substantive. First, we restyle their second variable ("level of competition among knowledge producing and validating organizations") as "degree of exclusive jurisdiction" to bring it in
line with Andrew Abbott's *The System of Professions* (1988). Second, we replace their third
variable ("reputational autonomy of knowledge producers") with "differential reputational authority," since it is not clear how reputational autonomy can vary independently
of lay exclusion (their first variable) and exclusive jurisdiction (their second). Fuchs and
Turner (1986:145) suggest that "reputational autonomy" is high when "particular scientific organizations or establishments exclusively control those symbolic standards of 'legitimate' knowledge production that determine which creative activities are acceptable as
'valid' and 'significant,' and, as a consequence, deserving of collegiate recognition." But
this seems only to rephrase "level of competition," their second variable.

the insulation of knowledge production from lay scrutiny, the degree of jurisdiction with regard to a subject matter, differential reputational authority, resource concentration, mutual dependence, task uncertainty, bureaucratic organization, and cognitive standardization. We can take these up in turn.

Insulation from lay scrutiny. No discipline will be perceived as mature in which work can be done (or effectively critiqued) by laity lacking the appropriate socialization and credentials. Barriers to external oversight are many, but vary considerably in efficiency: jargon, for instance, offers only marginal prophylaxis, while high degrees of theoreticity and methodological sedimentation offer much more. The amount of mathematical sophistication required in the harder sciences, to cite only one example, frustrates lay scrutiny in a way immature disciplines must sometimes envy.[6] (The idea of a laity is itself relative, of course, and in our context refers to people with college degrees or beyond. To them, work in immature disciplines is reasonably accessible; by contrast, work in mature disciplines reaches only fully socialized and credentialed audiences, and must be interpreted for lay persons by popularizers.)

Exclusive jurisdiction. To mature, a discipline must eventually eliminate effective competition as to knowledge of its subject matter. One of our concerns in this book has been jurisdictional battles over culture between interpretive and explanatory camps, and the mere existence of such disputes is emblematic of immaturity. Competition saps consumer confidence: where two (or more) conflicting parties might be right, none may be trusted.[7]

Differential reputational authority. Reputational inequalities in a dis-

6. Political scientist Samuel Huntington's persecution by mathematician Serge Lang nicely illustrates the problem. Proposed for election to the U.S. National Academy of Sciences, Huntington was opposed, presumably more for political than for epistemic reasons, by Lang, whose campaign nevertheless faulted Huntington's pretensions to mathematical formulation in his theories. Not only was Huntington's entire work embarrassingly open to scrutiny by a lay person like Lang, but was attacked precisely where it dared to mimic a more mature discipline, with regard to which Huntington rather than Lang was the lay person. See *The New York Times,* 29 April 1987, 1:1:6.

7. Achieving jurisdiction normally goes hand in hand with insulation from lay publics, but it is possible to imagine circumstances in which several putatively "expert" orientations vie with one another for control of terrain—a circumstance roughly approximated today in the relationship between graphanalysis and polygraph testing. Both procedures claim to see beneath the artifice of the presented self to lay bare its internal state, and their efforts in this regard could be seen as complementary, especially since they analyze quite different forms of evidence. Yet to view them this way would encourage unwanted confusion among consumers. The inability of either technique to definitively establish jurisdiction leaves both of them suspect, though polygraph testing is somewhat favored by its more abundant technology.

cipline provide elites with the authority to set standards for the rest of the community, to influence the general direction of investigation, and to systematically honor helpful contributions by hoi polloi. Were all investigators reputational equals, in contrast, inquiry might easily become Balkanized or idiosyncratic. Similarly, without an authority differential between senior scholars and neophytes, the former would be unable to set standards for or direct the work of the latter apart from wielding material incentives. The degree and patterning of reputational differentials is thus crucial to the issue of control in a discipline. Yet we need note an unusual feature of status allocation in mature disciplines: the degree to which it is collegially regulated (see Cole and Cole 1973). Thus hoi polloi, precisely because they know how to apply the standards set by elites, are equally capable of assessing innovations for their significance, and occasionally make substantial contributions themselves. This frustrates the normal urge among elites to reciprocally confer unmerited prestige. Thus though fundamental contributions by Swiss patent clerks and effective whistle-blowing by graduate students are somewhat rare in mature disciplines, they are also to be expected.

Resource concentration. The means of knowledge production may either be broadly available or restricted to the few. In general, the more costly they are, the more restricted; and the more restricted, the more they can be controlled by reputational elites. In experimental particle physics today, as remarked already, knowledge can only be generated by those with access to accelerators, and significant knowledge only by those with access to the newest and most expensive among them. For these scarce commodities, mechanisms of allocation must be devised, and these in turn concentrate control in groups of people with established reputations.

Mutual dependence. As suggested in chapter 5, investigators may have a greater or lesser need of taking one another's work into account, either competitively or cooperatively. Whitley (1984:88–89) sees dependence as involving analytically separable functional and strategic dimensions. Functional dependence refers to a need to incorporate "the specific results, ideas, and procedures of fellow specialists" in one's work, while strategic dependence refers to "the necessity of coordinating research strategies and convincing colleagues of the centrality of particular concerns to collective goals." This is "not just a technical matter of integrating specialist contributions . . . but involves the organization of programmes and projects in terms of particular priorities and interests. It is a political activity which sets the research agenda." Whitley suggests, for example, that in physics the requirement that significant research contribute to a theoretically integrated picture of the world entails strategic dependence, whereas in chemistry, where specialties often go their own way with little concern for overall coordination, it is less entailed. This difference can exist even when both fields show the same degree of functional dependence. Thus though the two dimensions are related, some independent variation is possible as well. In any event, Whitley argues that fields with high functional and strategic dependence are characterized by a strong sense of collective identity and by intense, nonsectarian, competition—qualities that diminish as these forms of dependence weaken.

Task uncertainty. Since all inquiry by definition occurs in novel circumstances and employs concepts and techniques that must in principle be capable of failure, the level of task uncertainty is high compared to that in many other occupations (see H. M. Collins 1985 for illustrations from the hard sciences). This places inherent limits on routinizing, and thus on bureaucratizing, the process. Nevertheless, within a somewhat narrowed range of variation, individual disciplines differ in the degree of task uncertainty they face. Again Whitley sees analytically separable dimensions as involved. On the one hand, "technical task uncertainty" concerns the unpredictability of one's methods and the exposure of one's results to multiple interpretation: "In fields where [it] is relatively high results will be ambiguous . . . and the use of technical procedures will be highly tacit, personal, and fluid. It will not be very obvious when particular methods should be used, nor when they have been applied successfully" (1984:121). Among the factors that reduce this form of uncertainty would be the purification, standardization, and stabilization of research materials, the reliable mechanization of assays and other diagnostics, community agreement over evaluative procedures (such as double-blind testing or significance levels), and so on. Essentially, this is the sedimentation of procedures to which Latour refers, and it applies to humanistic subjects as well, as when "standard" editions free of corruptions are sought. From our point of view, this factor is in turn partly dependent upon the poverty and perspicuousness of the niche being investigated. Strategic task uncertainty, on the other hand, refers to: "uncertainty about intellectual priorities, the significance of research topics and preferred ways of tackling them, the likely reputational payoff of different research strategies, and the relevance of task outcomes for collective intellectual goals" (1984:123). These are the sorts of problems that a "paradigm" is supposed to solve, but they may also be reduced by strong reputational inequalities.

Bureaucratization. In bureaucratically organized inquiry, senior investigators conceive of projects, find funding for them, and then apportion tasks among junior researchers, technicians, and clerical staff—who together with their equipment collectively constitute a laboratory. Directors of laboratories take on dual roles as researchers and managers: in the former capacity they conceive of integrated sets of tasks which, in the latter, they delegate and monitor. The results must then be drawn together so as to produce a research report, scholarly edition, or whatever. In a laboratory the division of labor will often proceed to a point where no single individual can master the full complement of necessary skills. Some of these will be complex and difficult enough to require specialists, but others may become routinized to the point that they can be performed by technicians or students, that is, by people of lesser theoretical scope. Differences of this sort generally correspond to the hierarchy of authority in a laboratory, with most being placed in the hands of those who shoulder the greatest relative task uncertainty.

Cognitive standardization. Cognitive standardization is perhaps too intimately bound up with technical task certainty to be separately operationalized. In any event, Fuchs and Turner (1986:147) mean by it the "standardization, formalization, and mathematization of knowledge." Along with all the preceding factors, it contributes to the perception of a field as mature, a perception that presumably influences the amount of resources available for inquiry, and thus its further bureaucratization and standardization.

This slightly modified version of Fuchs and Turner's model, though reasonably well specified by sociological standards, still represents only a rough sketch in which the variables are still somewhat vaguely conceptualized. Actually to be used, they would have to be operationalized independently of one another, the causal paths between them made clear, and further variables taken into account: it seems that today, for instance, the capacity of a field to provide technological spin-offs or otherwise ingratiate itself with engineers and the consumer public influences the flow of resources to it and thus its capacity for concentration. (Only resource-rich disciplines can experience concentration, since there is little to gather in poor ones.) By contrast, the inability of sociologists and psychologists to effectively increase, say, public literacy or scholastic achievement ensures they are kept on a relatively strict resource diet.

Though it seems to follow that English departments and divinity schools by and large lack laboratories because their "results" are not germane to building bridges, bombs, or other helpful gadgets, Fuchs and Turner introduce a relativist note of caution. Focusing on the issue of task uncertainty, they argue (1986:147) that this does not depend on "the intrinsic properties of specific subject matters, but instead [on] the structure of particular scientific organizations. In our view, it is the social structure of scientific organizations rather than the ontic structures of external reality that generates varying levels of task uncertainty." On this argument, what literary studies or theology lack to become mature disciplines (and produce technological dividends) is more bureaucratization. Indeed, medieval theology perhaps somewhat resembled a mature field both organizationally and cognitively, being more centrally administered, more standardized and formalized, and more dynamically connected to industries of spiritual engineering (beadhouses, penitential tribunals, and so on) than theology today. The impression that there is some essential difference between natural and supernatural phenomena would thus for Fuchs and Turner be an illusion fostered by current differences in the social organization of naturalistic and spiritualistic investigation. Were the tables turned and theology rebureaucratized, more potential might be seen in investigating the effects of collective prayer, say, than in researching nuclear fusion.

This argument is surely beneficial in that it deters us from too easily attributing organizational variation to features of subject matter that, after all, must largely be assumed rather than demonstrated. But since referential ecology should not be so easily ignored, we side with Whitley in suggesting that the "ontic structures of external reality" indeed influence task uncertainty. Strict relativism, it seems, has difficulty accounting for the formation of disciplinary consensus in highly competitive circumstances (see Cole 1992). The rapid waning of enthusiasm for cold fusion, despite the enormous prestige, wealth, and humanitarian acclaim that would have accrued to its discoverers and their backers, is not easily explained in a relativist framework, particularly since no one laboratory or group of scientists had the scope of control necessary to enforce the negative outcome. More likely, cold fusion simply behaved too mercurially and at too low a signal-to-noise ratio to merit further investment. Strict relativism also has difficulty accounting for certain aspects of the organization of theology during its more mature periods, since this field achieved reasonably high degrees of cognitive standardization only by jettisoning the collegial grounding of authority common in mature sciences. Orthodoxy was sustained by specialized bureaus staffed not by investigators of established repute but by "censors" whose position and power was based *outside* the community of active knowledge producers. The same, we expect, would be true of literary studies were they to become more mature today (as reflected anticipatorily, perhaps, in the program of F. R. Leavis and others for whom literature took on the stature of theology: see Lepenies 1988). Thus though relativism as a heuristic should be abandoned only if and when it breaks down sociologically, showing itself incapable of accounting for empirical variation, this does occasionally happen, and precisely at points where "external reality" contributes independently to task uncertainty.[8]

By adding this modicum of realism to the Fuchs-Turner model we can understand on the one hand why disciplines that are today thought immature can (or once did) vary somewhat on the basis of their differential organizational character, and on the other hand why they depart from our image of maturity whenever their referential niche continues to produce too high a level of task uncertainty—as we would argue both theology and hermeneutics do. As suggested before, the rich and mercurial phenomena that give rise to extreme uncertainty comprise niches that are poor sites for consensual investigation, and though a degree of maturity can be "forced" even in these circumstances—we refer again to medieval theology—the means necessary to insure it, in that they generally destroy the collegial grounding of authority, are apt to produce sclerosis rather than the epistemic payoff we expect of "sciences."

All the same, the thrust of Fuchs and Turner's argument is unaffected by the reservations we have entered: maturation is a complex process, but always occurs at the expense of the work autonomy of individual knowledge producers, who to advance their careers must become integrated into laboratories and other systems of cooperation and competition—the "many hands" of which Thomas Sprat wrote. Moreover, it is precisely this that gives them the organizational wherewithal to construct boundaries: by escaping from lay scrutiny and achieving jurisdiction, they finesse the difficulty faced by the scientists of Royal Society in having to honor virtuoso tastes, while by decreasing work autonomy they develop the control over output that prevents enchantment from reestablishing itself *within* the field of inquiry (as with Barkla, perhaps). Jurisdiction and control in turn are justified before the public by success in explanation, by technological spin-offs, and so on.

To put this in slightly different terms so as to connect it with our argument in chapter 5, the increasingly bureaucratized character of maturing disciplines combines with their authority structures, role differentiation, and insularity to create the conditions in which boundaries will be readily conceptualized and easily promoted, at least internally. The subsequent public struggle for clear differentiation from and superiority over other forms of inquiry—that is, for jurisdiction—is the external political manifestation of internal status consolidation and the

8. We might also note that the "scientific" investigation of many "spiritual" phenomena, as in contemporary Brazilian Spiritism, is usually more loosely organized than the harder sciences. As Hess (1991) indicates, Spiritists view the mimicking of normal science—both epistemically and organizationally—by Anglo-American parapsychologists as merely another manifestation of positivist blindness.

consensus it allows. Yet it would be a mistake to assign causal agency only to the internal developments: these cannot progress very far without public recognition and support.

We can now bring these reflections to bear on the study of culture, a field that seems comparatively immature—though how much so proves hard to measure. Scientometricians (scholars who study the organization and output of disciplines quantitatively) use citational practices as one way of measuring the organization of fields (for a review, see Todorov and Glanzel 1988). Mutual dependence, for instance, can be roughly gauged by the rapidity and frequency with which the average article in a field is cited. If the time between publication and citation is long or the frequency of citation low, it makes sense to argue that the average publication has not compellingly engaged the attention of other investigators. Consequently, when David Pendlebury was reported in *Science* (Hamilton 1991) to have found that on average only 2 out of each 1,000 articles published in scholarly journals of American literature in 1984 had been cited through 1988, the result seemed striking, since in contrast 908 of a 1,000 articles in the field of atomic, molecular, and chemical physics had been cited over the same period, while the averages for the whole database and for the social sciences, respectively, were 450 and 253. Pendlebury's results, if valid, would argue for a level of autonomy in literary knowledge production that might best be styled autistic: almost no one is registering anyone else's work. Yet citing practices vary widely from one discipline to another, and in all likelihood Pendlebury's figures for the humanities significantly understate the degree of mutual dependence in the less mature disciplines—as we argue in the appendix to this chapter.

The difficulty of developing a good measure for mutual dependence will be experienced with most of the factors in the Fuchs-Turner model. Suppose, for instance, we are interested in assessing the degree to which various disciplines (or subdisciplines) are insulated from lay scrutiny. We might imagine selecting representative journal articles and seeing whether they could be accurately paraphrased by an assortment of relatively well educated subjects.[9] But lacking such a study we must look to indirect measures, some of which will support our intuitions and some of which may not. For instance, insulation *should* roughly correlate with

9. Gilbert and Mulkay (1984) make the interesting, if ultimately unsatisfactory, argument that no one would ever agree on what an "accurate paraphrase" was, even in the hard sciences, because all scientists have idiosyncratic interpretations of one another's work. Consequently, there is no real consensus in science, on their view, but only a factitious overlooking of disagreement. They arrive at this conclusion, however, by constantly switching the level of specificity at which they expect agreement to be found.

the percentage of a discipline's university course offerings that demand prerequisites. Quick computations with a handy example (University of Michigan 1990) for arbitrarily selected fields yield: biology 79 percent, anthropology 23 percent, English 4 percent. Yet if we approach the subject from another direction, we find that the frequency with which doctoral programs are completed by people with bachelor's degrees outside the doctoral field—another plausible measure of insulation—would show English *most* insulated (23 percent "foreign" B.A.'s), biology next (29 percent), and anthropology a distant third (59 percent).[10] Perhaps we can explain away the discrepancy, and yet the latter figures might capture features of knowledge production, such as differentials in requisite cultural capital (possibly quite high in English), that we would want to take into consideration. In any case, neither measure would register the recent success of some literary theorists in upping their insulation—largely by introducing jargon, forming linkages with "difficult" philosophers such as Hegel and Heidegger, and increasing the scope of their references (and thus the capitalization of entry into the field).[11] Along with this increasing insulation from lay scrutiny, we find anticipated responses, such as efforts at popularization and a proliferation of uncomprehending middlebrow critiques. On the other hand, the generally low level of insulation in cultural inquiry is reflected in how often practitioners enter it without formal training: both Lévi-Strauss and Derrida, for instance, received training outside their current venue (see Lamont and Witten 1988), a phenomenon not uncommon in sociology itself until well into the 1950s (Turner and Turner 1989).

About at least one aspect of differential reputational authority, to take up yet another of our factors, we might be able to speak with greater confidence. If we assume that the authority gradient between professor and doctoral candidate is reflected in the capacity of the former to successfully recommend the dissertation topic, we find this more frequent in fields like physics and chemistry than in sociology or history (and, we suspect, in literary disciplines). Indeed, through a secondary analysis of

10. Figures developed from National Research Council (1967:252–253). Though the data here are somewhat old, they may actually be preferable because they avoid the distortions of the period of academic expansion that followed immediately on. In interpreting the percentages, we note that there is a high correlation ($r = .69$) between the number of doctorates granted in a field and its retention of B.A.'s. This might explain the low migration into English, a large field, and the high migration into anthropology, a small field.

11. Perhaps the easiest way to get a sense of this is to read the work of Marc Shell, whose range and depth of reference are perhaps unique among practicing literary scholars. Certainly there is no more stimulating contemporary practitioner of what Hesse called *das Glasparlenspeil* (see e.g. Shell 1991).

data collected by Bernard Berelson, Warren Hagstrom (1965:131) discovered quite large differences, with fewer than one out of ten of the historians and sociologists, but more than half of the physicists and chemists, believing they select most of their students' topics. Though one would appreciate student corroboration for these estimates, and worry that material incentives on occasion supplement epistemic authority, it seems probable that they accurately reflect not just different authority gradients but socialization for different degrees of autonomy in knowledge production. In most cultural disciplines, the advice of senior scholars to candidates no doubt more frequently resembles Cocteau's unhelpful "etonne moi!" than it does the relatively detailed blueprints that can be offered by mentors in more mature disciplines.

Of course the inability of senior scholars to direct the work of their juniors may reflect high task uncertainty just as much as weak authority. Since we have argued that culture (or the part of it that interests us) is difficult referential terrain and thus generates high task uncertainty, it would be particularly interesting to get a hold on this. Yet of all the Fuchs-Turner variables, uncertainty might be the most difficult to operationalize. Lodahl and Gordon (1972) infer greater "task predictability" for physics and chemistry than for sociology and political science from data on research and teaching, though it is hard to decide just what these mean. Alternatively, if we used the average time between launching a research project and submitting finished work for publication as an index, we would find with Harvey, Lin, and Nelson (1970) that it was longer for social than for natural scientists, though the difference is not striking. Such measures, though, seem quite unable to reflect our intuitive sense of the depth of variation—often dichotomized in terms of paradigmatic versus preparadigmatic field status. Perhaps looking at the frequency with which specific (and especially eponymous) research techniques are cited in the average article could capture something of technical task uncertainty, but the strategic variety remains bothersome. Here one might better point to singular instances, such as the difficulty Murdock's Human Relations Area Files has had in garnering allegiance to a reasonably standardized research protocol for ethnography, as evidence for our intuitions.

The bureaucratic organization of fields seems less problematic to measure because it must be roughly reflected in the prevalence of multiple authorship. Hagstrom (1965:129) borrows a table from Berelson indicating that in leading journals 83 percent of the chemistry articles, 47 percent of the psychology articles, and 3 percent of the English articles are multiply authored; while Hargens (1975) finds that though half his sample of chemists co-authored *all* their papers, this was true of only

4 percent of the political scientists. Indeed, with significant exceptions like archeology and survey research, inquiry into culture is by and large a solitary project: the laboratory organization which in mature disciplines can incorporate (and control) talented undergraduate students, graduates, and postdoctoral researchers (see Hagstrom 1965:130–138; Hargens 1975:15) simply does not exist. If, as Randall Collins (1975:495–496) has written, it is where "professors mediate the material aspects of their students' careers, via access to research equipment, publication, and job placement" that their "ideas are assured of continuous intellectual development," then this is much more true of mature than of immature forms of inquiry—issues of authority entirely aside.

With regard to cognitive standardization we occasionally face counterintuitive results: for instance, though most of us would assume there is less strategic task uncertainty in biochemistry than in sociology, and that this should lead to greater consensus about what constitutes worthy research proposals, Jonathan Cole (1983) found that NSF review panels in the two fields in fact showed the same degree of consensus. On the other hand, using a quite different measure, perhaps better geared to address standardization—the homogeneity of textbook subject matter and its sequencing—Levitt and Nass (1989) found significantly greater consensus in physics than in sociology, just as our intuitions would suggest.[12] Presumably the conflicting results here are due to differences between those areas of fields consolidated in textbooks and their research frontiers (with the former showing consensus differentials and the latter not). Clearly, however, the general absence of textbooks in fields like literary theory points to extremely low levels of standardization.

While we might bring further data to bear here, they would not substantially increase the precision of our description. Indeed, what we have considered seems apt to disguise large qualitative differences registered by practitioners. The conviction that disciplines like anthropology, sociology, and literary studies are immature enough to be deeply under the sway of fashion—though it may mistake what gets most talked about for what is actually happening—is frequently expressed. Consider the complaint by anthropologist Philip Salzman (1988), who sees his field as characterized by a

demi-decadal molting as the old theoretical/methodological/epistemological skin is shed and a bright new, totally different . . . anthropology emerges. . . . What we seem to have, in anthropology, is not so much progress, or even much in the way of discipline, but rather a cyclical kaleidoscope of the intellectual

12. Thanks to Paul DiMaggio for this reference.

imagination, lively certainly, insightful occasionally, well-meaning sometimes. But can we have any confidence that it is adding up to much of anything or going anywhere particularly noteworthy?[13]

Over the past twenty years, Salzman argues, four anthropological "styles" have supplanted one another: a processual anthropology associated with Firth, Barth, Swartz, Turner, and Tuden; French structuralism; Marxist anthropology; and the interpretive approach spearheaded by Geertz. Less critical analyses (e.g. Ortner 1984), while disagreeing on dates and particulars, paint a roughly similar picture. In accounting for it, Salzman points, as we have, to features of disciplinary organization. Unable to assess the empirical adequacy of one another's ethnographies and lacking the mutual dependence that would coordinate individual endeavors, anthropologists find they gain repute "not by methodological meticulousness, ethnographic groundedness, or analytic precision, but by exciting new approaches, innovative theories and previously untried models, or even . . . catchy slogans, different metaphors and trendy labels." Thus stature comes to rest on a form of innovation that is necessarily noncumulative, and a premium attaches to successful efforts to invent the anthropological project anew—a characteristic of fields whose development is governed by fashion.

Other observers would doubtless characterize the situation less drastically, but the basic thrust of Salzman's argument stands. In anthropology, as in all relatively immature forms of inquiry, the absence of strategic consensus means that ambitious scholars gain the broadest reputation by successfully forwarding a new program rather than by contributing to the old one(s). And here the allure of enchantment is apt to assert itself, for the more one's program conjures up as-yet-unimagined entities or processes, which is to say the more radically it opens for us a "whole new world," the more attention it is apt to receive both within anthropology and outside it. In fact, the more radical the program, the greater the likelihood it will be seen as applicable across cultural disciplines, perhaps promising, like psychoanalysis, to reorient all inquiry. Relatively unchecked by the confines of fields, specific enchanted visions thus spread across cultural disciplines, while the attendant expansion of reputational venues frees the innovator from the parochial control of the discipline of origin—should it be able to exercise any in the first place.[14]

13. Thanks to J. J. Errington for this reference.
14. In this regard we can quantify the broad influence of both Lévi-Strauss and Geertz. In a study of frequency of citation in journals covered by the *Arts & Humanities Citation Index*, Eugene Garfield (1986) found Lévi-Strauss roughly equal to Witt-

Perhaps one should say that these circumstances are preconditions for, rather than causes of, enchantment. Certainly sociology does not seem to have produced similarly influential cross-disciplinary innovations, though it is generated in organizational circumstances roughly similar to those of anthropology. Despite this poor showing, however, it is unsurprising that a recent monograph by Jonathan Turner and Stephen Turner (1990:197), after reviewing the institutional history and current organization of American sociology, should conclude that "sociology will, of course, continue to exist in some form—most likely as a collection of loosely integrated topics and subfields. But the hopes of . . . a scientific sociology are increasingly remote and unconstraining on individual students and sociologists as they make career choices. . . . These conditions are entrenched. And so . . . sociology . . . will remain the impossible science." This forecast is particularly interesting because postwar efforts to increase sociology's maturity, led by the Social Science Research Council and originally supported by foundation funds (supplanted later by large, if temporary, increases in federal support) appeared to point in a different direction. Yet the result of sociology's explosive growth, both in resources and number of practitioners, was, Turner and Turner (1990:139) argue, "an almost complete inability to consolidate symbolic resources around either a sense of a common professional community . . . or a common corpus and storehouse of knowledge"—or, in Whitley's terms, to lower strategic task uncertainty. With the dramatic collapse of funding in the midseventies, furthermore, research strategies that could thrive in resource-poor circumstances were relatively favored vis-à-vis quantitative and/or bureaucratically organized endeavors—and since many of these strategies were hostile to a more mature sociology (e.g. Gergin 1982; Denzin 1989; Seidman 1991b), the goal perhaps has even less support now than it did a generation ago.

It seems clear, then, that neither sociology nor anthropology has much prospect of increasing its strategic coherence and drawing boundaries between enchanted and disenchanted inquiry.[15] In fact to do so

---

genstein (1,691 and 1,642 citing articles respectively), and Geertz more referred to than Paul de Man (662 and 526). These are impressive comparisons, and the absolute values might be compared with Freud's 2,950 citing articles. (The average number of citing articles for the 101 most cited scholars—skewed badly upward by Lenin's showing—was 972. Some social science journals are covered in *A&HCI*, diminishing the purity of these numbers as indications of extradisciplinary impact.)

15. This does not imply that either field is failing to cumulate knowledge or to increase in theoreticity. In fact one might argue (see Black 1989 and Randall Collins 1989

in a world of reduced resources, recognizing the while that enchanted discourse is often less expensive to produce than explanatory, would appear somewhat suicidal. Yet we can point to two developments that, though by no means contradicting this judgment, encourage a pause before it is definitively rendered.

The first is the recent and unexpected growth of an explanatorily oriented sociology of culture. Until the mid-1960s this area—previously denominated "sociology of knowledge" and badly marginalized—had been stagnant for some time and promised to remain so.[16] Then, for reasons as yet little understood, the old literature was swept away and replaced by one both more research oriented and more strongly tied to central sociological concerns.[17] This development may itself turn out to be a fad, and in any event does not reveal a high degree of strategic consensus (like many areas of the social sciences today, the sociology of culture is itself divided into interpretive and explanatory camps, the former borrowing theoretical inspiration from semiotics and poststructuralism and the latter hewing to the more pedestrian strategies of the Anglo-American tradition), but it seems notable that at such a structurally inauspicious moment considerable interest in a naturalistic approach to culture has been evidenced.

A second countervailing factor is the increasing cross-disciplinarity of boundary-work between explanatory and interpretive strategies. To put this in a simple if slightly misleading form, the arguments involved seem to have become aligned with those between modernism and postmodernism (see Seidman 1991a). Thus the spread of terms like "deconstruction," of relativist sympathies, of linguistic metaphors, of interest in the discourse of power, and so on—as well as a sense that they are

---

for sociology) that significant strides have been made along both avenues. Nevertheless, these developments are neither visible to laypersons nor universally applauded within the fields themselves.

16. Of the reader edited by Curtis and Petras (1970), more than one-third was given over to "classic" statements then more than fifty years old, and three-quarters of the remainder to propaedeutic, metatheoretical, or otherwise nonempirical work. Of contemporary scholars included, the only one (besides Merton) who made a career in the area and whose work would remain in any updated reader was Diana Crane. Roughly the same could be said of the reader for the sociology of art and literature edited by Albrecht, Barnett, and Griff (1970).

17. Interest in culture seems to have developed with the growth of sociology in the late sixties and early seventies, but it surged thereafter and is being carried forward today by a notably young and female cadre of scholars. Peterson (1989) wonders whether the upsurge in interest reflects migration from declining subfields. For reviews of the literature, see Wuthnow and Witten (1988); Blau (1988); Peterson (1989); Lamont and Wuthnow (1990); as well as the review essays assembled by Peterson (1990).

all somehow bound up in a tidal cultural change—has caused strategic cleavages present in all cultural disciplines to be discussed in a similar vocabulary. Much earlier, we noted Morris Abrams's worry that the new literary theories, if broadly adopted, might make traditional literary history archaic; today, similar challenges are mounted in all relevant disciplines, and generally by means of the same set of concepts drawn from the same core texts. An unanticipated consequence of the spread of postmodernist vocabularies might thus be to awaken a sense of community among "modernists" across disciplines, forging links otherwise precluded by differences of focus.

It would be premature to speculate about the outcome of these developments, but we should note the part institutions will play. In our discussion of the Royal Society, we saw that neither virtuosi nor scientists formed insular groups: their activities were in fact more integrated than a Whiggish view of the development of science would find appropriate or plausible. The situation is similar today in that different epistemic registers—hermeneutic, ambiguous, and naturalistic—can be voiced from the same institutional locations: university departments of literature, communications, anthropology, sociology, and so on. (The range of registers used in any one venue contributes to the high degree of strategic task uncertainty occupants face.) The same degree of integration, however, is not found in journals, in that they generally favor one or the other register, which they are often launched explicitly to promote. Even here, however, bridges remain that connect potentially opposing camps: for instance, the journal *Theory, Culture, and Society* welcomes work in both an ambiguous and a naturalistic register (though perhaps not favoring extremes in either direction.) The continued viability of such venues restrains tendencies to insularity that might otherwise fracture existing departments—with a wedge already offered in the guise of new departments of "cultural studies" devoted largely to discourse in an ambiguous register. At the same time, neither naturalistic nor enchanted cultural inquiry has established much of an extradepartmental basis for its propagation. Thus there are few "institutes" that fund research, promote graduate training, and aim to reduce strategic or technical task uncertainty.[18] How the organizational framework for different forms of discourse develops will no doubt affect the future of enchantment: an increase in the internal homogeneity and external dif-

---

18. The recently formed sociology of culture section of the American Sociological Association, for instance, remains open to conflicting approaches, and though certain university departments, notably Princeton and the University of California, San Diego, offer strong programs in a naturalistic sociology of culture, its resource base remains poor.

ferentiation of journals or the development of insular institutes would no doubt signal a greater potential for reorganization of university departments, though their inertia remains immense.

Thus though the future of enchantment is somewhat clouded by the growth of a naturalistic sociology of culture and by the current homogeneity of the vocabulary of boundary-work, its institutional setting is for the time being guaranteed. Just as the natural sciences remained too institutionally weak to secure their boundaries until the middle third of the nineteenth century, so does naturalistic inquiry into culture today. Nor should eventual success, on the model of mature sciences, necessarily be anticipated. Perhaps it might be were cultural disciplines open, as archeology has been, to colonization by sedimented practices developed in mature arenas, but there simply are no cerebroscopes on the horizon. And perhaps it might be were the referential ecology of culture more tractable terrain, into which relatively simple, deep, and powerful insight might be had. But as it is, though enthusiasm for enchantment may be expected to wax and wane according to fashion, its social grounds remain promising.[19]

Perhaps we can illustrate and add nuance to this conclusion by examining a particular case: that of Michel Foucault's reception. Though himself contemptuous of disciplinary constraints, Foucault has become the focus of controversy, as boundaries are "worked" either to include or exclude him. Not unexpectedly, the excluders show allegiance to our naturalistic camp. For them, if we may take literary theorist Paisley Livingston's (1988:150–151 n. 2) view as representative: "Foucault's sweeping historical theses are oriented and supported by an unbridled metaphysical speculation whereby they are linked to an inordinate pro-

---

19. About fashions themselves, a bit more may be said. Recall Anne Harrington's argument from chapter 5 that enchantment is sometimes a response to ambient cultural and political conditions. If postmodern currents of thought at least indirectly encourage enchantment, and if we can detect in them a distinctly fin de siècle aesthetic—indeed, beyond philosophical sophistication there is not all that much to choose between Derrida and Huysmans, or between Baudrillard and Villiers de l'Isle Adam—then an understanding of this phenomenon would partly explain the current receptiveness of the ambient intellectual climate to enchantment. Unfortunately, fascination with "decadence" has been too infrequent to allow a firm sociological grip on it, though it is clearly encouraged by military defeat, perceived ideological exhaustion, and the radical insulation of intellectuals from practical politics—factors as germane today as in the 1890s. Historically, the original "mauve" taste culture was curdled by the First World War (see Green 1976), and (if we may generalize from one case) may be out of place in circumstances of social catastrophe and consequent engagement. Barring such shocks to the system, however, there seems little standing in the way of current tastes.

liferation of mythical entities, such as the "forces," "diagrams," "regimes," and "strata" that are posited as the unseen conditions behind the realities of human history." From this perspective, Foucault might reasonably be counted among our virtuosi. Includers, by contrast, find in him an innovator of major stature and a strong supporter of ambiguous registers, wherein what appears "mythical" to Livingston acquires greater substance.

Whatever one's position is, the *breadth* of Foucault's influence is clear from citation data. Among twentieth-century figures cited between 1976 and 1983 in journals covered by the *Arts & Humanities Citation Index,* for instance, Foucault ranks sixth, behind Freud, Barthes, Chomsky, Frye, and Eliot, and slightly ahead of a cluster including Lévi-Strauss, Heidegger, Derrida, and Wittgenstein (see Garfield 1986; Megill 1987).[20] And in the *Social Sciences Citation Index,* Foucault, after trailing Lévi-Strauss and Geertz in the first half of the 1980s, has surged ahead since then.[21] Impressive as these figures are, however, they don't speak to the *depth* of Foucault's influence, which would be better measured by his relative place in the canon of specific disciplines or subdisciplines. Here a slightly different picture emerges, though we can draw it only impressionistically. Foucault's deepest impact, it would seem, has been on New Historicist literary studies and interpretive social science. For the former he is clearly canonic, providing basic insights into the dynamics of power as expressed in discourse, while for the latter he contends for canonic status as offering one among numerous standpoints from which to combat positivism.[22] Yet despite this, and despite the volume of citation and expository or critical literature (Merquior 1991), he has had little influence on the "professional" research programs of disciplines like philosophy, history, and sociology (Rorty 1982:224; Megill 1987; Collins 1990).

In discussing Foucault's poor reception by traditional historians, for instance, Allan Megill (1987:119–121) speculates that the breadth and

20. Foucault ranks seventh if we include Lenin, whose position, however, is largely the result of high-volume citation in two Russian history journals (Garfield 1980; Megill 1987).

21. Between 1980 and 1985, Foucault was cited 871 times, as compared with 999 for Lévi-Strauss and 1,081 for Geertz. Between 1985 and 1990, the figures were 1662 for Foucault versus 979 for Lévi-Strauss and 1,443 for Geertz; and from 1990 to 1992, they were 531 versus 224 and 442.

22. The canonic status of Foucault for New Historicism is evident throughout Veeser's *The New Historicism* (1989). For interpretive social science, we note that Foucault, though not represented in the 1979 edition of Rabinow and Sullivan's reader, made the 1987 edition, having in the meantime been aggressively promoted by Rabinow (see Foucault 1984; Dreyfus and Rabinow 1982).

depth of a scholar's influence may often be inversely related (see also Lamont 1987). Breadth may be depend upon "an original and provocative world view"—something difficult to present today in the context of research that meets professional standards. Provocation often makes one both institutionally and epistemically marginal, too unorthodox to win tenure (though not to win over *tout Paris*). As Megill shows, after being acclaimed for his *Histoire de la Folie* in *Annales* in 1962, Foucault was ignored by "disciplinary" history until the 1970s, by which time, however, his poor opinion of traditional argumentative and evidentiary norms had become clear enough to crystallize his marginal status. Thus his work stands today outside the disciplinary boundary, though from that position it has been able to exert some influence on the strategic concerns of professional historians. Megill (1987:134) concludes that "though he is not *of* the discipline, he is important *to* it, partly because he has called attention to hitherto neglected fields of research, but mostly because he fosters a self-reflection that is needed to counteract the sclerosis, the self-satisfaction, the smugness that constantly threaten."

Foucault's mixed status in history—canonical for nonprofessionals like the New Historicists but a gadfly for the professionals—is replicated in sociology. His influence is currently strong in marginal domains like social (as opposed to sociological) theory and cultural studies, but weak in central ones like stratification and theory.[23] Efforts to change this, to "mainstream" him by redrawing boundaries, meet with opposition similar to that from the professional historians. A characteristic exchange is that between Mark Gottdiener (1990) and Randall Collins (1990). Gottdiener, responding to an earlier piece by Collins that minimized Foucault's contribution and stressed the cumulative character of sociology as a science, claims that: "most of the important and respected theorizing about present-day society takes place . . . outside of sociology. . . . The work of sociologists specializing in theory has been overshadowed by efforts of social theorists in philosophy, literary criticism, semiotics, Marxian political economy, and others" (1990:460), Foucault foremost among them. Thus failure to recognize him as a canonic figure and to "acknowledge the quasi-textual nature of society and its exo-semiotic dimensions of power and materialism . . . contributes to the persisting

23. Charles Lemert, a major interpreter of French contributions for American sociologists, includes Foucault in his edited volume on French sociology as "the contemporary nonsociological writer to have been taken most seriously by sociologists, if only at a distance" (1981:228). Lemert's critical study of Foucault (Lemert and Gillan 1982) treats him as a social theorist rather than a sociologist. On Foucault's place in cultural studies, see Lamont and Wuthnow 1990.

incapacity of sociological theory to contribute to new theoretical under-standing" (1990:461). Sociology is stagnating, in other words, because of its refusal to shift its boundaries.

Collins responds that, largely because of the marginality of sociology to French intellectual life from the 1920s until Bourdieu's recent ac-claim, Parisian intellectuals have produced an amateur sociology largely unaware of "what sociology has already achieved. . . . Where the ama-teurs have made useful contributions, it has not happened by theoretical breakthroughs so much as by taking ideas that parallel existing sociolog-ical ideas and applying them to fresh empirical materials" (1990:462). From this perspective, Foucault explored themes "already explicit in Durkheim, Mauss, and Goffman," while the advances he made with re-gard to them

put him into the theoretical debate on the microfoundations of macrosociology. But he couldn't go beyond a general assertion that there is a "microphysics of power" because he didn't know enough about organizational theory, empirical studies of real micro-interaction (mostly by American and British sociologists), or about political and military sociology at the macro level. This is a long detour for catching up with professional sociology. (1990:462)

Foucault's work thus faces a market segmented in a manner not unlike that of Derrida's (Lamont 1987): its "provocative new world-view" and antidisciplinary methods appeal where knowledge production is most autonomous and aimed at the broadest audiences, but are dismissed as amateur where mutual dependence is greater and reputational venues more circumscribed. The same segmentation of markets and reputa-tional venues was faced by the sciences in the late eighteenth and early-nineteenth centuries, as we saw, with academicians complaining about an amateurish "demi-savoir" that obviously had its own, broader, basis of support. Circumstances were altered as the harder sciences matured in part because knowledge production became too costly for amateurs to engage in it; they have not changed elsewhere because of the gener-ally low capitalization of inquiry. With little prospect of turning equally probable constructions of the world into unequally probable ones, stu-dents of culture will thus continue to face a segmented market, half of which rewards enchantment.

As we remarked in the introduction, then, the future of enchantment is secure in some places and insecure in others. Areas of cultural investi-gation where knowledge production is relatively autonomous, inexpen-sive, and aimed at lay acclaim prove most hospitable to it; mutually de-pendent, somewhat more expensive, and insular reputational venues prove least welcoming. In the boundary-work between these market segments, individuals from the slightly more mature locations see professional standards put at risk by amateurs, while individuals from less mature areas see important innovations being resisted by stagnant orthodoxies. It only remains to consider what, if anything, might be at stake here.[24]

Appendix: Measuring Mutual Dependence

The striking disparities David Pendlebury found in citation rates across disciplines have been questioned for specific fields: with regard to sociology, for instance (where Pendlebury found 77.4 percent of articles uncited), Lowell Hargens (1991:345) pointed out that a previous study (Peritz 1983) had found, using a sample of articles drawn from three prestigious journals and allowing eight years for citations to occur, that only 4 out of 150 had *not* been cited. Inquiring further into the discrepancy, Hargens and an associate "counted citations to 379 randomly selected articles and research notes published in a wide range of sociology journals" and found 43 percent cited within one year. This leads him to wonder whether there is not some flaw in the coding procedures used to develop Pendlebury's Institute for Scientific Information database.

It turns out, then, to be difficult to measure mutual dependence. Citations taken by themselves, as Susan Cozzens (1985) has shown, are a somewhat blunt instrument. She looked at two subfields—neuropharmacology and the sociology of science—and compared them not for rates of citation but for the specific ways in which citations were used. In the former subfield references were to specific results or procedures, while in the latter they were often diffuse and vague, suggesting that the degree of functional dependence is higher in neuropharmacology independent of citation rates. Thus there may be multiple senses in which citation practices across fields are noncomparable. Searching for some way to get around this, Hargens (1991:348) notes the role played by annual reviews and review journals in various disciplines (see also Subramanyam 1981:242–265). Presumably, reviews reflect the importance to a field of summing up recent research and presenting it in an easily digestible (as well as citable) form—a gesture that should reflect mutual dependence. Thus it seems indicative that in humanistic disciplines review articles, though by no means unknown, are not showcased

24. Since this was written, Fuchs (1992) has published an excellent book summarizing and extending our knowledge of the influence of community structure on cognitive production. It both supports and adds intriguingly to the conclusions we have reached here.

in vehicles devoted exclusively to them; whereas in the social sciences annual reviews are published in book format, and in the natural sciences, bimonthly (or more frequent) reviews are presented in journal format. Furthermore, the degree to which review journals are utilized can be measured in terms of an "impact factor"—the number of citations received by each item potentially citable. For various reasons, impact factors are no more comparable across fields than are other measure of citations, but a *ratio* of the impact of review journals to that of "primary journals"—those offering original research rather than reviews— escapes many of these difficulties and offers us the best way of tapping citations so as to measure comparative interdependence. To develop some systematic data, we looked at the ratio of the impact factor of the most cited review journal in selected fields to the average impact factor of the five most cited primary journals—those carrying original research reports rather than reviews. The results are presented in table 1.

Several features of the figures in table 1 may be commented upon. First, with the exception of those for sociology they show significant variation from year to year, suggesting that our time frame should be expanded before fine differences are subjected to interpretation.[25] Second, the ratios mask variation that might be important to detailed interpretation: for instance the mild surprise in the ranking of anthropology vis-à-vis sociology results not from the review journal of the former having greater impact (the averages are 0.915 and 1.339, respectively) but from its primary journals having less (0.928 vs. 1.834). Finally, the figures suggest we should revise downward an extrapolation Eugene Garfield—and noted by Subramanyam (1981) and Hargens (1991)—that review journals have an impact roughly five times greater than the leading primary journal. Indeed, none of our ratios reach this level, though using an average should widen the gap between primary journals and the leading review.

These fine points being noted, the figures seem a reasonable match for our intuitions. Taken as a rough index of comparative interdependence, they suggest this might be several times greater in the more mature than in the less mature sciences. It would, of course, be nice to have figures for the humanistic disciplines, but the absence there of review

25. In fact, the underlying data suggest considerable volatility in the impact factors of specific journals: for instance, in 1985 the leading review journal in physical chemistry (*Progress in Physical Organic Chemistry*) had an IF of 13.333, while its counterpart in 1987 (*Catalysis Review*) scored only 5.286. This indicates that the use of impact factors in order to measure short-term changes in journal stature may be misguided. For an instance, see the editor's note in *Current Anthropology* (Kuper 1990).

Table 1   Impact Ratios of Review Journals to Primary Journals, Selected Fields, 1984–1988

	1984	1985	1986	1987	1988	84–88 (average)
Physiology	3.506	4.025	4.872	2.646	2.659	3.542
Chemistry (physical)	2.822	4.075	2.443	1.994	2.916	2.850
Entomology	2.527	3.361	2.462	2.114	3.694	2.832
Astronomy and astrophysics	3.149	3.265	2.552	1.960	2.516	2.682
Psychology[a]	2.203	1.915	2.242	2.100	2.206	2.113
Anthropology (cultural)	1.405	0.964	1.144	0.822	0.743	1.016
Sociology	0.501	0.629	0.726	0.619	0.592	0.613

Note: The review journals selected are those with the highest impact factor for each year. The five highest-ranking primary journals (those that present full-length reports of original research and exclude both letters and reviews) are also selected yearly and averaged.

[a] Medically, clinically, and biologically oriented journals excluded.

Sources: SCI Journal Citation Reports and *SSCI Journal Citation Reports* (Philadelphia: Institute for Scientific Information, 1985–1989).

journals makes comparisons impossible. Further or better measures of mutual dependence can easily be imagined—circulation of preprints, frequency of specialty meetings and perceived value in attending them, for instance—but none of them appears to offer great advantages either in cross-field comparability or precision.

Conclusion: Between Science and Edification

Every discipline bears within itself the seeds of its own stultification.

Allan Megill (1987)

Any consideration of what is at stake in boundary struggles between enchanted and disenchanted discourse is conditioned by deep-seated beliefs about the aims of inquiry as they articulate with perceptions of how systems of knowledge production work. From Allan Megill's (1987) perspective, for instance, Foucault's status as gadfly to professional historians, beyond the pale but nevertheless influential, has the systemic advantage of hindering disciplinary ossification. Though perhaps somewhat slipshod and fantastical if evaluated by traditional standards, Foucault remains "good to think"—structuralism's old encomium—even within the discipline. Were he disparaged by historians as effectively as Immanuel Velikovsky was by cosmologists (see Bauer 1984), the overall output of the discipline would perhaps be diminished in quality. Of course Foucault's influence might have negative aspects as well, but any effort to assess these will be hobbled by the suspicion that not much is at stake.[1] Particularly in an immature discipline, what would count as damage in the first place? Returning to our seventeenth-century case, we might again wonder whether "science" was seriously handicapped by its failure to stigmatize virtuoso concerns. Was much lost? Perhaps one could point to the "waste" of roughly half of Newton's energies (but cf. Dyson 1988:48–50), yet beyond this one gets little sense of blight. For the most part (and quite unlike today), virtuosi seem to have been journeymen investigators whose energies, were they differently directed, might still have borne little fruit. The case seems so clear, and so in tune with our pluralist sympathies, that we are apt to overlook the implicit Whiggish assumption that the "scientists" were somehow bound to carry the day. Yet had virtuoso values come to dominate natural philosophy and perhaps long delayed (or entirely frustrated) the growth of science as we know it, our estimate might be different (if no less Whiggish).

---

1. For example, though some New Historicists seem no less slipshod in their use of historical materials than Foucault, having perhaps caught the habit from him, it is difficult to become very exercised about this when we consider their overall aims.

Thus the evaluative matrix in which we try to assess boundary-work is both perspectival and influenced by the relative maturity of the disciplines involved. For mature ones, the concern in positioning a boundary is to achieve the best compromise between accepting dubious ideas about the world and rejecting good ones. If the boundary is too capacious, worthless ideas will be entertained; if too circumscribed, profitable ones will be dismissed. Here an efficient balance is pressing because of the potential for mistakes to affect our lives: they make for flawed (or undiscovered) drugs, explosions in laboratories, serious squandering of tax monies, and so on. Yet an ideal boundary—one that would admit all good but exclude all bogus conceptions—is unachievable in practice because the craft knowledge involved in forging it is always too clumsy to yield perfect outcomes: no set of intuitions in the seventeenth century would have found it easy to exclude "blows invisible" while accepting meteorites. Thus one can strive only to maximize gain and minimize loss, though how this is to be done is not itself particularly clear.

But the issue is not just dubious conceptions: in mature disciplines the boundary we are concerned with has traditionally differentiated between reputable and disreputable errors in producing them. Reputable errors are, writes Harriet Zuckerman (1977:110), "those that occur in spite of investigators having lived up to prevailing methodological rules of the game and of having taken the normatively accepted procedural precautions. . . . In contrast, disreputable errors are those resulting from the neglect or violation of methodological canons and procedural precautions. Once spotted, they damage the standing and reputation of the scientist who has fallen into error." Disreputable error, she goes on to suggest, is similar to legal negligence. Even when mistakes are inadvertent, the investigator is held morally responsible for the damage that results. Research agendas that persist in disreputable error (or champion it as the way to "truth") will be stigmatized by the community and perhaps dubbed "pseudo-scientific."[2]

Unfortunately, as Durkheim ([1895]1964:71) indicated long ago while reflecting on the fate of Socrates, such a boundary will sometimes be unable to distinguish between disreputable error and worthwhile innovation. Indeed, if too restrictive and well-policed, it will ultimately stifle creative thought by threatening to judge it corrupt. A system of control strong enough to discourage Velikovsky from forwarding his

2. On the other hand, as we have already noted, even the most stringent adherence to approved norms does not guarantee a hearing for stigmatized subject matters, though it may improve their chances.

ideas might have discouraged Einstein as well: genius can only flourish when we provide social space for the fantastical at the same time—which leaves us to wonder whether efficacious boundaries are possible.[3] Yet a collapse of faith here, however cheered by iconoclasts like Feyerabend, would have little effect on everyday boundary-work, which must be performed if disciplines are to have integrity as strategies of inquiry and access to the resources they require.

But immature disciplines are in a sense *defined* by their inability to develop consensus about what might constitute disreputable error—at least beyond obvious issues like sloppiness and culpable ignorance.[4] Or perhaps we should say that even when agreement is reached in the abstract, there will be broad leeway in application: consider the Royal Society's motto *Nullius in verba* and its (lack of) effect on Aubrey. Further, as indicated, serious concern about this is thwarted by the reflection that little hangs in the balance: neither human lives nor huge sums are normally at stake, in part because where there is little mutual dependence to begin with, a putatively disreputable error will have little impact. Unlike the announcement of "polywater" by Deryagin (Zuckerman 1977:111), it will not cause a spate of laboratories to drop what they are doing and pursue what later will prove chimerical, a result of the experimenter inadvertently contaminating his samples: instead, the average research report will be consistently ignored. Yet, though individually innocuous, one might argue that candidates for disreputability, when viewed in sum, drain resources that on a prospectively Whiggish view would be better spent elsewhere.

These reflections suggest a general desideratum for a boundary stigmatizing anything as "error" (or even as a comparatively ineffectual means of establishing warrant): that it focus energies in productive ways

3. Some of the difficulties are illustrated by the reception of Edward Whitten's "superstring" theory in theoretical physics. Though Whitten is, according to John Horgan (1991:42), "widely viewed as the most brilliant physicist of his and quite a few other generations," complaints that his theory is "untestable" and a product of "mathematical smoke and mirrors," have been raised. Were suspicions of untestability—albeit a simple criterion somewhat removed from the complexities of craft knowledge—to evoke generalized horror and severe censure, superstring theory would presumably have been throttled before is was articulated. This would clearly be a bad thing, even though superstring theory may itself eventually prove bogus.

4. In disciplines like the contemporary creative arts even the idea of "error" can seem out of place. While "bad" art might be poorly executed or in questionable taste, we are unable to conceive of this resulting in "damage" for which the artist might be held morally responsible on analogy to negligence torts. That this is a recently developed and parochial viewpoint, not yet sufficiently established in Cincinnati, does little to diminish its hold upon us.

without significantly diminishing risk taking. At the same time, they make it clear why the "proper" boundary will not be a desperate concern of immature disciplines. But, granting this (and thus not taking ourselves too seriously), it still seems useful to speculate, employing the critical apparatus of earlier chapters, about the possible effects of more coherent boundaries on the study of culture. We concluded that virtuoso endeavors are often the cognitive equivalent of swidden agriculture: a cultural phenomenon is cultivated until it yields interpretive fruit, but then is abandoned for new ground, leaving avenues by which warrant might be gained unexplored. Were this virtuoso habit discouraged in favor of establishing naturalistic warrant, contributions of somewhat greater permanence might be made. For instance, when Lévi-Strauss explained the Oedipus myth as an unconscious resolution to a conundrum produced when the Greeks entertained both autochthonous and sexual modes of generation, we suggested that support for so radical an idea might be had by identifying similar myths among people—like the Trobrianders—who presumably face the same conundrum. In doing so, we appealed to a general principle whereby like causes are assumed to have like effects (and multiple examples, particularly from different times and places, to buttress one another).[5] A negative finding here would by no means preclude Lévi-Strauss's hypothesis, but a positive one would clearly lend it credence. Yet neither this warranting stratagem nor its underlying principle seems to have appealed to him: his explanation of Caduveo face painting, in overlooking gender differences in expressive style, also violated the stricture that like causes should have like effects. Again, the differences might somehow be accounted for, but no obligation to do so is registered.

The same is true of Geertz's analysis of the cockfight. Though the task he sets himself in this essay remains unclear—more of this in a moment—should it have to do with explaining why Balinese go to cockfights, then the issue of whether their pastime is singular and needs a particularistic explanation, or perhaps is more widespread and calls for comparative treatment, begs for attention it does not get. The authorization for particularistic inquiry would presumably be that Balinese fascination with cockfighting differs in significant respects from Iban, or Malay, or Filipino. If not, the problem is moot: without the effect being differentiated, the excuse to look for a unique cause does not arise. (Of

---

5. Of course the principle we appeal to here would be moot if the strategy of interpretation it is being used to "test" is so powerful that it cannot fail to find equivalents to the Oedipus myth among the Trobrianders—but this would seem another strike against the method rather than a support for it.

course it might, and in all probability would—the part cockfights play in Balinese life must differ *somehow*—but our point is merely that the lack of an excuse goes unnoticed.)

These examples are convenient because they illustrate the gulf of incomprehension that often separates interpretive and explanatory camps. Admirers of naturalistic norms are apt to feel that a basic principle of inquiry has been cavalierly ignored here, and thus to respond with the same sort of sarcasm Nehemiah Grew used in dismissing "miraculous" accounts of objects in the Royal Society's repository. Surely violating the "like causes" stricture offends our craft intuitions and perhaps should qualify as disreputable? Yet Geertz and Lévi-Strauss might be similarly frustrated at what must seem a willful disregard for their general aims (vague though these often are), to which the principle of "like causes" need not be immediately relevant. Could this knot of incomprehension be cut by the sort of agreement we outlined in chapter 6—one that would allow interpretive and explanatory inquiry to go separate but complementary ways, relying on different warranting standards? If this meant an end to enchanted discourse, what would virtuosi, and we ourselves, lose along the way?

Perhaps it is easier to arrive at an answer for Lévi-Strauss than for Geertz. Like Charles Taylor's inquiry into epochal changes in the realm of intersubjective meaning, Lévi-Strauss's structuralism discovers deep mechanisms at work in the production of culture; yet these are phenomena over which naturalistic canons have gained increasing jurisdiction, at least when a relatively long-lived tradition of research is sought. Though Lévi-Strauss accepts these canons in principle, however, they have little effect on his practice—despite the burden being neither very onerous nor apt to stifle creativity. As we noted, efforts were made (Hammel 1972; Sperber 1975; Swanson 1976) to "domesticate" structural inquiry so as to bring it more in line with naturalistic norms of warrant, and it is hard to see what damage was done in the process. Yet these efforts did not become institutionalized, with the consequence that naturalistic structural inquiry is today moribund. Similarly, though structuralism was appropriated for edifying aims as well, it seems in that context to have fallen before the march of fashion.[6] Thus though it showed itself capable of stimulating inquiry into both intent and meaning (and of winning Lévi-Strauss deserved acclaim), the permanent con-

6. The march began, of course, with Derrida's ([1967]1978) assault in "Structure, Sign, and Play in the Discourse of the Human Sciences," and can be traced through Culler's works (e.g. 1975; 1982).

tribution of structuralism has been small at least partly *because of* its virtuoso style.

With Geertz the matter is more complex. Like Oliver Sacks, he sometimes seems less interested in investigating the mechanisms beneath or behind culture than in exploring exotic "worlds" or states of being—an area where naturalistic inquiry would appear to have less claim. Perhaps Geertz and Sacks could be likened to painters who reject realist conventions on the assumption that unfaithfulness to surface features is sometimes the best way to a deeper verisimilitude. In this vein, a claim that cockfights are "stories the Balinese tell themselves about themselves" might be (both strictly and metaphorically) false and yet able to evoke, perhaps as an "objective correlative," an important aspect of Balineseness. The question then becomes whether one should seek warrant for this along a naturalistic or a hermeneutic avenue—a question Geertz would presumably decide in terms of the ends he has in mind for anthropological inquiry. But readers who look to him for unequivocal illumination on this front will, not unexpectedly, be frustrated. While he has declared an allegiance to some naturalistic values in quite certain terms,[7] observers like Hirschfeld (1986:35) have noted his frequent inattention to the bearing of naturalistic findings on his concerns, as well as a tendency to dismiss them in unflattering ways. But on the other hand, if Geertz hopes through anthropology to "enlarge the possibility of intelligible discourse between people quite different from one another" (1988:147), does his ambivalence itself become intelligible? Do we have here a role for which his ambiguous register might prove well suited?

Much rests on what we understand by "enlarge . . . intelligible discourse." Imagine prospective visitors to Bali, anxious to engage residents, but unable to fathom their insouciance about betting huge sums on cocks. Clearly these visitors would be well served by reading Geertz's discussion. On the other hand, they might be less well served if they went on to ask Balinese what they learn about their sensibility from the stories told by cockfights, or whether those who attend frequently learn more in result. Here bafflement rather than intelligible discourse is apt

---

7. In responding to an article by Michael Carrithers (1990), Geertz (1990:74) wanted to "have it on record" that he does not "believe that anthropology is not or cannot be a science, that ethnographies are novels, poems, dreams, or visions, that the reliability of anthropological knowledge is of secondary interest, or that the value of anthropological works inheres solely in their persuasiveness." Further, even while promoting a particularistic "local knowledge," he has admitted (1983) a crucial function for "experience distant" concepts such as those of science.

to be the consequence. Yet if to impose stricter standards of warrant here would presumably increase discursive intelligibility (as measured by a reduction in social blunders), it would also close off the prospect of enlarging not just the scope of discourse, but our ways of living in the world. Whether or not tuition in sensibility is a prime motive for attendance at fights, it is certainly a possible one and, for all we know, might be deeply in tune with Balinese life. It is in this sense that Geertz's interpretation might be strictly "false" while remaining somehow apt and an advance in edifying knowledge. Renato Rosaldo (1989:62) recently set for anthropology the goal of "apprehending the range of human possibilities in their fullest complexity," and this would not be easily accomplished by efforts that aspired only to naturalistic warrant—unless one wanted to view "human possibilities" as exhausted by those already plumbed.

Yet once we have slipped the moorings of naturalistic warrant in this way, it becomes unclear why we would want to keep anthropology—or at least this particular function for it—separate from imaginative genres like literature that also aim at expanding the repertoire of human possibilities. What would be the value of meeting stern demands for empirical warrant here? Why could not "the Balinese" be entities at once as imagined and as real as characters in George Eliot's novels? In this context Geertz's insistence (1990:74) that ethnographies are not "novels, poems, dreams, or visions," seems beside the point. Either one takes them to be aids to successful discourse between strangers, amenable to all sorts of pragmatic tests, or one takes them to be edifying guides to possible forms of life, which we would evaluate quite differently. In the latter case, imagined Balinese might actually be preferable to the real ones, while in the former they wouldn't. (Similarly, Sacks's "unfathomably weird twins" might have an advantage over the empirical variety were we anxious for an literary encounter with the Other.)

To make the same point from a slightly different angle: in the nineteenth century, as Lepenies (1988) has suggested, the issue of whether social life was to be understood through literature or through (what would soon become) the social sciences had not hardened into its recent form. Balzac's intention to offer a taxonomy of social types, for instance, represented as much a colonization of literature by "scientific" aspirations as the reverse (though in this domain the two had not yet really separated). Efforts today to blur genres pursue the original lack of differentiation. As Richard Rorty (1982:203) has written, "if we get rid of traditional notions of 'objectivity' and 'scientific method' we shall be able to see the social sciences as continuous with literature—as interpreting other people to us, and thus enlarging and deepening our sense of community. We shall see the anthropologists and historians as having made it possible for us—educated, leisured policy-makers of the West—to see any exotic specimen of humanity as also 'one of us.'" Yet, admitting the worth of humanizing peoples whose customs might otherwise be deemed peculiar or odious, the success of the project can still be judged by criteria whose difference always reconstitutes the boundaries just blurred. On the one hand, if we measure our success by the degree to which interpretations humanize exotic specimens—presumably by linking them to ourselves through fictions of relation—we enter directly upon aesthetic judgments. In this realm, as Taylor suggested, deeper and more discerning sensibilities will discover subtler and more interesting links between the apparently foreign and the familiar, showing us how, say, attending a cockfight is not all that different from reading Shakespeare or Flaubert, or (to borrow an example from Rorty) how Dewey is not all that different from Foucault. The more striking and unexpected the stratagems by which such comparisons are made, the more edified—and perhaps the more convinced the exotic specimen is "one of us"—we presumably will be.

By contrast, if our goal is to avoid blunders in direct encounters with the same exotic specimens, we will want "descriptions of situations which facilitate their prediction and control" (Rorty 1982:197). Of course such knowledge is sometimes in bad odor because of its instrumental character, but is none the less little different from the (perhaps less suspect) knowledge that allows one person to partner another in dance—prediction and mutual control being essential if the two are not to lurch about and cause one another embarrassment. Our encounters with exotic specimens would be evaluated similarly—by absence of unintended offense, by infrequency of furrowed brows, and so on. However much we free ourselves of the fetishes of epistemology and method, it will remain the case that "Deep Play" (in all likelihood) satisfies this second criterion less well than our edifying ones. Furthermore, it does so for reasons we can speak about straightforwardly in terms of better and worse "methods." Not to stigmatize the latter, however laudable in the "let one hundred flowers bloom" sense, would cost us pragmatic competence. And here we should note how ensnared Geertz becomes by his ambiguous register, since, awakened by this threat to our competence, we are apt to return to the edifying question and ask whether cockfights are *really* like Shakespeare or Flaubert for the Balinese. One could muster pedestrian tools here to suggest they are not, but in doing so would be as guilty of confusion as Geertz. No one will ever know what the cockfight *is like* for the Balinese because the phenomenon is rich enough to sustain indefinite, edifying construal—and efforts to close down discussion, for instance by calling for naturalistic warrant or by privileging Balinese construals over those of anthropological field-workers, would be unfortunate.

It seems, then, that in Geertz's case more coherent boundaries around edifying and naturalistic practices, to the exclusion of the enchanted middle, would yield more intelligible discourse on all fronts. Further, stultification does not much threaten, though along the way we perhaps lose the arena in which interpretive social science has aspired "to root out the various forms of scientism and positivism still so prevalent" (Bernstein 1983:173)—others would call this necrophobia—apparently by demonstrating superiority over naturalistic methods. Yet as both Fish and Rorty have suggested in other contexts, this project has always been vexed by its paradoxical expectation that, having driven naturalistic inquiry from the field by exposing its lack of foundations—indeed, a lack of foundations in general—interpretive science can slip into its shoes and *prove* itself the better guide to communicating across cultures, to learning from the Other, to coping with social upheaval, to illuminating the discourse of power, or whatever. It does so not by measuring itself against the instrumental criteria it has just dismissed—though surely these continue to lurk about—but by suggesting it has finally uncovered, as Rorty might put it, culture's *own language,* through which its previously obscure nature is revealed.

Of course it is a bit superfluous, given the conclusion of the previous chapter, to ruminate about these matters; yet it seemed worthwhile to sketch the various parameters involved and suggest how they operate concretely. As we indicated long ago, enchantment is itself an index of our pragmatic incompetence: we can only "buy" wonder, so to speak, in its currency. Mature sciences have managed to shed certain enduring disabilities into stigmatized fields, settling for short-term enchantment—and without necessarily becoming ossified in the process. Today's less-mature sciences might be able to do so too, were epistemic and organizational conditions more favorable.

Yet this is not something for or against which it makes much sense to argue.[8] In the end what matters is probably less the look of the referential terrain immediately ahead and the organizational forms we might develop to deal with it, than the alternative moral profiles we can take

---

8. In roughly analogous circumstances, Paul Roth (1987:244–245) concludes that "the debate on choice of frameworks is not a matter of appealing to some higher standard of rationality, some algorithm for choosing the most rational from among competing systems of beliefs; it is a choice of how one wants to live one's life."

on through a decision to be scientist, virtuoso, or edifier. Producers of knowledge select their particular epistemic register in part because it allows a way of being in the world that has moral or aesthetic appeal, as Hirsch has already suggested. Though "rational" assessments might affect our choice—we can reject naturalism after measuring its repressive weight, its often astonishing ability to confuse our prejudices with the structure of the world (Seidman 1991b), or reject ambiguous registers out of concern for our competence—more commonly we simply choose what feels right to us as a vocation, what fits our sensibility.

Gerald Holton (1973) has suggested that science itself is partly an expressive activity through which we give vent to quite abstract aesthetic prejudices—for continuity over discreteness, for instance. Thus though an existing picture of the world might trouble us because it seemed rife with anomalies . . . it might also simply offend our sense of how the world *ought* to be. (Einstein, as we noted, never became comfortable with the Copenhagen interpretation of quantum mechanics.) And just as Mallarmé found it difficult to account for the harmonies he discovered among words, we are hard-pressed to explain why the world "looks better" to us conceptualized one way than another. But it does.

For Lévi-Strauss, the world looks better when Orphic, when it speaks a language upon which to pattern our own and from which to learn some humility. Like many other (but not all) contemporary virtuosi, he seeks to knit together the orders of words and things, of meaning and materiality, so as to avoid a disenchanted world where, as Weber had it, things no longer signify but merely happen—where, as we might say, the discourse of edification is no longer able to ground itself in nature. Weber himself was not pleased with this prospect: though its cold intellectual necessity appealed to his ascetic tendencies, its potential for flatness and spiritual monotony troubled his mystical and aristocratic side (see Mitzman [1970] 1985).

In the seventeenth century Weber's ambivalence was not yet called for. Nature, no less than myth, could still be read for the message "writ obscurely" in it. In a sense, the cabinets of curiosities gathered by virtuosi underwrote this Orphic promise, since their contents established the enchantment of the world, its connection to domains beyond our ken. Clearly, members of the Royal Society did not foresee that their motto would eventually be applied to Nature itself, so that its book, when opened, would have *nullius in verba*—no text. Today, virtuoso students of culture stand between us and a similar disappointment: that culture also has no text, no meaning, *of its own*. From their perspective, to disenchant culture, to split it into intention and meaning, into naturalistic and edifying domains, would leave us to choose between a banausic,

Bibliography

Abbott, Andrew. 1988. *The System of the Professions: an essay on the division of expert labor.* Chicago: University of Chicago Press.

Abrams, M. H. 1977. The Deconstructive Angel. *Critical Inquiry* 3:425–438.

Ackermann, Robert J. 1985. *Data, Instruments, and Theory: a dialectical approach to understanding science.* Princeton: Princeton University Press.

Affergan, Francis. 1986. Animal Anthropology of Cockfighting in Martinique. *Cahiers Internationaux de Sociologie,* 33:109–126.

Albrecht, Milton, James Barnett, and Mason Griff. 1970. *The Sociology of Art and Literature: a reader.* New York: Praeger.

Alexander, Jeffrey. 1987. *Twenty Lectures: sociological theory since World War II.* New York: Columbia University Press.

Alexander, Jeffrey, and Steven Seidman, eds. 1990. *Culture and Society: contemporary debates.* Cambridge and New York: Cambridge University Press.

Altick, Richard. 1978. *The Shows of London.* Cambridge, Mass.: Belknap Press of Harvard University Press.

Ashworth, William B. Jr. 1991. Remarkable Humans and Singular Beasts. In Joy Kenseth, ed., *The Age of the Marvelous.* Dartmouth, New Hampshire: Hood Museum of Art.

Atran, Scott. 1990. *Cognitive Foundations of Natural History: towards an anthropology of science.* Cambridge and Paris: Cambridge University Press and Editions de la Maison des Sciences de l'Homme.

Aubrey, John. [1696] 1784. *Miscellanies upon Various Subjects.* London: W. Ottridge.

Barclay, James. 1980. *A Stroll through Borneo.* London: Hodder and Stoughton.

Barkla, C. G.. 1925. The J Phenomenon in X-rays, Part 1. *Philosophical Magazine* 49:1033–1055.

Bauer, Henry H. 1984. *Beyond Velikovsky: the history of a public controversy.* Urbana and Chicago: University of Illinois Press.

Becker, Howard. 1963. *Outsiders: studies in the sociology of deviance.* New York: The Free Press.

Beisel, Nicola. 1990. Class, Culture, and Campaigns against Vice in Three American Cities, 1872–1892. *American Sociological Review* 55:44–62.

Bergesen, Albert. 1984. Social Control and Corporate Organization. In Donald Black, ed., *Toward a General Theory of Social Control.* New York: Academic Press.

Bernstein, Richard. 1983. *Beyond Objectivism and Relativism.* Philadelphia: University of Pennsylvania Press.

Black, Donald. 1989. *Sociological Justice.* New York and Oxford: Oxford University Press

Blau, Judith. 1988. Study of the Arts: a reappraisal. *Annual Review of Sociology* 14:269–292.

Blau, Peter. 1977. *Inequality and Heterogeneity*. New York: The Free Press.

Bloom, Harold. 1983. *Kaballah and Criticism*. New York: Continuun.

Bloomfield, Leonard. 1930. *Sacred Stories of the Sweetgrass Cree*. Bulletin 60, Anthropological Series 11, National Museum of Canada. Ottawa: Ackland.

Bloor, David. 1991. *Knowledge and Social Imagery*. Second edition. Chicago: University of Chicago Press.

Bodgan, Robert. 1988. *Freak Show: presenting human oddities for amusement and profit*. Chicago: University of Chicago Press.

Booth, Wayne. 1974. *Modern Dogma and the Rhetoric of Assent*. Notre Dame: University of Notre Dame Press.

———. 1977. Preserving the Exemplar. *Critical Inquiry* 3:407–423.

Bourdieu, Pierre. 1984. *Distinction: a social critique of the judgement of taste*. Trans. Richard Nice. Cambridge, Mass.: Harvard University Press.

Brandt, Jason. 1987. Review of Sacks, *The Man Who Mistook His Wife for a Hat*. *The Journal of Nervous and Mental Diseases*. 175:118–119.

Brown, Richard Harvey. 1987. *Society as Text: essays in rhetoric, reason, and reality*. Chicago: University of Chicago Press.

Butler, Judith. 1990. Sexual Inversions. A paper presented to the "Foucault/Sexuality/Foucault" Conference, University of Michigan.

Calhoun, Craig. 1991. Morality, Identity, and Historical Explanation: Charles Taylor on the sources of the self. *Sociological Theory* 9:232–263.

Campbell, Donald. 1974. Evolutionary Epistemology. In Paul Schlipp, ed., *The Philosophy of Karl Popper*, vol. 1 La Salle, Ill.: Open Court.

———. 1986. Science's Social System of Validity-Enhancing Collective Belief Change and the Problems of the Social Sciences. In D. Fiske and R. Shweder, eds., *Metatheory in Social Science*. Chicago: University of Chicago Press.

Carrithers, Michael. 1990. Is Anthropology Art or Science? *Current Anthropology* 31:263–271.

Clifford, James. 1988. *The Predicament of Culture: twentieth-century ethnography, literature, and art*. Cambridge, Mass.: Harvard University Press.

Clifford, James, and George Marcus, eds. 1986. *Writing Culture: the poetics and politics of ethnography*. Berkeley: University of California Press.

Cole, Jonathan, and Stephen Cole. 1973. *Social Stratification in Science*. Chicago: University of Chicago Press.

Cole, Stephen. 1983. The Hierarchy of the Sciences? *American Journal of Sociology* 89:111–139.

———. 1992. *Making Science: between science and nature*. Cambridge, Mass.: Harvard University Press.

Collin, Finn. 1985. *Theory and Understanding: a critique of interpretive social science*. Oxford: Basil Blackwell.

Collins, H. M. 1985. *Changing Order: replication and induction in scientific practice*. Beverly Hills: Sage Publications.

Collins, H. M., and T. J. Pinch. 1982. *Frames of Meaning: the social construction of extraordinary science*. London: Routledge and Kegan Paul.

Collins, Randall. 1975. *Conflict Sociology*. New York: Academic Press.

———. 1979. *The Credential Society: an historical sociology of education and stratification*. New York: Academic Press.

———. 1989. Sociology: Proscience or Antiscience? *American Sociological Review*. 54:124–139.

———. 1990. Reply: Cumulation and Anti-Cumulation in Sociology. *American Sociological Review* 55:462–463.

Cooter, Roger. 1984. *The Cultural Meaning of Popular Science: phrenology and the organization of consent in nineteenth-century Britain.* Cambridge and New York: Cambridge University Press.

Cozzens, Susan B. 1985. Comparing the Sciences: citation context analysis of papers from neuropharmacology and the sociology of science. *Social Studies of Science* 15:127–153.

Crapanzano, Vincent. 1986. Hermes Dilemma: the masking of subversion in ethnographic description. In Clifford and Marcus, *Writing Culture.*

Crease, Robert P., and N. P. Samios. 1989. Cold Fusion Confusion. *New York Times Magazine.* Sept 24.

Crews, Frederick. 1986. *Skeptical Engagements.* New York: Oxford University Press.

Crutchfield, James P, J. Doyle Farmer, Norman H. Packard, and Robert B. Shaw. 1986. Chaos. *Scientific American* 255:46–57.

Cuddihy, John M. 1974. *The Ordeal of Civility.* New York: Basic Books.

Culler, Jonathan. 1975. *Structualist Poetics: structuralism, linguistics, and the study of literature.* Ithaca: Cornell University Press.

———. 1982. *On Deconstruction: theory and criticism after structuralism.* Ithaca: Cornell University Press.

Curtis, James, and John Petras. 1970. *The Sociology of Knowledge: a reader.* New York: Praeger.

Darnton, Robert. 1968. *Mesmerism and the End of the Enlightenment in France.* Cambridge, Mass.: Harvard University Press.

Darwin, Charles. 1872. *The Expression of the Emotions in Man and Animals.* London: J. Murray.

de Man, Paul. 1979. *Allegories of Reading.* New Haven: Yale University Press.

Denzin, Norman K. 1989. *Interpretive Biography.* Newbury Park, Calif.: Sage.

Derrida, Jacques. [1967] 1978. Structure, Sign, and Play in the Discourse of the Human Sciences. In *Writing and Difference,* trans. Alan Bass. Chicago: University of Chicago Press.

DiMaggio, Paul. 1987. Classification in Art. *American Sociological Review* 52:440–455.

Dogan, Mattei, and Robert Pahre. 1990. *Creative Marginality: innovation at the intersections of social sciences.* Boulder: Westview Press.

Donoghue, Denis. 1981. *Ferocious Alphabets.* Boston: Little, Brown.

Douglas, Mary. 1966. *Purity and Danger.* London: Routledge and Kegan Paul.

Dreyfus, Hubert L. 1980. Holism and Hermeneutics. *Review of Metaphysics* 34:3–23.

Dreyfus, Hubert, and Paul Rabinow, eds. 1982. *Michel Foucault: beyond structuralism and hermeneutics*. Chicago: University of Chicago Press.

Durkheim, Emile. [1895] 1964. *The Rules of the Sociological Method*. New York: The Free Press.

Dyson, Freeman. 1988. *Infinite in All Directions*. New York: Harper and Row.

Erikson, Kai. 1966. *Wayward Puritans*. New York: Wiley.

Esposito, Joseph. 1977. *Schelling's Idealism and Philosophy of Nature*. Lewisburg: Bucknell University Press.

Fish, Stanley. 1980. *Is There a Text in this Class? the authority of interpretive communities*. Cambridge, Mass.: Harvard University Press.

———. 1989a. *Doing What Comes Naturally: change, rhetoric, and the practice of theory in literary and legal studies*. Durham: Duke University Press.

———. 1989b. Commentary: The Young and the Restless. In Veeser, *The New Historicism*.

Fisher, Donald. 1990. Boundary Work and Science. In Susan Cozzens and Thomas Gieryn, eds., *Theories of Science in Society*. Bloomington and Indianapolis: Indiana University Press.

Fiske, Donald, and Richard Shweder, eds. 1986. *Metatheory in the Social Sciences*. Chicago: University of Chicago Press.

Fort, Charles. 1919. *The Book of the Damned*. New York: Boni and Liveright.

Foster, George. 1967. *Tzintzuntzan*. Boston: Little, Brown.

Foucault, Michel. 1984. *The Foucault Reader*. Ed. Paul Rabinow. New York: Pantheon.

Fowlie, Wallace. 1953. *Mallarmé*. Chicago: University of Chicago Press.

Freud, Sigmund. 1966. *The Complete Introductory Lectures on Psychoanalysis*. Ed. and trans. James Strachey. New York: W. W. Norton.

Fuchs, Stephan. 1992. *The Professional Quest for Truth: a social theory of science and knowledge*. Albany: State University of New York Press.

Fuchs, Stephan, and Jonathan Turner. 1986. What Makes a Science "Mature"? patterns of organizational control in scientific production. *Sociological Theory* 4:143–150.

Gallie, W. B. 1964. *Philosophy and Historical Understanding*. New York: Schocken Books.

Gans, Herbert. 1974. *Popular Culture and High Culture: an analysis and evaluation of taste*. New York: Basic Books.

Garfield, Eugene. 1980. Is Information Retrieval in the Arts and Humanities Inherently Different from that in Science? The Effect that ISI's Citation Index for the Arts and Humanities Is Expected to have on Future Scholarship. *Library Quarterly* 50:40–57.

———. 1986. The 250 Most-Cited Authors in the *Arts & Humanities Citation Index*, 1976–1983. *Current Contents* 48:3–10 (Dec. 1)

Geertz, Clifford. 1973. *The Interpretation of Cultures*. New York: Basic Books.

———. 1983. *Local Knowledge: further essays in interpretive anthropology*. New York: Basic Books.

———. 1984. Distinguished Lecture: Anti Anti-Relativism. *American Anthropologist* 86:263–278.

———. 1988. *Works and Lives: the anthropologist as author.* Stanford: Stanford University Press.

———. 1990. Reply to Carrithers. *Current Anthropology* 31:274.

Geertz, Clifford, ed. [1971] 1974. *Myth, Symbol, and Culture.* New York: W. W. Norton and Company.

Gergen, Kenneth J. 1982. *Toward Transformation in Social Knowledge.* New York: Springer-Verlag.

Giere, Ronald N. 1988. *Explaining Science: a cognitive approach.* Chicago and London: University of Chicago Press.

Gieryn, Thomas F. 1983a. Boundary-work and the Demarcation of Science from Non-science: strains and interests in the professional ideologies of scientists. *American Sociological Review* 48:781–795.

———. 1983b. Making the Demarcation of Science a Sociological Problem: boundary-work by John Tyndall, Victorian scientist. In R. Laudan, *The Demarcation between Science and Pseudo-Science.*

Gilbert, G. N., and Michael Mulkay. 1984. *Opening Pandora's Box: a sociological analysis of scientific discourse.* Cambridge: Cambridge University Press.

Gilovich, Thomas, Robert Valone, and Amos Tversky. 1985. The Hot Hand in Basketball: on the misperception of random sequences. *Cognitive Psychology* 17:295–314.

Glanvill, Joseph. 1668. *A Philosophical Endeavor in the Defence of the Being Of Witches and Apparitions.* London: E. Cotes.

Gleick, James. 1987. *Chaos: Making a New Science.* New York: Viking.

Golding, John. 1988. The Triumph of Picasso. *New York Review of Books* 35:12 (21 July).

Goody, Jack. 1977. *The Domestication of the Savage Mind.* Cambridge: Cambridge University Press.

Gottdiener, Mark. 1990. The Logocentrism of the Classics. *American Sociological Review.* 55:460–462.

Gould, Stephen Jay. 1989. *Wonderful Life: the Burgess Shale and the nature of history.* New York: Norton.

Graves, Robert. 1955. *The Greek Myths.* New York: George Braziller.

Green, Martin. 1976. *Children of the Sun: a narrative of "decadence" in England after 1918.* New York: Basic Books.

Griswold, Wendy, 1981. American Character and the American Novel: an expansion of reflection theory in the sociology of literature. *American Journal of Sociology* 86:740–765.

Grunbaum, Adolf. 1984 *The Foundations of Psychoanalysis: a philosophical critique.* Berkeley: University of California Press.

Hagstrom, Warren. 1965. *The Scientific Community.* New York: Basic Books.

Hahn, Roger. 1971. *Anatomy of a Scientific Institution: the Paris Academy of Sciences, 1666–1803.* Berkeley: University of California Press.

Hall, Marie Boas. 1984. *All Scientists Now: the Royal Society in the nineteenth century*. Cambridge: Cambridge University Press.

Hamilton, David P. 1991. Research Papers: Who's Uncited Now? *Science* 251:25.

Hammel, Eugene. 1972. The Myth of Structural Analysis: Lévi-Strauss and the Three Bears. *Addison-Wesley Modular Publications* 25.

Hargens, Lowell. 1975. *Patterns of Scientific Research*. Washington: American Sociological Association.

———. 1991. Impressions and Misimpressions about Sociology Journals. *Contemporary Sociology* 20:343–349.

Harrington, Anne. 1991. Interwar German Psychobiology: Between Nationalism and the Irrational. *Science in Context* 4:429–447.

Harris, Marvin. 1964. *The Nature of Cultural Things*. New York: Random House.

———. 1979. *Cultural Materialism*. New York: Random House.

Harvey, William, Nan Lin, and Carnot Nelson. 1970. Some Comparisons of Communication Activities in the Physical and Social Sciences. In Carnot Nelson and Donald Pollack, eds., *Communication among Scientists and Engineers*. Lexington, Mass.: D. C. Heath.

Hawley, F. Frederick. 1989. Cockfight in the Cotton: A moral crusade in microcosm. *Contemporary Crises* 13:129–144.

Headland, Thomas, Kenneth Pike, and Marvin Harris. 1990. *Emics and Etics: the insider/outsider controversy*. Newbury Park: Sage.

Hess, David J. 1991. *Spirits and Scientists: ideology, Spiritism, and Brazilian culture*. University Park: Pennsylvania State University Press.

Hirsch, E. D. 1967. *Validity in Interpretation*. New Haven: Yale University Press.

———. 1976. *The Aims of Interpretation*. Chicago: University of Chicago Press.

Hirschfeld, Lawrence. 1986. Hermeneutics and Some Lessions from Anthropology. *Contemporary Sociology* 15:34–37.

Holton, Gerald. 1973. *The Thematic Origins of Scientific Thought: Kepler to Einstein*. Cambridge, Mass.: Harvard University Press.

Hoppen, K. Theodore. 1976. The Nature of the Early Royal Society. *British Journal of the History of Science* 9:1–24, 243–273.

Horgan, John. 1991. The Pied Piper of Superstrings. *Scientific American* 265:5:42–47.

Houghton, Walter E. 1942. The English Virtuoso in the Seventeenth Century. *Journal of the History of Ideas* 3:51–73, 190–219.

Humphreys, Paul. 1989. *The Chances of Explanation: causal explanation in the social, medical, and physical sciences*. Princeton: Princeton University Press.

Hunter, Michael. 1975. *John Aubrey and the Realm of Learning*. New York: Science History Publications.

———. 1981. *Science and Society in Restoration England*. Cambridge: Cambridge University Press.

———. 1982. *The Royal Society and Its Fellows: 1660–1700*. British Society for the History of Science Monograph. N.p.

———. 1989. *Establishing the New Science: the experience of the early Royal Society*. Woodbridge: Boydell Press.

Idel, Moshe. 1989. *Language, Torah, and Hermeneutics in Abraham Abulafia*. Trans. Menahem Kallus. Albany: State University of New York Press.

Impey, Oliver, and Arthur MacGregor. 1985. *The Origins of Museums: the cabinet of curiosities in sixteenth- and seventeenth-century Europe*. Oxford: Clarendon Press.

Jameson, Fredric. 1981. *The Political Unconscious*. Ithaca: Cornell University Press.

Jones, W. T. 1961. *The Romantic Syndrome: toward a new method in cultural anthropology and history of ideas*. The Hague: M. Nijhoff

Juhl, P. D. 1980. *Interpretation, an essay in the philosophy of literary criticism*. Princeton: Princeton University Press.

Kael, Pauline. 1991. The Doctor and the Director. *New Yorker Magazine* February 11.

Kenseth, Joy. 1991a. The Age of the Marvelous: an introduction. In Kenseth, ed., *The Age of the Marvelous*.

Kenseth, Joy. 1991b. "A World of Wonders in One Closet Shut." In Kenseth 1991.

Kenseth, Joy, ed. 1991. *The Age of the Marvelous*. Dartmouth, N. H.: Hood Museum of Art.

Kermode, Frank. 1967. *The Sense of an Ending*. New York: Oxford University Press.

———. 1979. *The Genesis of Secrecy: on the interpretation of narrative*. Cambridge, Mass.: Harvard University Press.

Kirk, G. S. 1975. *Myth*. Cambridge: Cambridge University Press.

Knapp, Steven, and Walter Benn Michaels. 1982. Against Theory. In W. J. T. Mitchell, ed., *Against Theory*. Chicago: University of Chicago Press.

Krauss, Lawrence M. 1986. Dark Matter in the Universe. *Scientific American* 255:58.

Kuper, Adam. 1990. Editorial. *Current Anthropology* 31, preceding p. 337.

Lamont, Michèle. 1987. How to Become a Dominant French Philosopher: the case of Jacques Derrida. *American Journal of Sociology* 93:584–622.

Lamont, Michèle, and Marsha Witten. 1988. Surveying the Continental Drift: the diffusion of French social and literary theory in the United States. *French Politics and Society* 6:17–24.

Lamont, Michèle, and Robert Wuthnow. 1990. Betwixt and Between: recent cultural sociology in Europe and the United States. In George Ritzer, ed., *Frontiers of Social Theory: the new synthesis*. New York: Columbia University Press.

Lansang, Angel. 1966. *Cockfighting in the Philippines*. Baguio City: Catholic School Press.

Latour, Bruno. 1987. *Science in Action.* Cambridge, Mass.: Harvard University Press.

Latour, Bruno, and Steve Woolgar. 1979. *Laboratory Life: the social construction of scientific facts.* Beverly Hills and London: Sage Publications.

Laudan, Larry. 1983. The Demise of the Demarcation Problem. In Laudan, *The Demarcation between Science and Pseudo-Science.*

———. 1984. *Science and Values.* Berkeley: University of California Press.

———. 1987. Progress or Rationality? The Prospects for Normative Naturalism. *American Philosophical Quarterly* 24:19–31.

Laudan, Rachel, ed. 1983. *The Demarcation between Science and Pseudo-Science.* Working Papers in Science and Technology, 2:1. Blacksburg: Center for the Study of Science in Society, Virginia Polytechnic Institute and State University.

Lemert, Charles. 1981. *French Sociology: rupture and renewal since 1968.* New York: Columbia University Press.

Lemert, Charles, and Garth Gillan. 1982. *Michel Foucault: social theory and transgression.* New York: Columbia University Press.

Lepenies, Wolf. 1988. *Between Literature and Science: the rise of sociology.* Trans. R. J. Hollingdale. Cambridge and Paris: Cambridge University Press and Editions de la Maison des Sciences de l'Homme.

Leplin, Jarrett. 1984. Truth and Scientific Progress. In Leplin, ed., *Scientific Realism.* Berkeley: University of California Press.

Levine, Donald. 1986. The Forms and Functions of Social Knowledge. In Fiske and Shweder, *Metatheory in the Social Sciences.*

Lévi-Strauss, Claude. 1955. *Tristes Tropiques.* Paris: Plon.

———. 1963a. *Structural Anthropology.* Trans. C. Jacobson and B. G. Scheopf. New York: Basic Books.

———. 1963b. Réponses à quelques questions. *Esprit* 322:628–653.

———. 1966. *The Savage Mind.* Chicago: University of Chicago Press.

———. 1969. *The Raw and the Cooked.* Trans. John Weightman and Doreen Weightman. New York: Harper and Row.

———. 1973. *From Honey to Ashes.* Trans. John Weightman and Doreen Weightman. New York: Harper and Row.

———. 1974. *Tristes Tropiques.* Trans. John Weightman and Doreen Weightman. New York: Atheneum

———. 1976. *Structural Anthropology,* Vol. 2. Trans. Monique Layton. New York: Basic Books.

———. 1978. *The Origin of Table Manners.* Trans. John Weightman and Doreen Weightman. New York: Harper and Row.

———. 1979. *Myth and Meaning.* New York: Schocken Books.

———. 1981. *The Naked Man.* Trans. John Weightman and Doreen Weightman. New York: Harper and Row.

———. 1988. *The Jealous Potter.* Trans. Benedicte Chorier. Chicago: University of Chicago Press.

Levitt, Barbara, and Clifford Nass. 1989. The Lid on the Garbage Can: constraints on decision-making in the technical core of college-text publishers. *Administrative Science Quarterly* 34:190–207.

Ley, Willy. 1963. *Watchers of the Skies*. New York: Viking.

Lieberman, Saul. 1962. *Hellenism in Jewish Palestine*. New York: Jewish Theological Seminary of America.

Lieberson, Jonathan. 1984. Interpreting the Interpreter. *The New York Review of Books* 31:4 (15 March).

Livingston, Paisley. 1988. *Literary Knowledge: humanistic inquiry and the philosophy of science*. Ithaca and London: Cornell University Press.

Lodahl, Janice, and Gerald Gordon. 1972. The Structure of Scientific Fields and the Functioning of University Graduate Departments. *American Sociological Review* 37:57–72.

Lukes, Steven. 1977. Some Problems about Rationality. In Bryan Wilson, ed., *Rationality*. Oxford: Basil Blackwell.

MacGregor, Arthur. 1985. The Cabinet of Curiosities in Seventeenth-Century Britain. In Impey and MacGregor, *The Origins of Museums*.

Malinowski, Bronislaw. [1935] 1965. *Coral Gardens and Their Magic*. Vol. 1: *Soil Tilling and Agricultural Rites in the Trobriand Islands*. Bloomington: University of Indiana Press.

Mallarmé, Stephane. 1945. *Oeuvres complète*. Paris: Gallimard.

Marcus, George, and Michael Fischer. 1986. *Writing Culture: an experimental moment in the human sciences*. Chicago: University of Chicago Press.

Margolis, Joseph. 1990. Reconciling Realism and Relativism. In Herbert Simons, ed., *The Rhetorical Turn: invention and persuasion in the conduct of inquiry*. Chicago: University of Chicago Press.

Marvin, Garry. 1984. The Cockfight in Andalusia, Spain: images of the truly male. *Anthropological Quarterly* 57:60–70.

Megill, Allan. 1987. The Reception of Foucault by Historians. *Journal of the History of Ideas* 48:117–141.

Merquior, José G. 1991. Notes on the American Reception of Foucault. *Stanford French Review* 15:25–35.

Miller, J. Hillis. 1976. Ariadne's Thread: repetition and the narrative line. *Critical Inquiry* 3:57–77.

Mitzman, Arthur. [1970] 1985. *The Iron Cage: an historical interpretation of Max Weber*. New Brunswick and Oxford: Transaction Books.

Nagel, Thomas. 1979. What Is It Like to Be a Bat? In *Mortal Questions*. Cambridge and New York: Cambridge University Press.

National Research Council. Office of Scientific Personnel. Research Division. 1967. *Doctorate Recipients from United States Universities, 1858–1964: sciences, humanities, professions, arts; a statistical report*. Washington: National Academy of Sciences.

Needham, Rodney. 1978. Evasive Fantasies. In *Primordial Characters*. Charlottesville: University of Virginia Press.

Newman, S. 1987. Review of Sacks, *The Man Who Mistook His Wife for His Hat*. *The British Journal of Psychiatry* 150:281.

Nicki, R. M. 1983. Psychophysiology and Aesthetics. In Anthony Gale and John Edwards, eds., *Physiological Correlates of Human Behavior*, Vol. 2: *Attention and Performance*. New York: Academic Press.

Nicolson, Marjorie Hope. 1965. *Pepys' Diary and the New Science*. Charlottesville: University of Virginia Press.

Nimuendajú, Curt. 1952. *The Tukuna*. Ed. Robert Lowie and trans. William Hohenthal. University of California Publications in American Archeology and Ethnology, vol. 45. Berkeley: University of California Press.

Olmi, Giuseppe. 1985. Science—Honour—Metaphor: Italian cabinets of the sixteenth and seventeenth centuries. In Impey and MacGregor, *The Origins of Museums*.

Ortner, Sherry. 1984. Theory in Anthropology since the Sixties. *Comparative Studies in Society and History* 26:126–166.

Pace, David. 1986. *Claude Lévi-Strauss*. London: ARK Paperbacks.

Park, Katherine, and Lorraine Daston. 1981. Unnatural Conceptions: the study of monsters in sixteenth- and seventeenth-century France and England. *Past and Present* 92:20–54.

Paulson, William. 1988. *The Noise of Culture: literary texts in a world of information*. Ithaca: Cornell University Press.

Pecora, Vincent. The Limits of Local Knowledge. In Veeser 1989.

Peritz, Bluma. 1983. Are Methodological Papers More Cited than Theoretical or Empirical Ones? The Case of Sociology. *Scientometrics* 5:211–218.

Perlmutter, David. 1991. The Language of the Deaf. *The New York Review of Books* 38:6 (28 March) 65–72.

Peterson, Richard A. 1989. La Sociologie de l'art et de la culture aux Etats-Unis. *L'Annee Sociologique* 39:153–179.

———. 1990. Symposium: The Many Facets of Culture. *Contemporary Sociology* 19:498–523.

Pettit, Philip. 1975. *The Concept of Structuralism*. Berkeley: University of California Press.

Pfungst, Oscar. [1911] 1965. *Clever Hans: the horse of Mr. Von Osten*. Trans. Carl Rahn, ed. Robert Rosenthal. New York: Holt, Rinehart and Winston.

Polanyi, Michael. 1958. *Personal Knowledge: towards a post-critical philosophy*. Chicago: University of Chicago Press.

Powell, Anthony. 1948. *John Aubrey*. New York: Scribners

Rabinow, Paul, and William Sullivan, eds. 1979. *Interpretive Social Science*. Berkeley: University of California Press.

———. 1987. *Interpretive Social Science: a second look*. Berkeley: University of California Press.

Radway, Janice. 1984. *Reading the Romance: women, patriarchy, and popular literature*. Chapel Hill: University of North Carolina Press.

Richards, Robert J. 1987. *Darwin and the Emergence of Evolutionary Theories of Mind and Behavior*. Chicago: University of Chicago Press.

Ricoeur, Paul. 1971. The Model of the Text: meaningful action considered as a text. *Social Research.* 38:329–362.
———. 1974. *The Conflict of Interpretations.* Don Idhe, ed. Evanston: Northwestern University Press.
Ringer, Fritz. 1969. *The Decline of the German Mandarins: the German academic community, 1890–1933.* Cambridge, Mass.: Harvard University Press.
Rorty, Richard. 1979. *Philosophy and the Mirror of Nature.* Princeton: Princeton University Press.
———. 1982. *The Consequences of Pragmatism.* Minneapolis: University of Minnesota Press.
Rosaldo, Renato. 1989. *Culture and Truth: the remaking of social analysis.* Boston: Beacon Press.
Roseberry, William. 1982. Balinese Cockfights and the Seduction of Anthropology. *Social Research* 49:1013–1028.
Roth, Paul A. 1987. *Meaning and Method in the Social Sciences.* Ithaca and London: Cornell University Press.
Rudwick, Martin J. S. 1985. *The Great Devonian Controversy: the shaping of scientific knowledge among gentlemanly experts.* Chicago: University of Chicago Press.
Russell, Collin. 1983. *Science and Social Change in Britain and Europe: 1700–1900.* New York: St. Martin's Press.
Sacks, Oliver. 1974. *Awakenings.* Garden City, N.J.: Doubleday.
———. 1985. *The Man Who Mistook His Wife for a Hat.* New York: Summit Books.
———. 1989. *Seeing Voices: a journey into the world of the deaf.* Berkeley: University of California Press.
Sacks, Oliver, and Robert Wasserman. 1987. The Case of the Colorblind Painter. *New York Review of Books* 34:18 (19 November).
Salzman, Philip C. 1988. Fads and Fashions in Anthropology. *Anthropology Newsletter* 29:1,31 (May).
Scholem, Gershom. 1974. *Kabbalah.* Jerusalem: Keter Publishing.
Schneider, Mark. 1979. Goethe and the Structuralist Tradition. *Studies in Romanticism* 18:453–478.
———. 1987. Culture-as-text in the Work of Clifford Geertz. *Theory and Society* 16:809–839.
———. 1991. Review of David Harvey, *The Condition of Postmodernity. Contemporary Sociology.* 20:5
Seidman, Stephen, 1991a. The End of Sociological Theory: the postmodern hope. *Sociological Theory* 9:131–146.
———. 1991b. Postmodern Anxiety: the politics of epistemology. *Sociological Theory* 9:180–190.
Seung, T. K. 1982. *Structuralism and Hermeneutics.* New York: Columbia University Press.
Sewell, Elizabeth. 1960. *The Orphic Vision.* New Haven: Yale University Press.

Shankman, Paul. 1984. The Thick and the Thin: on the interpretive theoretical program of Clifford Geertz. *Current Anthropology* 25:261–270.

Shapin, Steven, and Simon Schaffer. 1985. *Leviathan and the Air-Pump: Hobbes, Boyle and the experimental life*. Princeton: Princeton University Press.

Shell, Marc. 1991. Marranos (Pigs), or From Coexistence to Toleration. *Critical Inquiry* 17:306–335.

Shweder, Richard A. 1977. Likeness and Likelihood in Everyday Thought: magical thinking in judgments about personality. *Current Anthropology* 18:637–648.

Shweder, Richard, and Roy D'Andrade. 1980. The Semantic Distortion Hypothesis. In R. A. Shweder, ed., *Fallible Judgment in Behavioral Research*. New Directions for Methodology of Social and Behavioral Science, No. 4. San Francisco: Jossey-Bass.

Skinner, Quentin, ed. 1985. *The Return of Grand Theory in the Human Sciences*. Cambridge: Cambridge University Press.

Sklar, Robert. 1975. *Movie-Made America: a cultural history of the American movies*. New York: Randon House.

Sperber, Dan. 1975. *Rethinking Symbolism*. Trans. Alice Morton. Cambridge: Cambridge University Press.

———. 1985. *On Anthropological Knowledge*. Cambridge and Paris: Cambridge University Press and Editions de la Maison des Sciences de l'Homme.

Sperber, Dan, and Deirdre Wilson. 1986. *Relevance: communication and cognition*. Oxford: Basil Blackwell.

Starr, Paul. 1982. *The Social Transformation of American Medicine*. New York: Basic Books.

St. Aubyn, Frederic. 1969. *Stephane Mallarmé*. New York: Twayne.

Steiner, George. 1967. Orpheus with his Myths. In *Language and Silence*. New York: Atheneum.

Stewart, Larry. 1992. *The Rise of Public Science: rhetoric, technology, and natural philosophy in Newtonian Britain, 1660–1750*. Cambridge: Cambridge University Press.

Subramanyam, Krishna. 1981. *Scientific and Technical Information Resources*. New York and Basel: Marcel Dekker.

Sutherland, Stuart. 1985. Review of Sacks, *The Man Who Mistook His Wife for a Hat*. *Nature* 318:609 (19/26 December).

Swanson, Guy. 1976. Orpheus and Star-Husband: meaning and the structure of myths. *Ethnology* 15:115–133.

Taylor, Charles. [1971] 1979. Interpretation and the Science of Man. In Rabinow and Sullivan, *Interpretive Social Science*.

———. 1989. *Sources of the Self: the making of modern identity*. Cambridge: Harvard University Press.

TenHouten, Warren, and Charles Kaplan. 1973. *Science and Its Mirror Image: a theory of inquiry*. New York: Harper and Row.

Thomas, Keith. 1971. *Religion and the Decline of Magic*. New York: Charles Scribner's Sons.

————. 1983. *Man and the Natural World*. London: Allen Lane.

Thomas, L. L., J. Kronenfeld, and D. Kronenfeld. 1976. Asdiwal Crumbles: a critique of Lévi-Strauss on myth. *American Ethnologist* 3:147–174.

Thompson, Robert Farris. 1973. Yoruba Artistic Criticism. In Warren d'Azevedo, ed., *The Traditional Artist in African Societies*. Bloomington: University of Indiana Press.

————. 1987. Personal communication.

Thompson, Stith. [1929] 1966. *Tales of the North American Indians*. Bloomington: University of Indiana Press.

————. [1946] 1977. *The Folktale*. Berkeley: University of California Press.

Todorov, R., and W. Glanzel. 1988. Journal citation measures: a concise review. *Journal of Information Science* 14:47–56.

Toulmin, Stephen. 1970. Reasons and Causes. In R. Borger and F. Cioffi, eds., *Explanation in the Behavioural Sciences*. Cambridge: Cambridge University Press.

Turner, Jonathan, and Stephen Turner. 1990. *The Impossible Science: an institutional analysis of American sociology*. Newbury Park, Calif.: Sage.

Tversky, Amos, and Daniel Kahneman. 1983. Extensional versus Intuitive Reasoning: the conjunction fallacy in probability judgment. *Psychological Review* 90:293–315.

University of Michigan. 1990. *The University of Michigan Bulletin*. Ann Arbor: N.p.

van den Daele, Wolfgang. 1977. The Social Construction of Science: institutionalization and definition of positive science in the latter half of the seventeenth century. In E. Mendelsohn, P. Weingart, and R. Whitley, eds., *The Social Production of Scientific Knowledge. Sociology of the Sciences Yearbook*. 1:27–54.

Veeser, H. Aram, ed. 1989. *The New Historicism*. New York and London: Routledge.

Vickers, Brian. 1984. Analogy versus Identity: the rejection of occult symbolism, 1580–1680. In Brian Vickers, ed., *Occult and Scientific Mentalities in the Renaissance*. Cambridge: Cambridge University Press.

Walters, Ronald G. 1980. Signs of the Times: Clifford Geertz and historians. *Social Research* 47:537–556.

Watson, Graham. 1989. Definitive Geertz. *Ethnos* 54:23–30.

Weber, Max. 1946. *From Max Weber*. H. H. Gerth and C. W. Mills, eds. Oxford: Oxford University Press.

————. 1968. *Economy and Society*. Guenther Roth and Charles Wittich, eds. New York: Bedminster Press.

Webster, Charles. 1982. *From Paracelsus to Newton: magic and the making of modern science*. Cambridge: Cambridge University Press.

Werblowsky, R. J. Zwi. 1962. *Joseph Karo, lawyer and mystic*. London: Oxford University Press.

Westfall, Richard. [1958] 1973. *Science and Religion in Seventeenth-Century England*. Ann Arbor: University of Michigan Press.

Westrum, Ron. 1978. Science and Social Intelligence about Anomalies: the case of meteorites. *Social Studies of Science* 8:461–493.

———. 1982. Crypto-Science and Social Intelligence about Anomalies. *Zetetic Scholar* 10:89–101.

Whitehead, Alfred N. 1925. *Science and the Modern World.* New York: Macmillan.

Whitley, Richard. 1984. *The Intellectual and Social Organization of the Sciences.* Oxford: Clarendon Press.

Winch, Peter. [1958] 1963. *The Idea of a Social Science and Its Relation to Philosophy.* London: Routledge and Kegan Paul.

Woolgar, Steve. 1988. *Science, the Very Idea.* Chichester, Sussex: Ellis Horwood; London and New York: Tavistock Publications.

Wright, W. G. 1981. On the Boundaries of Science in Seventeenth-Century England. In E. Mendelsohn and Y. Elkana, eds., *Sciences and Cultures. Sociology of the Sciences Yearbook* 5:77–100.

Wuthnow, Robert. 1980. The World Economy and the Institutionalization of Science in Seventeenth-Century Europe. In Albert Bergesen, ed., *Studies of the Modern World System.* New York: Academic Press.

———. 1987. *Meaning and Moral Order: explorations in cultural analysis.* Berkeley: University of California Press.

Wuthnow, Robert, and Marsha Witten. 1988. New Directions in the Study of Culture. *Annual Review of Sociology* 14:49–67.

Wynne, Brian. 1976. C. G. Barkla and the J Phenomenon: a case study in the treatment of deviance in science. *Social Studies of Science* 6:307–347.

———. 1979. Between Orthodoxy and Oblivion: the normalization of deviance in science. In Roy Wallis, ed., *On the Margins of Science.* Sociological Review Monograph No. 27. Keele: University of Keele Press.

Zuckerman, Harriet. 1977. Deviant Behavior and Social Control in Science. In Edward Sagarin, ed., *Deviance and Social Change.* Beverly Hills and London: Sage Publications.

Index

Abbott, Andrew, 172n
Abrams, M. H., 28, 147, 186
Abulafia, Abraham, 51
Ackermann, Robert J., 31n, 121n
Action: meaningful, textual character of, 73–76; rational, intentional structure of, 39, 46–47, 166
Alexander, Jeffrey, 64n, 81n
Allen, Woody, 151n
Altick, Richard, 129
Amateur inquiry, 140, 190–91
Anthropology, 28, 116, 182–83, 200–201; semiotic, 55–56, 65, 72, 199; structural, 83–84, 95, 112, 198
Ashmole, Elias, 130n
Atran, Scott, 147n
Aubrey, John, 1, 1n, 6, 10, 14, 19, 21–22, 134–35, 196
Authorial intention. *See* Determinate meaning.
Authority, reputational. *See* Reputational authority.
Azande magic, 114–15

Bacon, Francis, 130, 133, 140
Balinese cockfights. *See* Cockfights.
Balzac, Honoré de, 200
Bandele, 70, 71
Barclay, James, 66n
Barkla, C. G., 120–21, 122n
Barthes, Roland, 112
Barzun, Jacques, 68n
Bauer, Henry H., 194
Becker, Howard, 125
Beisel, Nicola, 124
Bentham, Jeremy, 61, 62
Berelson, Bernard, 181
Bergeson, Albert, 124
Bernstein, Richard, 40, 202
Black, Donald, 184n
Blake, William, 60, 112, 146, 166
Blau, Judith, 125, 185n
Bloom, Harold, 51
Bloomfield, Leonard, 103n

Bloor, David, 9n
Blows Invisible, 1, 24
Bogdan, Robert, 8n
Booth, Wayne, 78n, 145
Boundaries: blurring of, 79, 81n, 201; between enchanted and disenchanted inquiry, 2, 26, 116, 121–23, 138, 141, 178, 194; sociological interest in, 124. *See also* Boundary work; Social control
Boundary-work, 117–22, 132, 187–91, 194–95. *See also* Boundaries; Social control
Bourdieu, Pierre, 166n, 190
Boyle, Robert, 132, 171
Breton, André, 43, 58, 60, 60, 72
Brown, Richard Harvey, 77n
Butler, Judith, 81n
Butler, Samuel, 132n

Cabinets of curiosities, 54, 82, 129–32, 136, 203
Caduveo face painting, analysis of, 85–89, 197
Cagliostro, Count Allessandro di, 139
Calhoun, Craig, 25n
Campbell, Donald, 5
Carné, Marcel, 108
Carrithers, Michael, 199n
Castaneda, Carlos, 79
Cervantes, Miguel de, 168
Chaos: in myth, 89–90, 157; study of, 33, 163
Clifford, James, 81
Cockfights, analysis of, 60–68, 197
Codability of culture. *See* Culture.
Coded messages, 50, 57, 71, 87, 105, 112
Cognitive science, 114–15. *See also* Disciplines; Science(s)
Cognitive standardization, 176, 182
Cole, Jonathan, 174, 182
Cole, Stephen, 118, 174, 177
Collin, Finn, 39, 46, 57n, 150n, 169